The make-buy decision has been central to questions of organising and the pursuit of efficiency since Coase set out the Theory of the Firm in 1937. In recent times, however, we have come to care more about *how* we make or buy, and with *whom* we engage to do so. This comprehensive new book provides an in-depth and up-to-date analysis of social procurement, delving deep into the multiple perspectives and foundations of how procurement matters, and the social outcomes that can be achieved when we use procurement to make a difference.

Janine O'Flynn, *Professor, The University of Melbourne, Australia*

In one of the most comprehensive texts on social procurement to date, Barraket, Keast, and Furneaux provide a thorough exploration of this expanding trend that stretches across government, civil society, and for-profit sectors. Combining country comparisons, theoretical insights, and boundary analysis, they offer a unique inside look at the possibilities and challenges of this much understudied avenue to social value creation.

Janelle A. Kerlin, *Associate Professor, Georgia State University, USA*

This book provides us at last with a thorough analysis of commissioning, purchasing and procurement from the perspectives of social procurement, social value and public value. Combining theoretical and practical insights, it will be invaluable for researchers and practitioners alike.

Tony Bovaird, *Emeritus Professor, The University of Birmingham, UK*

Social Procurement and New Public Governance

In recent years, the search for innovative, locally relevant and engaging public service has become the new philosophers' stone. Social procurement represents one approach to maximising public spending and social value through the purchase of goods and services. It has gained increasing attention in recent years as a way that governments and corporations can amplify the benefits of their purchasing power, and as a mechanism by which markets for social enterprise and other third-sector organisations can be grown.

Despite growing policy and practitioner interest in social procurement, relatively little conceptual or empirical thinking has been published on the issue. Taking a critically informed approach, this innovative text examines emerging approaches to social procurement within the context of New Public Governance (NPG), and examines the practices of social procurement across Europe, North America and Australia.

Considering both the possibilities and limitations of social procurement, and the types of value it can generate, this book also provides empirically driven insights into the practicalities of "triple bottom line" procurement, the related challenges of measuring social value and the management of both the strategic and operational dimensions of procurement processes. As such it will be invaluable reading for all those interested in social services, public governance and social enterprise.

Jo Barraket is Professor and Director of the Centre for Social Impact Swinburne at Swinburne University of Technology, Australia.

Robyn Keast is Professor and Chair of the Collaborative Research Network: Policy and Planning for Regional Sustainability, Southern Cross University, Australia.

Craig Furneaux is Lecturer at The Australian Centre for Philanthropy and Nonprofit Studies, Queensland University of Technology, Australia.

Routledge Critical Studies in Public Management
Edited by Stephen Osborne

The study and practice of public management has undergone profound changes across the world. Over the past quarter century, we have seen:

- increasing criticism of public administration as the over-arching framework for the provision of public services,
- the rise (and critical appraisal) of the "New Public Management" as an emergent paradigm for the provision of public services,
- the transformation of the "public sector" into the cross-sectoral provision of public services, and
- the growth of the governance of inter-organizational relationships as an essential element in the provision of public services.

In reality these trends have not so much replaced each other as elided or co-existed together—the public policy process has not gone away as a legitimate topic of study, intra-organizational management continues to be essential to the efficient provision of public services, whist the governance of inter-organizational and inter-sectoral relationships is now essential to the effective provision of these services.

Further, whilst the study of public management has been enriched by contribution of a range of insights from the "mainstream" management literature, it has also contributed to this literature in such areas as networks and inter-organizational collaboration, innovation and stakeholder theory.

This series is dedicated to presenting and critiquing this important body of theory and empirical study. It will publish books that both explore and evaluate the emergent and developing nature of public administration, management and governance (in theory and practice) and examine the relationship with and contribution to the over-arching disciplines of management and organizational sociology.

Books in the series will be of interest to academics and researchers in this field, students undertaking advanced studies of it as part of their undergraduate or postgraduate degree and reflective policy makers and practitioners.

1 **Unbundled Government:**
A critical analysis of the global
trend to agencies, quangos and
contractualisation
*Edited by Christopher Pollitt and
Colin Talbot*

2 **The Study of Public
Management in Europe and
the US:**
A competitive analysis of national
distinctiveness
Edited by Walter Kickert

3 **Managing Complex
Governance Systems**
Dynamics, self-organization and
coevolution in public investments
*Edited by Geert Teisman, Arwin van
Buuren and Lasse Gerrits*

4 **Making Public Services
Management Critical**
*Edited by Graeme Currie, Jackie
Ford, Nancy Harding and Mark
Learmonth*

5 **Social Accounting and Public
Management**
Accountability for the
common good
*Edited by Stephen P. Osborne and
Amanda Ball*

6 **Public Management and
Complexity Theory**
Richer decision-making in
public services
*Mary Lee Rhodes, Joanne Murphy,
Jenny Muir and John A. Murray*

7 **New Public Governance,
the Third Sector, and
Co-Production**
*Edited by Victor Pestoff, Taco
Brandsen and Bram Verschuere*

8 **Branding in Governance and
Public Management**
Jasper Eshuis and Erik-Hans Klijn

9 **Public Policy beyond the
Financial Crisis**
An international comparative study
Philip Haynes

10 **Rethinking Public-Private
Partnerships**
Strategies for turbulent times
*Edited by Carsten Greve and
Graeme Hodge*

11 **Public-Private Partnerships
in the USA**
Lessons to be learned for the
United Kingdom
Anthony Wall

12 **Trust and Confidence in
Government and Public
Services**
*Edited by Sue Llewellyn, Stephen
Brookes and Ann Mahon*

13 **Critical Leadership**
Dynamics of leader–follower
relations in a public organization
*Paul Evans, John Hassard and
Paula Hyde*

14 **Policy Transfer and Learning in
Public Policy and Management**
International contexts, content
and development
*Edited by Peter Carroll and Richard
Common*

15 **Crossing Boundaries in
Public Management and
Policy**
The international experience
*Edited by Janine O'Flynn, Deborah
Blackman and John Halligan*

16 **Public–Private Partnerships in the European Union**
Christopher Bovis

17 **Network Theory in the Public Sector**
Building new theoretical frameworks
Edited by Robyn Keast, Myrna Mandell and Robert Agranoff

18 **Public Administration Reformation**
Market demand from public organizations
Edited by Yogesh K. Dwivedi, Mahmud A. Shareef, Sanjay K. Pandey and Vinod Kumar

19 **Public Innovation Through Collaboration and Design**
Edited by Christopher Ansell and Jacob Torfing

20 **Strategic Management in Public Organizations**
European practices and perspectives
Edited by Paul Joyce and Anne Drumaux

21 **Organizational Reputation in the Public Sector**
Branding, identity, and images of government
Edited by Arild Wæraas and Moshe Maor

22 **Making Governments Accountable**
The role of public accounts committees and national audit offices
Edited by Zahirul Hoque

23 **The Professions, State and the Market**
Medicine in Britain, the United States and Russia
Mike Saks

24 **Social Procurement and New Public Governance**
Jo Barraket, Robyn Keast and Craig Furneaux

Social Procurement and New Public Governance

Jo Barraket, Robyn Keast
and Craig Furneaux

Routledge
Taylor & Francis Group

LONDON AND NEW YORK

First published 2016
by Routledge
2 Park Square, Milton Park, Abingdon, Oxon OX14 4RN

and by Routledge
605 Third Avenue, New York, NY 10017

First issued in paperback 2020

Routledge is an imprint of the Taylor & Francis Group, an informa business

Copyright © 2016 Jo Barraket, Robyn Keast and Craig Furneaux

The right of Jo Barraket, Robyn Keast and Craig Furneaux to be identified as authors of this work has been asserted by them in accordance with sections 77 and 78 of the Copyright, Designs and Patents Act 1988.

British Library Cataloguing in Publication Data
A catalogue record for this book is available from the British Library

Library of Congress Cataloging-in-Publication Data
Barraket, Jo.
   Social procurement and new public governance / Jo Barraket,
Robyn Keast and Craig Furneaux. — 1st Edition.
      pages cm. — (Routledge critical studies in public management)
   Includes bibliographical references and index.
   1. Social integration.   2. Public administration.   3. Organizational
change.   I. Keast, Robyn   II. Title.
   HM683.B37 2016
   658.7'2—dc23
   2015021521

ISBN 13: 978−0−367−73759−7 (pbk)
ISBN 13: 978−0−415−85855−7 (hbk)

Typeset in Bembo
by Apex CoVantage, LLC

To Robert Handelsmann, Bryan Wharton and Millie Wharton Calhoun, and Gayleen, Jonathan, Josiah and Jannah Furneaux, for their patience; for giving us the support, time and space needed to develop this project; and for all the coffee.

Contents

List of figures		xiii
List of tables		xiv
Preface		xv
Acknowledgements		xvii
Abbreviations		xviii
Notes on authors		xix

1   Introduction   1

What is social procurement? 4
Understanding social procurement: our approach 7
Making sense of social procurement: structure of the book 9
References 10

2   Socio-economic and political drivers of social procurement   13

Introduction 13
Drivers for current social procurement approaches 13
Conclusion 27
References 27

3   Historical and contemporary developments in social procurement   34

Introduction 34
Early history of procuring for social outcomes: differential approaches 34
Approaches to social procurement 37
New approaches to social procurement: benefits and limitations 44
Conclusion 45
Note 46
References 46

4   Institutional and resource enablers of social procurement   50

Institutional perspectives on social procurement 50
Conceptualising institutional enablers of social procurement 52
Conclusion 64
References 65

5 Social procurement and the corporate sector 70
   Corporate social responsibility and its evolution 70
   Positioning CSR in the social procurement typology 74
   Conclusion 84
   Notes 84
   References 84

6 Governing beyond government: third-sector and
   next-practice networks 89
   Introduction: governance in transition 89
   Governance modes: prominent typologies 90
   Third-sector governance in transition 91
   Next-practice networks: navigating and negotiating 97
   Conclusion 100
   References 101

7 Assessing and measuring social value 106
   Introduction 106
   Drivers of interest in social value measurement 107
   Approaches to defining social value in social procurement 110
   *Approaches to prioritising and assessing social value in social
       procurement processes 112*
   Measurement challenges 116
   Conclusion 118
   Note 119
   References 119

8 Theoretical implications and practical portents 124
   Introduction 124
   *New public governance, public value and hybridity: creating new
       spaces and imperatives for social procurement 125*
   Macro-analysis and institutional theory 129
   Meso-accounts: network theory and beyond 130
   Micro-analyses and the role of agency 131
   Theorising social procurement: an integrative approach 133
   Conclusion 136
   References 137

9 Conclusion 142
   References 144

   Index 145

Figures

4.1 Institutional elements of a social procurement environment   52
8.1 Structure, agency and social procurement   134

Tables

1.1   Summary of the types of social procurement and their
      implications for procurement practice   6
4.1   Typology of social procurement   55
4.2   Social procurement actors and the roles they typically undertake   59
4.3   Resource types and their functions in the emergence of social
      procurement   64
5.1   Main approaches to CSR   71
5.2   Typology of social procurement   75
5.3   Internal and external aspects of CSR (summarised from
      European Commission 2001)   76
5.4   Intent and impact of environmental (waste water)
      regulation on firms   79
5.5   Compliance responses and their effects   80
6.1   Governance modes   90
7.1   Approaches to determining and prioritising social value in
      social procurement and commissioning processes   113

Preface

Social procurement is gathering momentum as government, community and business sectors all search for new ways to achieve their social and economic objectives through revised purchasing activities. The case for social procurement both as a public policy and as a public service delivery mechanism in the New Public Governance (NPG) context seems clear: social procurement objectives and practices place strong emphasis on relationships that cut across multiple traditional boundaries, respond to growing demands for cost sharing and accountabilities, and necessarily expand governance participation. Emergent practice suggests that social procurement can facilitate innovation and lend a strong eye to sustainability. Yet the implementation challenges are great.

Grounded in complex networks of relationships and sometimes competing institutional logics, NPG provides fertile conditions for the next round of social procurement to be navigated and take shape. Done well, social procurement not only supports NPG but also can provide a common signifier around which these networks and service supply chains interact and integrate. However, such success is by no means guaranteed and the contingencies of successful implementation for social procurement need to be explored.

Consequently, there is now growing attention directed towards social procurement, with high expectations placed on this set of approaches as a way forward in delivering high-value public and social outcomes. But comprehensive application of social procurement requires new ways of working, new performance measurement and investment tools, and new skill sets. Social procurement policy and practice will need to develop quickly to keep up with growing expectations and rising pressure from various stakeholders.

Much is being written about new developments in social procurement, though this is largely embedded in the "grey literature" of government and practice reports and in specific procurement practice journals. A comprehensive knowledge set is needed: bringing together historical background material and providing fresh analytical frameworks to capture the new elements required for operation within NPG. This new book is addressed to this challenge. It presents the start of a conversation that requires further debate to better understand the function and drivers of contemporary purchasing as an expression of and response to the demands of NPG. It is a most welcome and much needed contribution that will be of interest to all serious students of, and researchers in, the fields of social procurement and of the delivery of public services.

Professor Stephen P. Osborne
Chair in International Public Management
Director of the Centre for Service Excellence
University of Edinburgh Business School, Scotland

Acknowledgements

A number of people were instrumental in the preparation of this book. Janelle Weissman, Kristy Walters and Dr. Sharine Barth provided assistance with desktop research. Emily Foenander and Blake Blain assisted with formatting and proofing the manuscript. Sinead Waldron and the editorial team at Routledge were exemplary in their support for the book's progress and getting the final copy to print. We particularly thank Professor Stephen Osborne for contributing his thoughts via the preface, and Professor Tony Bovaird and two anonymous reviewers for their comments on the original proposal.

Abbreviations

ABIs	Area-based initiatives
BSL	Brotherhood of St Laurence
CB	Cost benefit
CBA	Cost-benefit analysis
CEIS	Community Enterprise in Scotland
CIC	Community Interest Company
CSR	Corporate social responsibility
EMB	Ethnic minority businesses
EU	European Union
ICT	Information and communication technologies
ISO	International Standards Organisation
NGO	Non-government organisation
NHS	National Health Service
NPG	New public governance
NPM	New public management
PA	Public administration
PCC	Parramatta City Council
PFI	Private finance initiative
PTEP	The Public Tenant Employment Program
SEN	The Social Enterprise Networks
SMEs	Small to medium enterprises
SROI	Social return on investment
SVA	Social Ventures Australia
UK	United Kingdom
UNEP	United Nations Environment Programme
VfM	Value for money
YCC	Yarra City Council

Notes on authors

Jo Barraket is Professor and Director of Centre for Social Impact Swinburne at Swinburne University of Technology in Melbourne, Australia. Her research interests include social enterprise and the relationships between government and third-sector organisations in public policy processes.

Robyn Keast is a professor at Southern Cross School of Business and Tourism and Chair of the Collaborative Research Network: Policy and Planning for Regional Sustainability. Her research portfolio is focused on public sector governance, in particular networked arrangements and collaborative practice.

Craig Furneaux is a lecturer at The Australian Centre for Philanthropy and Nonprofit Studies, Queensland University of Technology. His research focuses on social innovation in the social economy.

1 Introduction

In 1844, a group of weavers in Rochdale, England, realised the power of collective purchasing to improve social equity for their families and communities by establishing the first modern consumer cooperative (Birchall, 1994). As well as giving rise to the international cooperative movement, this act shed light on the politics of purchasing and the capacity of civil society to effect social change through economic action, which has resonated in subsequent fair trade and ethical consumption movements. The socio-political power of purchasing is not confined to civil society or individual consumers; it has historically been employed in public programs across a number of jurisdictions (McCrudden, 2004) and is experiencing renewed attention in contemporary approaches to public governance (Bovaird, 2006; Erridge, 2007). Developments in corporate behaviour are also drawing attention to the social effects – both regressive and progressive – of purchasing and supply chains of private for-profit firms and the function of double or triple bottom line value creation in future approaches to global growth (Porter & Kramer, 2011). Despite their different starting points, each of these discussions seeks to address the nature of value that is produced through purchasing decisions and supply chain relationships that operate across boundaries within and between sectors.

Commissioning, purchasing and procurement are often treated as interchangeable in practitioner and policy texts about social procurement (Furneaux & Barraket, 2014). In broad terms, commissioning may be understood as the processes by which needs are assessed and then services provided, whereas purchasing focuses on the more technical aspects of how particular goods or services are acquired (Murray, 2009). Procurement is related to purchasing, but further involves higher order decisions regarding the inclusion and use of third-party suppliers (Furneaux & Barraket, 2014). Throughout this volume, we are variously concerned with commissioning, purchasing and procurement practices because each of these forms part of common understandings of social procurement.

From the actions of individual consumers and citizen collectives through to the practices of political and corporate institutions, interest in the effects of commissioning, purchasing and procurement in stimulating social value creation is growing. This volume examines current developments in social-purpose purchasing, with a particular focus on institutional and organisational approaches to procurement. As part of emerging repertoires of new public governance, social procurement practices are both constituted in and reflective of the changing landscape of public value and accountabilities in complex multi-actor operating environments. We are thus primarily concerned in this book with the relationship between current interests in social procurement and developments in theories and practice of public governing. Collective actors from all sectors form part of the mosaic of new public governance (NPG) and are thus considered throughout our discussion in relation to their roles in social procurement discourses, frameworks and practices.

Through different lenses, the value produced through social procurement is variously understood to be "public" (Jørgensen & Bozeman, 2007), "shared" (Porter and Kramer, 2011) or "social" (Nicholls, Sacks, & Walsham, 2006). Each demands attention not just to the transactional consequences of new procurement processes, but also to the spaces produced through these processes to leverage resources that increase systems-wide change (Mendel & Brudney, 2014). For clarity, we refer throughout this book to "public value" as resources and actions that combine enriching the public sphere with delivery of "what the public values" (Benington & Moore, 2011, p. 43). Social value is an underdeveloped concept, which has been linked in popular debates to the value created by the third sector and social programs (Mulgan, 2010; Wood & Leighton, 2010). While we consider the amorphous nature of social value and the possibilities and challenges this creates for procuring it in Chapter 7, our discussion of social value and social impacts generally refers to the creation of public value that is particularly concerned with social and environmental equity. Of course, what constitutes public and social value is contingent rather than fixed and thus subject to contestation. This is reflected in both the literatures and social procurement practices canvassed in this book.

Emerging discourses of social procurement reflect currently popular sentiments evident across multiple domains – including public policy and administration, commerce and third-sector management – about the perceived inherent ideals of aligning routine actions and processes with the creation of positive social impacts. In practice, social procurement also represents one approach to maximising public spending benefits in an era of NPG (Osborne, 2006, 2010). In seeking to deliver social impacts, social procurement activities also raise new questions about the nature and measurement of public value. This volume introduces the concept of social procurement and examines social procurement practice across multiple jurisdictions in Europe, North America, and Australia. Taking a critically informed approach, we consider the possibilities and limitations of social procurement, what is driving new inflections of these practices, and the types of value they generate in different contexts. We further consider the challenges of contemporary social procurement in terms of the new approaches, skill sets and relationships these demand. This text makes theoretical contributions to policy studies and third-sector management, increasing knowledge of the complexities of governing through networks and, more specifically, managing the hybrid organisations emerging from NPG and its network emphasis. It provides empirically driven insights into the practicalities of double or "triple bottom line" procurement, as well as the related challenges of measuring social value and managing both the strategic and operational dimensions of new procurement processes. The book will be of interest to scholars and advanced students in public sector and third-sector management, social entrepreneurship, and policy studies. It will also be of use to public and private sector professionals engaged in the design, implementation, management and evaluation of social procurement activities.

Public policy trends stimulated by new public management (Hood, 1995) and more recent developments in network governance (Considine, 2005; Kickert, Klijn, & Koppenjan, 1997; Sørensen & Torfing, 2005) have placed increasing importance on the role of non-government actors in delivering policy outcomes. Within this context, the potential policy functions of civil society in general and third-sector organisations – such as social enterprises, charities and mutuals – in particular, have gained increasing attention in many developed economies over the past 15 years. Growing government reliance on third-sector providers to devise innovative responses to complex societal needs has demanded that attention be paid across all sectors to how best to stimulate markets in which the third sector is active. At the same time, dwindling tax bases, the changing needs of ageing populations, and increased public reliance on government interventions during economically tumultuous times have illuminated the importance of making the most out of public sector spending, encouraging a shift towards procurement based on achieving multiple outcomes in addition to maximising financial value. This reflects a related trend towards recognising that procurement has a strategic, as well as an operational, function to play in new governance regimes. This expanded role includes understanding the potential for procurement to stimulate social and environmental value creation, while simultaneously meeting financial bottom lines.

This text seeks to examine emerging approaches to social procurement within the context of NPG. In recent years, the search for innovative yet locally relevant and engaging public service delivery forms has become the new philosophers' stone. Consequently, a myriad of models has emerged as mechanisms facilitating the design, and implement direct service delivery through for example, the prime provider model (O'Flynn et al., 2014), collaborative models (Huxham, 1996; Keast, Brown, Mandell, & Woolcock, 2004), systems of care (Winters & Terrell, 2003), consortia and collective impact models (Kania & Kramer, 2011), and the growing emphasis on co-produced, value-added approaches (Bovaird, 2007; Osborne & Strokosch, 2013; Pestoff, 2006), as well as those which leverage the consumer-/market focus such as quasi commercial ventures, social enterprises and community-business partnerships (2003). While these models are diverse in function and form, many are located at the intersection between public and citizen (or civil society) co-engagement. Emerging models have also been accompanied by new mechanisms – including financing instruments such as social impact bonds and outcomes-based grants and contracts – each with its own operating logics and demanding new skills and competencies for successful execution. The proliferation of new models and their associated instruments has created new opportunities to tailor responses to social and economic problems. They have, on the one hand, provided operating spaces for greater deliberation and, on the other, raised challenges of coordination and action amongst actors who speak different operational languages.

NPG encompasses multi-actor settings, as mechanisms for realising integrated and committed public service delivery (Bovaird, 2007; Osborne & Strokosch, 2013). Further, NPG acknowledges the residual presence, interplay and therefore, influence of multiple governance modes. NPG scholars thus argue not for recognition of a purely "new" governance regime, but rather that a more encompassing hybrid assemblage is necessary to both explain and enable the current operating context (Koppenjan, 2012). NPG offers practitioners an alternative perspective to shape public governance and service delivery in a post-New Public Management (NPM) era. It builds on the "interpretive turn" in policy studies (Rhodes, 2007) in which public policy design and delivery has been recognised as a relational process involving multiple government and non-government actors (Kooiman, 2003). In this book, we suggest that current approaches to social procurement are both constituted in these relational arrangements and produce "boundary objects" (Star & Griesemer, 1989), or integrative devices through which multiple and diverse actors make sense of new shared practice.

As a domain in which practice appears to be exceeding theory, emerging approaches to social procurement also raise new questions about the role of private actors in the legitimation of and accountability for public value creation. While there is a rich vein of literature of the effects on public policy and public management of privatisation consistent with NPM (Brignall & Modell, 2000; Christensen & Lægreid, 2001; Considine, 2001), these analyses typically position government institutions and professionals at the centre of the equation. We know less about the implications for public value creation where accountability and legitimation functions are stretched and governmental institutions are decentred in policy arrangements. Social procurement presents one interesting field of practice in which to examine these issues. While current discussions of social procurement focus on public service delivery, social procurement activities are also taking place in private production, in areas such as new housing estate developments and ethical consumer goods. Beyond public policy, emerging practices by private – third-sector and for-profit – actors not stimulated by governments suggest that the boundaries of the public sphere are changing.

What is social procurement?

In its broadest sense, *social procurement* refers to generating social value through the purchase of goods and services. It has gained increasing attention from policy makers and third-sector leaders in recent years as a way that governments can amplify the benefits of their purchasing power, and as a mechanism by which markets for social enterprise and other "for benefit" organisations can be expanded. Attention to social procurement through purchasing from such organisations by the corporate sector is at an embryonic stage. However, corporations playing a role in affirmative action through "minority supplier" initiatives has a long history in North America (McCrudden, 2004), while sustainable development imperatives of the 1990s provided a precursor for business practices meeting double (environmental and financial) bottom line objectives (Salzmann, Ionescu-Somers, & Steger, 2005). As we explore later in this text, some corporate entities have recently identified social procurement as a mechanism for increasing their corporate social responsibility, recognising that there is a business case to be made for purposefully stimulating diverse supply chains.

Despite growing interest in social procurement across all sectors, relatively little has been written on the topic (for exceptions, see Bovaird, 2006; Erridge, 2007; Erridge & Greer, 2002; Munoz, 2009) and limited attempts to define the term (Arrowsmith, 2010; Furneaux & Barraket, 2014). In this volume, we recognise that social procurement occurs through a variety of discrete activities, including those that seek to produce social value through direct and indirect means.

In addition to the types of activities that are constitutive of social procurement, current interests in social procurement form part of a wider discursive shift towards both taming and claiming intangible value for the public sphere. Drawing on Newman & McKee's (2005) analysis of new governance in a different policy setting, we observe that emergent discourses of social procurement construct "the social" as both a site of governance problems and a potential source of solutions. Elsewhere defined as an example of "horizontal policies" (Arrowsmith, 2010), social procurement combines the instrumental activity of procurement with the strategic intent of generating social value in response to identified societal needs, such as local employment creation and development of the third sector. In so doing, this approach emphasizes both the interdependence of social and economic policy domains and the interrelatedness of policy actors from government, civil society and the private sector in generating social value. As Bovaird (2006) suggests, the need for joint working across sectors characteristic of NPG gives rise to new types of market relationships and new thinking about the "public value added" of public procurement processes and, indeed, of private procurement whose effects interact with the public sphere.

While not a new activity, renewed thinking about social procurement is gaining legitimacy in public policy, with recent developments – such as the UK's Public Services (Social Value) Act 2012 and the Council of Australian Governments' formalisation of the National Partnership Agreement on Indigenous Economic Participation – giving institutional weight to the practice within the public sector. While social procurement has received attention from policy makers as part of a broader suite of new approaches to public value-adding, it has also been advocated for by third-sector leaders as an important mechanism for opening up markets and mobilising resources in support of third-sector and hybrid organisations – in particular, social enterprises – and the missions they seek to fulfil (Nicholls et al., 2006). Alongside philanthropic and government grants, and open market trading through social enterprise, social procurement is an important source of income for the third sector (HM Treasury, 2007). Beyond providing income, social procurement is also important for the third sector and other for-benefit organisations as a means of resourcing mission fulfilment, as well as a mechanism for achieving a range of social objectives for a purchaser, whether this be a government, private for-profit or third-sector organisation (Barraket & Weissman, 2009; Burkett, 2010).

While social procurement has been predominantly constructed as a public policy lever, creating social value through purchasing decisions is not limited to the public sector. As previously discussed, some corporate businesses are now exercising their purchasing power to fulfil their own corporate responsibility objectives. Within the third sector, there is growing discussion about the mission fulfilment potential of strengthening ethical supply chains, by increasing organisation to organisation purchasing within the sector, and by expanding purchasing relationships with other forms of social business. As discussed in further detail in subsequent chapters, different approaches to social procurement seek to generate social value through direct and indirect means, resulting in the use of different practices and instruments. Table 1.1 outlines the variety of approaches to social procurement considered in this volume and their implications for procurement practice.

Table 1.1 Summary of the types of social procurement and their implications for procurement practice

	Type of Social Procurement	Focus	Outcome	Implications
Type 1	...**from** third sector	Procurement **of** social programs, **from** third sector, **with** a public good	Direct	Competitive tendering of social goods/ services
Type 2	...**of** social outcomes	Procurement **of** public works **with** an additional social benefit	Indirect	Multiple outcomes (both hard and soft) achieved in a single contract
Type 3	...% of services **from** social benefit suppliers	Procurement **of** traditional goods/ services **from** diverse suppliers	Direct	Shifts away from competitive tendering to positive discrimination. Issues here in relation to competition policy
Type 4	...of **ethical** goods	Procurement **of** goods and services **from** social benefit suppliers	Direct or indirect	Focus on social value chain

Understanding social procurement: our approach

Social procurement is, on the one hand, a set of identifiable empirical practices and, on the other, the expression of a set of ideas related to the nature of value creation in complex systems. In this volume, we examine empirical examples of social procurement and their implications for practice of those engaged with it. We also contend, however, that social procurement operates discursively as a "boundary spanning space", which assists in rendering governable the terrain that operates at the interface between actors, authority and accountabilities in NPG arrangements. In broad terms, and as discussed in detail in Chapter 8, boundary objects are ". . . artefacts that enable or constrain knowledge sharing across boundaries . . ." (Spee & Jarzabkowski, 2009, p. 226), providing symbolic mechanisms for sense-making about practice between different types of actors.

The analysis presented in subsequent chapters is broadly informed by a comparative approach and deliberative understanding of policy design and implementation. Comparative analysis can take place at the macro, meso and micro levels. Our analysis of drivers of social procurement is located at the macro level, based on consideration of broad socio-political trends influencing public policy and private purchasing practice across world regions. The consideration of social procurement practices presented here draws primarily on meso and micro comparators, considering policy frameworks and organisational strategies that inform social procurement, as well as the micro-processes and outcomes of social procurement within specific geographic and socio-political contexts. As is traced throughout the discussion, there are iterative relationships between levels, with micro-practices both illuminating and manifesting normative agendas produced in and through macro institutions.

Although the narrative of globalisation and the permeability of traditional borders inform conceptual propositions regarding both new public governance and contemporary corporate responsibility, the nation state remains a useful unit for comparative analysis, because much of the delivery and administration of public programs and regulation of business initiatives continues to occur at this level. In this sense, "The nation-state remains an arena of contestation, where social struggles and social rights are won and lost and where governments strive for national legitimacy" (Kennett, 2001, p. 2). Further, socio-cultural, political and historical experiences differ markedly from nation state to nation state and thus give rise to different institutional arrangements and organisational practices in which policy regimes and business practices are embedded. This suggests that a comparative approach can help illuminate not just what, but how, different policy and business logics are produced and enacted in different national and subnational contexts.

Throughout the discussion, we focus primarily on comparative developments in social procurement in the UK (with a predominant, but not exclusive, focus on England), the United States, Canada and Australia. There are two reasons for this selection. The first relates to common experiences of policy design and implementation. Despite having different welfare regimes, political systems and policy actors, considerable policy transfer has occurred amongst these countries since the post-war era. This has ranged from contextually nuanced interpretations of particular policy interventions through to more bald "cut and paste" approaches to policy transfer. Meso and micro-analyses of particular examples of policy transfer allow us to examine the relationship between context and program success. These analyses also provide us with insights into the "illogics of policy logics" where they are transposed onto one setting from another, and the potential for perverse outcomes that this can produce. Thus the comparative approach adopted throughout the following discussion seeks to disrupt the reader's cultural and contextual expectations, in order to trace both the commonalities and differences in comparative experiences of what, on the surface, appears to be a relatively universal set of propositions for policy design and implementation. Of course, developments in social procurement are not confined to the countries focused on here. Social procurement initiatives have been adopted in South Korea and South Africa, for example see McCrudden, (2007). These experiences contribute to a comparative understanding of the development of social procurement practices and discourses and are thus considered in subsequent chapters.

In addition to its comparative approach, this volume is grounded in a deliberative approach to policy analysis. Deliberative policy analysis, which is part of the "interpretive turn" in policy studies (Rhodes, 2007), may be broadly aligned with a constructivist framework, which is concerned with the constructedness of narratives of truth and fact that present in policy discourses. The purpose here is not to dismiss the empirical foundations of policymaking, but to examine the ways in which these are both influenced by, and influential upon, the wider institutional, political and social contexts in which they develop. As Fischer (2003) suggests, the core objective of deliberative analysis is to explicate the relationship between the empirical and the normative in public policy discourses. Citing Majone (1989), Fischer observes that policy arguments are typically structured as ". . . a complex blend of factual statements, interpretations, opinion and evaluation. . ." (2003, p. 222). In this sense, the empirical – or the facts of policy – are interwoven with the values – or the norms – of political leaders, policymakers and the institutions they inhabit. Thus, policy is produced in a dialectical relationship between the discursive and the non-discursive, with each dependent on the other for its existence (Atkinson, 2000, p 212).

A deliberative approach to policy analysis is predicated on an understanding of policy as cultural product. That is, rather than viewing policies simply as tools for instrumental, goal-oriented rational action, this approach views public policies as communicative modes through which human meaning is expressed (Yanow, 2000). The implication of understanding policy in this way is that the focus of analysis is not simply on what policy says, but how it is expressed. This approach thus " . . . entails an analytic focus on ways in which policy and implementing agency language, legislative and implementory acts, and the physical objects through which these are enacted (e.g. their programmatic vehicles and/or the buildings that house them) communicate meanings to various policy-relevant publics" (Yanow, 2003, p. 229). As Yanow (2003) suggests, the metaphor of culture encourages us to view policy discourses as being embedded within their wider societal contexts. Just as effective comparative policy requires engagement with the socio-cultural contexts of particular national systems, so too does a deliberative approach emphasise the situatedness of policy prescriptions within a wider set of institutional norms and practices that inform social, economic and political experience.

Just as NPG approaches presume increased permeability of the traditional boundaries between policy domains and policy actors, so too does the analysis of new governance require some recasting of accepted boundaries between intellectual traditions. Throughout this text, theoretical propositions derived from sociology, policy studies and critical management theory provide our analytical starting points. Yet it is both impossible and undesirable to examine recent developments in social procurement and social value creation more broadly without employing the disciplinary lenses of political theory, economics, entrepreneurship and innovation studies, and accountancy, each of which provide insights into conceptualising and explicating the logic and effects of recent trends in this field. Without making claims to true interdisciplinarity, our discussion borrows from the literature of each of these disciplines in its articulation of the evolution of ideas and practice of social procurement and social value creation.

Making sense of social procurement: structure of the book

As cultural product, social procurement practices are embedded in their socio-political and historical contexts. Across a variety of jurisdictions, purchasing and supply chain development to produce social outcomes has been initiated – in different contexts and with different drivers – by civil society, public institutions and private for-profit firms. In Chapters 2 and 3, we consider the history of social procurement and its contemporary practice, as well as the wider socio-political, economic, technological and geographic developments that inform these.

NPG ascribes new agency and accountabilities to a variety of state and non-state actors. In Chapter 5, we look particularly to contemporary trends in corporate citizenship and its influence on corporate social procurement both within and beyond activities prescribed by policy and regulation. We note that corporations have been instrumental in transnational transfers of practice that have directly influenced policy development to support social procurement in some jurisdictions. In Chapter 6, we examine more broadly the impacts and future implications of layered modes of governance on actors participating in social procurement. We suggest that NPG gives rise to a complex operating environment for those charged with the responsibility for procuring and delivering social services and outcomes, and identify core elements that can be mixed to achieve these.

New practices in social procurement and related policy instruments stimulate both practical and conceptual questions about the nature of social value and its measurement. In Chapter 7, we explore these questions in detail, and canvass the practical implementation challenges of existing approaches to measuring social value for social procurement. We observe that the institutional logics that underpin new approaches to social procurement demand new – and thus far, largely unrealised – dialogues between "upstream" purchasers of services, providers and "downstream" beneficiaries of the value created.

The practical and conceptual issues canvassed throughout the volume flag tensions in accounting for both structure and agency in theorising social procurement in particular and emergent practice in NPG more broadly. In Chapter 8, we synthesise theoretical accounts that have explanatory power when accounting for new developments in social procurement and propose understanding new discourses of social procurement as integrative devices that facilitate merging and provide new spaces for innovation in practice amongst NPG actors. We conclude the discussion in Chapter 9 with a review of our core arguments and observations and a discussion of implications for future research and practice.

References

Arrowsmith, S. (2010). Horizontal policies in public procurement: A taxonomy. *Journal of Public Procurement, 10*(2), 149–186. doi:10.1017/cbo9780511576041.006

Atkinson, R.A. (2000). Narratives of policy: The construction of urban problems and urban policy in the official discourse of British government 1968–1998. *Critical Social Policy, 20*(2), 211–232. doi:10.1177/026101830002000202

Barraket, J., & Weissman, J. (2009). *Social procurement and its implications for social enterprise: A literature review.* (Working Paper No. CPNS48). Retrieved from http://eprints.qut.edu.au/29060/ (Accessed 28th May 2015)

Benington, J., & Moore, M.H. (2011). *Public value: Theory and practice.* Hampshire, UK: Palgrave Macmillan.

Birchall, J. (1994). *Co-op: The people's business.* Manchester, UK: Manchester University Press.

Bovaird, T. (2006). Developing new forms of partnership with the "market" in the procurement of public services. *Public Administration, 84*(1), 81–102. doi:10.1111/j.0033–3298.2006.00494.x

Bovaird, T. (2007). Beyond engagement and participation: User and community coproduction of public services. *Public Administration Review, 67*(5), 846–860. doi:10.1111/j.1540–6210.2007.00773.x

Brignall, S., & Modell, S. (2000). An institutional perspective on performance measurement and management in the "new public sector." *Management Accounting Research, 11*(3), 281–306. doi:10.1006/mare.2000.0136

Burkett, I. (2010). *Financing social enterprise: Understanding needs and realities.* Brisbane: Foresters Community Finance. Retrieved from www.foresters.org.au/site/DefaultSite/filesystem/documents/Financing%20Social%20Enterprise%20finalemail.pdf

Christensen, T., & Lægreid, P. (2001). New public management: The effects of contractualism and devolution on political control. *Public Management Review, 3*(1), 73–94. doi:10.1080/14616670010009469

Considine, M. (2001). *Enterprising states: The public management of welfare-to-work*. Cambridge, UK: Cambridge University Press.

Considine, M. (2005). *Making public policy: Institutions, actors, strategies*. Cambridge, UK: Polity Press.

Erridge, A. (2007). Public procurement, public value and the Northern Ireland unemployment pilot project. *Public Administration, 85*(4), 1023–1043. doi:10.1111/j.1467–9299.2007.00674.x

Erridge, A., & Greer, J. (2002). Partnerships and public procurement: Building social capital through supply relations. *Public Administration, 80*(3), 503–522. doi:10.1111/1467–9299.00315

Fischer, F. (2003). *Reframing public policy: Discursive politics and deliberative practices*. Oxford, UK: Oxford University Press.

Furneaux, C., & Barraket, J. (2014). Purchasing social good(s): A definition and typology of social procurement. *Public Money & Management, 34*(4), 265–272. doi:10.1080/09540962.2014.920199

HM Treasury. (2007). *The future role of the third sector in social and economic regeneration: Final report*. (Report No. CM7189). Retrieved from http://hm-treasury.gov.uk

Hood, C. (1995). The "new public management" in the 1980s: Variations on a theme. *Accounting, Organizations and Society, 20*(2–3), 93–109. http://doi.org/10.1016/0361–3682(93)E0001-W

Huxham, C. (1996). Collaboration and collaborative advantage. In C. Huxham (Ed.), *Creating collaborative advantage* (pp. 1–18). London: Sage Publications.

Jørgensen, T.B., & Bozeman, B. (2007). Public values: An inventory. *Administration & Society, 39*(3), 354–381. doi:10.1177/0095399707300703

Kania, J., & Kramer, M. (2011). Collective impact. *Stanford Social Innovation Review, 94*. Retrieved from www.ssireview.org/articles/entry/collective_impact (Accessed 28th May 2015)

Keast, R., Brown, K., Mandell, M., & Woolcock, G. (2004). Network structures: Working differently and changing expectations. *Public Administration Review, 64*(3), 363–371. doi:10.1111/j.1540–6210.2004.00380.x

Kennett, P. (2001). *Comparative social policy: Theory and research*. Buckingham: Open University Press.

Kickert, W.J.M., Klijn, E.-H., & Koppenjan, J.F.M. (1997). *Managing complex networks: Strategies for the public sector*. London: Sage Publications.

Kooiman, J. (2003). *Governing as governance*. Thousand Oaks, CA: Sage Publications. Retrieved from http://site.ebrary.com/lib/alltitles/docDetail.action?docID=10369672 (Accessed 28th May 2015)

Koppenjan, J.F.M. (2012). *The new public governance in public service delivery reconciling efficiency and quality*. The Hague: Eleven International Publishing.

Majone, D. (1989). *Evidence, argument, & persuasion in the policy process*. Chelsea, MI: Yale University Press.

McCrudden, C. (2004). Using public procurement to achieve social outcomes. *Natural Resources Forum, 28*(4), 257–267. doi:10.1111/j.1477–8947.2004.00099.x

McCrudden, C. (2007). *Buying social justice: Equality, government procurement, & legal change*. Oxford, UK: Oxford University Press.

Mendel, S.C., & Brudney, J.L. (2014). Doing good, public good, and public value. *Nonprofit Management and Leadership, 25*(1), 23–40. doi:10.1002/nml.21109

Mulgan, G. (2010). Measuring social value. *Stanford Social Innovation Review, 8*(3), 37–43. Retrieved from http://csi.gsb.stanford.edu/measuring-social-value (Accessed 28th May 2015)

Munoz, S.A. (2009). Social enterprise and public sector voices on procurement. *Social Enterprise Journal*, *5*(1), 69–82. doi:10.1108/17508610910956417

Murray, J.G. (2009). Towards a common understanding of the differences between purchasing, procurement and commissioning in the UK public sector. *Journal of Purchasing and Supply Chain Management*, *15*, 198–202.

Newman, J., & McKee, B. (2005). Beyond the new public management? Public services and the social investment state. *Policy & Politics*, *33*(4), 657–673. doi:10.1332/030557305774329181

Nicholls, J., Sacks, J., & Walsham, M. (2006). More for your money: A guide to procuring from social enterprises. Retrieved from www.socialenterprise.org.uk/data/files/publications/sec_procurement_guide_final_06.pdf

O'Flynn, J., Dickenson, H., O'Sullivan, S., Gallet, W., Currie, K., Pettit, M., . . . Robinson, T. (2014) *The prime provider model: An opportunity for better public service delivery, social policy*. (Working Paper No. 18). University of Melbourne (May 2014) Melbourne: Brotherhood of St Laurence.

Osborne, S.P. (2006). The new public governance? *Public Management Review*, *8*(3), 377–387. doi:10.1080/14719030600853022

Osborne, S.P. (2010). Delivering public services: Time for a new theory? *Public Management Review*, *12*(1), 1–10. doi:10.1080/14719030903495232

Osborne, S.P., & Strokosch, K. (2013). It takes two to tango? Understanding the co-production of public services by integrating the services management and public administration perspectives. *British Journal of Management*, *24*, S31–S47. doi:10.1111/1467–8551.12010

Pestoff, V. (2006). Citizens and co-production of welfare services: Preschool services in eight European countries. *Public Management Review*, *8*(4), 503–519. doi:10.1080/14719030601022882

Porter, M., & Kramer, M. (2011). The big idea: Creating shared value. *CFA Digest*, *41*(1), 12–13. Retrieved from https://hbr.org/2011/01/the-big-idea-creating-shared-value/ (Accessed 28th May 2015)

Rhodes, R.A.W. (2007). Understanding governance: Ten years on. *Organization Studies*, *28*(8), 1243–1264. doi:10.1177/0170840607076586

Salamon, L. (2003). *The resilient sector: The state of nonprofit America*. Washington, DC: Brookings Institution Press.

Salzmann, O., Ionescu-Somers, A., & Steger, U. (2005). The business case for corporate sustainability: Literature review and research options. *European Management Journal*, *23*(1), 27–36. doi:10.1016/j.emj.2004.12.007

Sørensen, E., & Torfing, J. (2005). The democratic anchorage of governance networks. *Scandinavian Political Studies*, *28*(3), 195–218. doi:10.1111/j.1467–9477.2005.00129.x

Spee, A.P., & Jarzabkowski, P. (2009). Strategy tools as boundary objects. *Strategic Organization*, *7*(2), 223–232. doi:10.1177/1476127009102674

Star, S.L., & Griesemer, J.R. (1989). Institutional ecology, 'translations' and boundary objects: Amateurs and professionals in Berkeley's museum of vertebrate zoology, 1907–39. *Social Studies of Science*, *19*(3), 387–420. doi:10.1177/030631289019003001

Winters, N., and Terrell, E. (2003). Case management: The linchpin of community-based systems of care. In A. Pumaiega, & N. Winters (Eds.), *The handbook of child and adolescent systems-of-care: The new community psychiatry* (pp. 171–202). San Francisco, CA: Jossey Bass.

Wood, C., & Leighton, D. (2010). *Measuring social value: The gap between policy and practice*. London: Demos.

Yanow, D. (2000). *Conducting interpretive policy analysis*. Thousand Oaks, CA: Sage Publications.

Yanow, D. (2003). Accessing local knowledge: Policy analysis and communities of meaning. In M.A. Hajer, & H. Wagenaar (Eds.), *Deliberative policy analysis* (pp. 228–246). Cambridge, UK: Cambridge University Press.

2 Socio-economic and political drivers of social procurement

Introduction

To understand what is driving interest in social procurement, this chapter considers the wider social, economic and political contexts in which different approaches to social procurement have evolved, focusing particularly on the contemporary conditions shaping resurgent interest in its development. We start this chapter by setting out and discussing some of the key drivers for the current emphasis on social procurement as a significant policy and practice strategy. The next section isolates the drivers for the present-day emphasis on social procurement and, in so doing, provides further insights into the different forms and practices they may now take. This chapter provides the context for developments in social procurement, which are then reviewed in more specific detail in Chapter 3.

Drivers for current social procurement approaches

Many of the earlier drivers for social procurement inform and shape current social procurement practices, including addressing the persistence in disadvantage caused by poverty, ethno-religious inequality, migration and social isolation, as well as securing social order. Times have also changed; globalisation, the rise of new technologies, instant communication and the internet have transformed the way people communicate and connect. Coupled with these factors are a growing array of challenging issues, such as the mass movement of migrant groups into new countries, the persistent socio-economic inequality of some groups despite increased global wealth, and growing fiscal constraints on national economies, that are straining the resources of governments and highlighting the inability of governments alone to solve these intractable as well as more emergent issues. These are but a few of the changes transforming societies around the world and informing the adoption of alternative procurement processes.

Changing faces: changing places

Societies are becoming more aged, culturally diverse and blended, with single-parent families replacing the nuclear units as the main form of social organization in many jurisdictions (AIHW, 2011; Olson, 2011). In some countries, such as Australia and the United Kingdom (UK), there is a continuing pattern of relocation away from small country and inland regional towns to larger cities located on the coast (Beer et al., 2005; Cambridge Econometrics and Institute for Employment Research, 2012). Elsewhere in the world there are significant transnational migrations occurring – for economic, political and social reasons – creating large flows of people across previously impervious national boundaries. It is argued that this mobility, coupled with a loss of familial contact, exacerbates the breakdown of community strength and values (Mackay & Conn, 1993; Edgar, 2001; Shucksmith, 2012) and adds to a growing disconnection amongst people, communities and states (Madanipour, 1998). On the growing inequality between people and places, Dorling et al. (2008, p. 12) commented, "Already wealthy areas have tended to become disproportionately wealthier. There is evidence of increasing polarisation, where rich and poor now live further apart".

Layered on top of this growing locational disconnection has been a noticeable emphasis on individualism characterized by self-interested, opportunistic actions at the expense of broader society or collective value (Bauman, 2000; Gottlieb, 1999; Van Lange, De Cremer, Van Dijk, & Van Vugt 2007; Rose, 1999). This situation has been facilitated, even brokered, by the growing focus on the marketization of services, which is argued to have turned citizens from recipients or contributors to services to customers, with the associated higher service expectations (Ryan, 2001) or to competitors for services (Petrella, 1996). Hardy's (1998) earlier warning that not only does excessive self-interest corrupt, but "... it also has no regard for duty or responsibility" (p. 136) seems even more pertinent today. At the same time, there is ample evidence of collective generosity in response to disasters and other social issues. Younger generations, in particular, are also demonstrating a strong environmental consciousness in their purchasing preferences and behaviours.

Citizens are also generally better educated, and have faster and more direct access to information as a result of both the ongoing developments and decreasing costs of information and communication technology (ICT). These mechanisms have enabled more instantaneous access to a greater range of information. People can also conduct their business online, undertake education and training, disperse assets and infrastructures, monitor transport flows and conduct safety checks, and can even manage and monitor remote agriculture more economically (Plunkett Foundation and Carnegie UK Trust, 2012; Queensland Government, 2007). ICT is increasingly used as a tool for supporting core social service delivery, such as tele-health, electronic case records, data sharing and joined-up back office services (Ozanne & Rose, 2013), and to source funds to support social and environmental initiatives. In view of the benefits of advanced ICT, around the world there is a strong agenda supporting provision of higher-speed broadband for all sectors, including the non-profit arena (OECD, 2007; Department of Broadband, Communication and the Digital Economy, 2009). The growing role and sophistication of online service delivery, e-commerce and other advances in ICT systems also provides opportunity for the wider deployment and better integration of procurement processes, including online applications and contract management/monitoring systems.

While technological advancement has provided benefits and opportunities, it also presents challenges for governments, communities and citizens. Citizens and communities are increasingly wired up and linked in, but there are still groups in society who are not a part of this digital progress, perpetuating inequalities (Van Dijk & Hacker, 2003; Parker-Oliver & Demiris, 2006). ICT advances have also led to increased expectations of government and government representatives and demands for more immediate contributions of representatives and their departments. As Homeshaw (1995) explained at the beginning of the e-government movement:

> Knowing what services are available in other jurisdictions makes people less tolerant of the services supplied locally at high costs. The growth of citizen on-line democracy networks is also changing voters' tolerance of incompetent and self-serving politicians.
>
> (p. 104)

Armed with this new information, and with increased political sophistication, interest groups have grown more organized and vocal, while generally remaining focused on narrow interests (Gerber, 1999; Osborne, 2006). Alongside the greater pressure on governments to perform is a growing doubt in their ability to deliver the types and quality of services required, or to address the new as well as intractable social issues.

Globalisation

Contemporary society is also shaped by ongoing, rapid and intertwined changes in economic, technological, political and cultural factors. Combined, these changes are referred to as *globalisation*. Globalisation denotes an increased movement of people, goods and services, capital and ideas and has led to a growing global economy. It is often conceptualized by the notion of a "borderless world" permeating the relative independence of nations in determining domestic economic and social policies (Kanter, 2003).

The forces of globalisation have long been a feature of society, generating both progressive and regressive outcomes. However, current conditions have amplified their impact and reach (Daft, 2010), leading not just to the internationalisation of business but also to some social problems. For example, globalisation has facilitated the migration of manufacturing to areas using exploitative labour practices to produce cheap material goods for high resale profit. The penetration of global political and economic conditions on domestic policies is also a factor in the growing numbers of refugees and increased international migration (Kazi, 2011). Similarly, the increasing use of ICT, globally integrated banking systems and company outsourcing have all contributed to the loss of guaranteed incomes and job security in many communities as well as undermined the capacity of domestic policies to respond (Kanter, 2003). As Beck (1992) notes, problems such as environmental degradation that have very real local consequences are global in nature, exceeding boundaries between nation states and related frameworks for regulating practice, such as domestic legislation. Alphonse, George and Moffat (2008) further observe that globalisation has created an environment for a decreased role of the state and led to the need for increased corporate involvement: ". . . resulting in gross inequalities, injustices and marginalisation of various vulnerable groups" (p. 1).

The structural forces of globalisation thus aggravate social disadvantage and poverty and continue to push some individuals and communities to the margins of society, limiting access to resources, services and justice, resulting in social exclusion that is costly in both a personal and economic sense (Parkinson, 1998).

Changing economic conditions and policy approaches

One of the main consequences of globalisation and its liberal trading practices has been its encroachment upon the relative independence of nations in determining their domestic economic, public and social policies. However, as many writers note, although globalisation has no doubt affected government operations, it has not translated into a decline in government autonomy (Held, McGrew, Goldblatt & Perraton, 1999), with most governments continuing to be major providers and procurers of public goods and holders of large budgets (Brammer & Walker, 2007; Islam & Siwar, 2013). Nonetheless, fuelled by economic downturn, increased demands and a growing neoliberal political ideology that championed ". . . the primacy of individual freedom of choice, market security, laissez faire and minimal government" (McDonald, 2006, p. 63), most governments adopted a new public management (NPM) approach, characterized by market principles of privatisation such as increased contractual regulation and competition. On top of this, the ongoing global economic downturn has had a major impact, with many governments pursuing policies of fiscal austerity to decrease spending debt and reduce state service delivery costs (Schui, 2014). On this point Shucksmith (2012) notes, some members of the European Union (EU) have entered into agreements (fiscal pacts) to prevent their governments from spending to boost demand. Shucksmith (2012) goes on to provide as an example, the UK's Coalition Government announcing in its 2010 Spending Review spending cuts of £81 billion over a four-year period, later extending the period of reduced spending to 2016–17 in its 2011 Autumn Statement.

Since 2010, Australian federal and state governments have also implemented "efficiency strategies" in the form of agency budget cuts, recruitment freezing and caps on staffing levels and wages increases (Elliott, 2013). The collective effect of this suite of reforms was a projected loss of more than 50,000 public administration and community sector positions. MacDermott and Stone (2013) in their review of the Australian "austerity" reforms identify multiplier effects of lost productivity in the form of depleted workforce capability skills and an inability to design and deliver quality services, including the ability to adequately compose and manage contracts.

While these economic developments do not threaten the overall sovereignty or autonomy of states, they point to a structural transformation in which government's role and power in economic and social policy development, as well as service provider and procurer, is increasingly shared with other sectors (ARNOVA, 2010).

Changing social and public policies

Despite the persistent message of "fiscal crisis" within so-called developed nations, it is apparent that many countries continue to generate increased financial wealth and that many of their citizens engage in productive and relatively enjoyable lifestyles. Nonetheless, socio-economic inequities – between nations and within national citizenries – have generally increased rather than decreased over the past decade (Heathcote, Perri &Violante, 2010; Fletcher & Guttmann, 2013), although tax transfers in some nations mitigate this (Brzozowski, Gervais, Klein & Suzuki, 2010). Within many developed economies, there remains a considerable minority of people who continue to experience significant exclusion, because of either economic or social problems. These include workforce participation barriers, crime, preventable health issues and entrenched and intergenerational welfare dependency. In Australia, for instance, despite 30 years of continued economic growth, 5% to 13% of the population do not share this prosperity (AIHW, 2013). The social impacts of this exclusion are of increasing concern to economists because the ramifications are seen to affect the overall productivity of the nation. As the Australian Institute of Health and Welfare (2013) notes:

> As any economist will tell you, one of the main contributors to productivity is participation. Higher participation and lower unemployment means higher economic output and living standards. But after a decade of strong economic growth, Australia struggles to eliminate long-term unemployment, and the related issues of intergenerational disadvantage.
>
> (p. 26)

Many other countries also wrestle with social problems resulting from several decades of social, technological and economic change, including problems of entrenched and intergenerational unemployment, poverty, low community participation and fractured social relationships. The response to these social issues has been a return to the "social" or "community" as both a mechanism and location for solutions to these intractable problems (Adams & Hess, 2001; Labonte, 2004). Social exclusion was one of the first renewed "community driven" responses and has been widely used to capture the growing experience and evidence of embedded disadvantage, such as that expressed in the foregoing discussion (European Commission, 1992).

Social exclusion refers to processes in which individuals or entire groups of people are systematically blocked from rights, opportunities and resources (e.g., housing, employment, healthcare, civic and democratic participation) that are normally available to members of society and are considered to be foundations of social cohesion (Sommerville, 1998; de Haan, 1998). Exclusion not only generates individual isolation and groups left behind by economic progress but also, left unattended, can fuel general disaffection, with wider socio-political and economic effects.

As the concept of social exclusion became popularised in policy and development discourses in the 1990s, it was transferred and adopted worldwide (Percy-Smith, 2000; Labonte, 2004). However, the broad application of the term has resulted in differential foci and applications (Sen, 2000). For example, within continental Europe, the social policy approach to social exclusion tended to focus on labour market exclusion (Geyer, 1999), whereas in some other jurisdictions – Australia, new Zealand and the UK, for example – the term was applied more widely to denote a range of social issues and responses (Arthurson & Jacobs, 2004). For some commentators, these diverse applications have made it a contested concept, which has undermined its utility for social change (Sen, 2000).

A related term, *social inclusion*, has also been used as a policy concept stressing the importance of being part of a society (European Foundation 1995, p4, cited in de Haan 1998, p. 26). Social inclusion has often been presented as opposite of exclusion (Silver, 2010; Labonte, Hadi & Kauffmann, 2011) simply mirroring the intent of social exclusion, whereas others argue that the term and approach has its own distinctive logic, with features clustered around notions of being part of something bigger (Friendly and Lero, 2002; Hayes, Gray and Edwards, 2008). Sounding a warning, however, Sen (2000) notes that there is a predilection towards assuming all forms of inclusion are inherently good, overlooking the potential for problematic forms of inclusion.

Despite their methodological and conceptual limitations, notions of social exclusion and inclusion are considered to be more useful than some of the earlier community-derived modes, such as social cohesion and social capital, particularly as they get at the "grit of human relations" (Silver, 1994, p. 6) and offer a new set of lenses through which to examine and respond to large-scale social issues (Labonte, 2004).

Overcoming the effects of social exclusion and building a more inclusive society is a goal with universal political appeal. Conservative thinkers contend that social inclusion facilitates self-reliance, strengthens national economic performance and reduces waste and duplication in public spending. Those on the left of politics highlight the social benefits such as poverty reduction, human dignity and well-being. As a consequence, achieving greater social inclusion became a key political imperative informing national and regional development globally (Arthurson & Jacobs, 2004). For example, the Copenhagen Declaration on Social Development (United Nations, 1995, chapter 1, resolution 1, annex 1) explicitly set out a social inclusion agenda. At the national level, a number of countries (e.g., the UK, Canada and Australia) institutionalised social inclusion into polices, as well as in the creation of specialist bodies and units. The concept and its application, however, have remained politically volatile and readily subject to shifting political ideologies and agendas. An example of this political volatility is that on 18 September 2013, after only a few weeks in power, the new Australian conservative Coalition Government under Prime Minister Tony Abbott, disbanded the Australian Social Inclusion Unit created by the former Labour Government in 2007.

Around the time that social exclusion/inclusion as a global central policy strategy was being abandoned, other strategies, including that underpinned by the notion of "Big Society", emerged (Blond, 2009; Cabinet Office, 2010). At the foundation of the Big Society was a set of principles and practices to facilitate the "release" of communities and community resources from the power of government and return significant economic power to them through the establishment of mutualised or cooperative forms of organisation (Alcock, 2010; Thompson, 2011), which are intended to counterbalance corporate (neo-liberal) power. This has given rise to, for example, spin-outs from the public sector of primary and community care providers structured as social enterprises, as well as opening the door for larger private providers in the National Health Service (Roy, Donaldson, Baker & Kay, 2013).

Many ideas pursued under the Big Society banner, such as shrinking government and outsourcing to private providers, have for some time now been part of the government reform arsenal. What was introduced under the Big Society mantra was a discourse supporting citizen empowerment and community to justify policy changes, such as austerity measures, that have served to disempower community organisations by reducing their capacity and, in some extreme situations, replacing community organizations with voluntary bodies (Elliott, 2013). Also encapsulated within the Big Society framework is a redistribution of public funds to private (for profit and not for profit) service providers and the weakening of the capacity of the public sector to respond to issues or provide leadership. The Big Society experiment has been previously declared failed by a number of commentators and has been variously critiqued for its empty rhetoric, its emphasis on small government rather than big society, and for lack of translation of its community-centric vision from the halls of government to the communities it exhorted (Kisby, 2010; Scott, 2011). Despite a lack of public engagement with the first Big Society agenda, David Cameron's recently elected Conservative Party has retained a stated commitment to Big Society in its Manifesto (Conservatives, 2015). This new iteration references community participation but, resonant of earlier social inclusion agendas, is substantively focused on individual participation through skills development, volunteering and advancing societal tolerance for diversity.

Despite their various foci and criticisms – both popular and academic – this suite of community-centric policy strategies (i.e., social exclusion/inclusion, social capital, social enterprise and the Big Society) all provide a useful way to draw policy attention to the questions of inequality and have highlighted the need for new ways to engage with "wicked" problems (Rittel & Webber,

1973), bringing to the fore ideas of co-production and alternative procurement models as legitimate and necessary ways forward (Pestoff, Brandsen & Verschuere, 2012).

Wicked problems

Exacerbating the pressing policy and service provision challenges previously noted is the fact that many of the problems to be resolved are complex and interrelated and therefore often do not respond to conventional solutions. These complex social problems are referred to as "messes" (Ackoff, 1974) and increasingly "wicked" issues (Rittel & Webber, 1973), symbolising a situation in which issues are imperfectly understood, defy precise definition, do not have clear linear solutions and, when unravelled, have various components found to be tightly interdependent (OECD, 1996; Clarke & Stewart, 1997). It was argued that in these conditions "Realities constantly confound, wicked problems linger, others metamorphose, and well-tried solutions suddenly provide unanticipated or perverse consequences" (Ryan, 2003, p. 11).

A further confounding feature of these complex, intractable social problems is that they are cross-cutting; that is, they do not fit into neat functional boundaries of government departments or organizational units. Instead they demand cross-departmental, cross agency and often cross-sectoral responses. Governments, and most large organizations, are typically poorly set up to deal with these new challenges or the wicked issues because of their largely hierarchical structures, routinized practices and defined boundaries of action and accountability. Such characteristics make these entities, in their current forms, unsuitable to address the multiple needs and growing demands of their constituencies and, in particular, develop and sustain boundary-spanning service arrangements. This realisation of the need to "work-together" led to significant emphasis on more joined-up and horizontal service models, such as partnerships, networks and collaborations, which show no signs of decreasing and demand substantially different types of working relationships and, therefore, procurement arrangements (6 et al., 1999; Kickert, Klijn & Koppenjan, 1997; Stewart, 2002; Keast, 2011).

There is also a growing view that previous government approaches to procuring and providing services through "grants and individual welfare and support services" are no longer appropriate or sustainable. Some commentators, such as Pearson (1999), talk passionately and persuasively about the negative impacts of "welfarism" on individuals and communities, especially dispossessed communities. Others take a more economic stance, arguing the need for a change in the role of government from "provider" to "enabler" – focused on the stimulation of economic policy as driver for more sustainable social outcomes. At the same time, the role and functioning of social sector organizations has also come under closer scrutiny, with many expressing concerns at the financial sustainability and perceived lack of accountability for outcomes under previous funding models (ARNOVA, 2010; Australian Productivity Commission, 2010).

Taken together these changes in the broader social, political and economic context have knock-on implications for government, third and private for-profit sectors and forecast changes in terms of their relationships, modes of service delivery and relative independence.

Changing sectors

Government

For the past century governments have been the dominant force in the procuring and provision of larger scale or universal public and social services, with the private sector and particularly the non-profit community sector playing a support function (Tierney, 1970; Kendall & Knapp, 1993; Hall, 2011). Despite the effects of NPM, such as downsizing and contracting out, and, more recently, austerity policies, governments will continue to be the leading procurer of social services. What will change are the processes and procedures for how these services are purchased, with whom and under what conditions.

In response to the dual challenges of fiscal restraint and increased demand noted earlier, public administrators at all levels are experimenting with creative, alternative means to purchase and deliver quality services more efficiently and economically. This experimentation is occurring in both the internal and external operations of government. Internally there have been internal purchaser–provider splits, creating quasi-markets within and between departments, as well as the leveraging of technology to create more economical and efficient "joined-up back-room" processes, including for example, the use of procurement cards for small cost, routine purchases (McCue & Gianakis, 2001). Goldsmith & Eggers (2004) also highlighted the adoption by the US government of a suite of projects to better understand and evaluate internal needs against the capacity of existing contracts to deliver, as well as enhancing the skills of the public service to manage and monitor contracts.

Externally, the greater awareness of the capacity of, and the need for, other sectors to contribute to public and social service delivery, and thus defray some of the costs and risks, has led to a greater use of the third sector and, increasingly, private for-profit firms as a service delivery arm of government. Ostensibly, these new arrangements are often couched as "partnerships", signalling a new relationship between government and private actors. However, the prevailing competition policy has shifted procuring arrangements from arm's length grants to more competitive tendering and much tighter contracts, placing deliverables under increased scrutiny. Moreover, as McBratney and McGregor-Lowndes' (2012) study of Australian national- and state-level contracts has highlighted, these contracts now place greater levels of accountability on providers, particularly third-sector organisations, often more than governments apply to their own internal processes. Clearly for partnerships to function contracts are needed that meet the specified accountability requirements, but in a way that preserves and even builds sustained service supply chains across sectors (Lund-Thomsen & Costa, 2011).

Alongside competition policy has been a strong emphasis on integration, and particularly collaboration, as a way to link up services for greater efficiency and effectiveness as well as provide more innovative service delivery models (6 et al., 1999; O'Flynn, 2009; Keast, 2011). At the 2010 ARNOVA conference on research related to third-sector and voluntary action, the dual policy focus of competition and collaboration was widely discussed, concluding that the tensions between the two approaches continued to reflect the service delivery challenges occurring within and across sectors (ARNOVA, 2010). Despite their differences it could be argued that rather than being in conflict, competition and collaboration, if designed and managed well, can co-exist and even operate in synchronisation to deliver enhanced models and outcomes. On this, Ham (2012) contends that problems occur when the policy positions are pushed too far in each direction, without checks and balances. A more forward-looking approach to service delivery and procurement is called for or, as Ham (2012) notes, "The wrong kind of integration may emerge unless policy-makers think two or three steps ahead" (p. 2). Bryson (1988) also stressed the need for the community and government sectors to adopt more strategic approaches to their policy development and service implementation. In so doing, he highlighted the importance of dialogue, particularly around values and purposes, as crucial to establishing coherent pathways for intervention, or at least understanding how different elements were likely to work together or not. More recently, Joyce, Bryson and Holzer (2014) reiterated the need for strategic management capability (i.e., thinking, design and planning) for broader public sector organisations to "... be better at anticipating surprises and preparing for them (p. 4), particularly given the expanded and complex supply chain now in place for service provision.

Community services and the third sector

Over recent decades, the third sector – particularly non-profits delivering community services – has been subject to a number of changes that have reshaped the nature and method of its services delivery and how these are funded and procured, as well as the sector's relationships with government, and increasingly the private for-profit sector (ARNOVA, 2010). Initially these changes centred on an exponential increase in government expenditure for a wide range of specialist support services. More recently, with the adoption of market-based ideology, there has been a shift from grant-based funding of specialist services to the transfer of many "traditional" government services using competitive tendering principles and process. With competitive contracting has come greater performance specificity in the contracts, an expansion of complex compliance processes and regulations, and heightened accountability requirements (ARNOVA, 2010; McBratney & McGregor-Lowndes, 2012). Beyond competitive tendering, new financing instruments – such as social impact bonds, discussed further in Chapter 3 – seek to mobilise new resources and new actors in support of delivering social value (Jackson, 2013; Joy & Shields, 2013; McHugh, Sinclair, Roy, Huckfield & Donaldson, 2013).

Along with these funding changes has been a transfer of risk for performance from government to private (third-sector and for-profit) contractors.
Also emerging from the marketization orientation is the need for new business models as third-sector organisations face and cope with the reality of a
highly competitive environment, including a growth in the number of private for-profits entering the service field (Phillips, 2007; ARNOVA, 2010). To
survive and be sustainable, third-sector organisations are being challenged to
collaborate more, as well as scale up through processes such as mergers and
amalgamations, and form short-term strategic alliances and partnerships with
previous competitors or new bodies (Deloitte, 2009). On the surface, these
structural and business model reforms and the associated procurement changes
appear sensible and necessary, with the economic argument for sectoral adaptation gaining ground. For many commentators, however, the reforms and
associated procurement changes forecast real problems in terms of the loss of
the communitarian ethos of the sector and ongoing feasibility of third-sector
organisations as civil society "advocates" and "watch-dogs" (Lyons, 2001). The
challenge then for the sector is to develop alternative resourcing models and/or
develop sufficient capacity to ensure a level of self-sufficiency and control over
current and future procurement processes.

Alongside the structural developments are a number of internal challenges
for third-sector organisations, which are likely to increasingly affect the way in
which services are designed and the capacity of the sector to deliver. The community services sector workforce is predominately female and has historically
been paid less than other industries (Walsh, 1993; Oster, 2003; AIHW, 2011).
Adding to the pressures is an undersupply of suitably qualified workers, and
many of the existing workers are nearing retirement age or have been attracted
to better paying industries, such as mining, tourism (see, for example, in the
housing and homelessness sector, Keast, Waterhouse, Murphy & Brown, 2011),
or to the private for-profit agencies entering the service domain. As demands
for social services increase, the sector is responding with the introduction of a
range of policies and strategies to improve current salary and conditions and
to enhance the existing qualification framework (AIHW, 2011, p. 314). It is
also being proactive, exploring the development of a range of new skills and
resources to facilitate and support capacity in more innovative alternative forms
of business (ARNOVA, 2010), as well as enhancing contracting capabilities to
make them more resilient and self-sufficient.

Private for-profit sector

Ongoing market-based policy developments have also expanded opportunities for the private for-profit sector to become more involved in the provision of public services, including social services. This has occurred as a result
of the accelerated competitive tendering process and the ability of for-profits
to quickly direct spare capacity to the production of high-quality, competitive applications as well as meet government requirements for heightened

accountability, with their size also allowing them negotiation strength (Williams, 2012). It has been noted that, in several countries, private for-profit businesses now outnumber third-sector suppliers in social services provision (Ryan, 1999; Lyons, 2001; ARNOVA, 2010). Despite their profits going to private owners or shareholders, most of these emergent bodies do exhibit a service ethos. Nonetheless, their entrance into the service delivery space, frequently as government-preferred providers, has caused tensions with their third-sector counterparts, as previously noted (Phillips, 2007). The adoption of compulsory competitive tendering also allowed governments to be more specific in the determination of contracts, including the incorporation of social value in procurement as part of a growing corporate social responsibility (CSR) agenda related to, for example, environmental and social issues (McCrudden, 2007). In this way, as Matten and Moon (2008) contend, governments have sought to use business CSR as a way to bolster their decreased capacity to address growing social service demands.

As well as co-option by government, the business sector has also accelerated its attention to CSR as a mechanism to self-regulate their activities and the activities of supply-chain nodes to ensure products and processes conform to social and environmental expectations (Meehan & Bryde, 2011). To operationalise this approach a well-accepted business model is in place that calls for "... actions that appear to further some social good, beyond the interests of the firm and that which is required by law" (McWilliams, Siegel & Wright, 2006, p. 4). The incorporation of CSR principles in both business and government arenas is an increasingly common practice, and is being manifest in procurement policies well beyond the early emphasis on employment and environment to include such diverse areas as national industrial policy, support for small business, ethical business, local development and participation of workers with a disability. However, while businesses have commercial acumen, they often lack expertise in the determination of appropriate interventions or initiatives as well as an informed capacity to assess social benefits. Therefore, it is argued that the most effective CSR outcomes will be derived from a closer alignment between business and their recipients, transferring both resources and capacity, and changing the systems of power and entitlement. Such a transformation will not come easily and will require behavioural and skill adjustments from all parties, including a shift from traditional "hard procurement" practices to a more sustained relational approach (Walker & Hampson, 2008; Keast, Waterhouse, Brown & Mandell, 2005).

Taken together, the changes identified previously demonstrate a deepening level of interaction and intersection between the three sectors. Moreover, it is widely argued that the increased scale, scope and efficiency of outcomes derived from these emergent *hybrid* arrangements between the sectors are necessary to secure ongoing quality public and social service provision. This blurring of the boundaries between organisations and sectors is increasingly referred to as a shift from government to governance (Stoker, 1998; Rhodes, 1996), increasingly now referred to as *new public governance* (NPG) to better reflect the plurality of engagement and complexity of interactions (Osborne, 2010; Koppenjan, 2012). In this model, collaborative relationships, pragmatic deliberation and democratic structures and processes are the foundations to collective outcomes and enhanced social value (Bovaird, 2007). Therefore, the traditional "hard" approach to procurement, based on highly competitive and contested short-term relationships, cheapest versus economic best value, is not appropriate (Walker & Hampson, 2008; Kalubanga, 2012). Untempered, this sort of model invites a confrontational approach that is not helpful to sustained relationships, and the high level of specificity in hard contracts can work against the sharing of resources, innovations and the achievement of mutually satisfying "win/win" outcomes – all key integrating elements. It is argued that the addition of a relational element to procurement also offers a more effective and sustainable way forward, beyond pure reliance on regulations and contracts (Walker & Hampson, 2008; Erridge, 2007). Bovaird (2007) encapsulates this view as follows:

> They can be broadly located within a relational approach that seeks to generate public value by building social capital between sectors and recognising the social value added by particular approaches to goods and services provisio.

(p. 97)

As Barraket and Weissman (2009) expand, this means that successful and sustained implementation of social procurement requires more than the judicious application of the technical rules of procurement; it is also dependent on the nature and quality of the relationships between the purchasers and providers. However, Brammer and Walker's (2007) comparative study of national governments revealed that the practice of "... deeply embedded relational processes of procurement ..." (p. 24) were rare, pointing to the need for changes in practise and processes.

Changes in procurement: foci and practices

As we see out the second decade of the 21st century there is a renewed and amplified interest in sustainable procurement at local, national and international levels (Meehan & Bryde, 2011; Lund-Thomsen & Costa, 2011). This is in part being driven by stronger stakeholder pressure for greater transparency of environmental and societal actions, and a growing recognition of the need to secure "best value" rather than "lowest cost" outcomes. These aspects, when coupled with internal drivers for competitiveness through enhanced organizational efficiencies, reduced waste and certainty of supply chain, have led to a more strategic and deliberate use of purchasing and purchasing relationships (Kalubanga, 2012).

Sustainability in the current context therefore refers not just to addressing current economic, social and environmental issues but also to the development and use of mechanisms that look after the future. Thus, sustainable procurement is also centred on advancing the range of processes and decisions that are made in the development of procurement contracts up and down the supply chain. In this way sustainable procurement has somewhat of a developmental orientation and is focused on building sustainability considerations into contracts and supporting activities that encourage and facilitate sustainable outcomes.

Despite its currency, the scope and complexity of sustainable procurement is proving to be a somewhat confusing concept that has been difficult to operationalise, particularly as it draws from three, often distinct, policy domains: state, market and community (McCrudden, 2004; Brammer & Walker, 2007; Lund-Thomsen & Costa, 2011). It has been contended that the fuzziness of the term has implications for the creation of appropriate processes and contracts. Furthermore, a lack of empirical basis to the claims of sustainable procurement is thought to undermine both the term's usefulness and the development of suitable implementation tools (Brammer & Walker, 2007; Lund-Thomsen & Costa, 2011). Partly in response to the need to overcome this implementation issue, the use of procurement to deliver innovations in processes, products and service has resurfaced (Edler & Uyarra, 2013). There is substantial support for the role of innovation in creating both the demand- and supply-side innovations to aid in the procurement of social value (for a review of the contemporary literature on this issue see Rolfstam, Hommen, Edler, Tsipouri & Rigby, 2005; Rolfstam, Phillips & Bakker 2011). These benefits notwithstanding, the designation of public procurement of innovation has not been easy to achieve, with many challenges yet to be overcome in order to provide the suite of alternative mechanisms required to fully implement social or sustainable procurement (Edler & Uyarra, 2013).

This repositioning of procurement from a peripheral to a core strategic function of organisations, requiring both internal and external management (Callender & Matthews, 2000), brings with it changes in the types of skills and competencies needed to function in this new operating environment (HM Treasury, 2010; Goldsmith & Eggers, 2004). Specifically discussing the public sector, but equally relevant in the third-sector arena, Edler and Uyarra (2013) point to a potential lack of leadership, capacity and resources for the procurement function, particularly with respect to the new forms of contracts. Some sectors have been able to respond by introducing improved training and specialist skills development, as well as a growing professionalisation of the role (e.g., Chartered Institute of Purchasing and Supply). For social procurement to function and prosper, capacity and capability must be shared across the supply chain. This shared approach requires a change in current practices and, unless they are internalised across all procurement partners, the aspirations for social/public procurement will not be delivered. In many organizations it likely will not be the lack of procedures and systems that limit social procurement but rather the cultural and behavioural changes that are necessary to go forward together.

Conclusion

The foregoing discussion does not isolate and discuss the full array of drivers and challenges shaping the current context for social procurement or those likely to affect its developments in the future. Nonetheless, the review does show that the current appetite for social procurement is informed and shaped by numerous factors, many of which have their genesis in earlier times and provide part of the foundation for current models. In contemporary society the unprecedented combination of accelerating change, escalating complexity and hyper-connectivity has brought forward new issues to be addressed, requiring new combinations of partners and resources, more hybrid organizational forms and, as a consequence, different sets of skills and behaviours.

This chapter highlights the growing complexity of the operating environment for social procurement and participating actors. In so doing it also reinforces the understanding that contemporary social procurement is no longer an add-on element: it is a strategic and integral part of the social policy and service delivery armoury. In Chapter 3, we examine in greater detail specific developments in social procurement practice in light of this shift.

References

6. P., Leat, D., Seltzer, K., & Stoker, G. (1999). *Governing in the round: Strategies for holistic government*. London: Demos.

Ackoff, R. L. (1974). *Redesigning the future*. New York: Wiley.

Adams, D., & Hess, M. (2001). Community in public policy: Fad or foundation. *Australian Journal of Public Administration, 60*(2), 13–23. doi: 10.1111/1467–8500.00205

Alcock, P. (2010). Building the Big Society: a new policy environment for the third sector in England. *Voluntary Sector Review, 1*(3), 379–389. http://doi.org/10.1332/204080510X538365

Alphonse, M., George, P., & Moffatt, K. (2008). Redefining social work standards in the context of globalization: Lessons from India. *International Social Work, 51*, 145–158. doi: 10.1177/0020872807085855

Arthurson, K., & Jacobs, K. (2004). A critique of the concept of social exclusion and its utility for Australian social housing policy. *Australian Journal of Social Issues, 39*(1), 25–40. Retrieved from: http://search.informit.com.au/documentSummary;dn=837706214763794;res=IELHSS

Association for Research on Non-Profit Organisations and Voluntary Action (ARNOVA). (2010). *Public policy for nonprofits: A report on ARNOVA's symposium of October 2010*. Retrieved from: http://c.ymcdn.com/sites/www.arnova.org/resource/resmgr/Publications/ARNOVA_Symposium_on_Public_P.pdf (Accessed 28th May 2015)

Australian Institute of Health and Welfare (AIHW). (2011). *Australia's welfare 2011: Australia's Welfare Series* (Report No. 10). Canberra, Australia: AIHW.

Australian Institute of Health and Welfare (AIHW) (2013). *Australia's welfare 2013: Australia's Welfare Series* (Report No. 11, Cat. No. AUS 174). Canberra, Australia: AIHW.

Australian Productivity Commission. (2010). *Contribution of the not-for-profit sector: Research report*. Canberra: Australian Productivity Commission.

Barraket, J., & Weissmann, J. (2009). *Social procurement and its implications for social enterprise: A literature review*. (Working Paper No: CPNS 48). Brisbane, Queensland: Queensland University of Technology.

Bauman, Z. (2000). *Liquid modernity.* Cambridge, UK: Polity Press.

Beck, U. (1992). *Risk society: Towards a new modernity.* London: Sage Publications.

Beer, A., Clower, T., Haughton, G., & Maude, A. (2005). Neoliberalism and Institutions for Regional Development in Australia. *Geographical Research, 43*(1), 49–58.

Blond, P. (2009, February). Rise of the Red Tories. *Prospect Magazine,* 32–36. Retrieved from http://www.obamagrams.com/pdf/4c%20-%20Prospect%20-%20P%20Blond%20-%20 2-2009.pdf (Accessed 28th May 2015)

Bovaird, T. (2007). Beyond engagement and participation: User and community co-production of public services. *Public Administration Review, 67*(5), 846–860. doi: 10.1111/j.1540–621 0.2007.00773.x

Brammer, S., & Walker, H. L. (2007). *Sustainable procurement practice in the public sector: An international comparative study.* (Working Paper No. 281). Retrieved from School of Management University of Bath website: http://opus.bath.ac.uk/281/ (Accessed 28th May 2015)

Bryson, J. M. (1988). A strategic planning process for public and nonprofit organizations. *Long Range Planning, 21*(1), 73–81. doi:10.1016/0024–6301(88)90061–1

Brzozowski, M., Gervais, M., Klein, P., & Suzuki, M. (2010). Consumption, income, and wealth inequality in Canada. *Review of Economic Dynamics, 13*(1), 52–75. doi:10.1016/j. red.2009.10.006

Cabinet Office. (2010). *Building the Big Society.* Retrieved from www.gov.uk/government/ uploads/system/uploads/attachment_data/file/78979/building-big-society_0.pdf (Accessed 28th May 2015)

Callender, G., & Matthews, D. L. (2000). Government purchasing: An evolving profession? *Journal of Public Budgeting, Accounting & Financial Management, 12*(2), 272–290.

Cambridge Econometrics and Institute for Employment Research. (2012). *Working futures 2010–2020: Report for the UK commission for employment and skills* (1st ed.). London: Commission for Employment and Skills.

Clarke, M., & Stewart, J. (1997). *Handling the wicked issues: A challenge for government.* In LOGOV Discussion Paper, Institute of Local Government Studies, University of Birmingham.

Conservatives. (2015). *The Conservative party manifesto 2015.* Retrieved from https://s3-eu-west-1.amazonaws.com/manifesto2015/ConservativeManifesto2015.pdf

Daft, R. (2010). *Organization theory and design* (10th ed.). Mason, OH: South-Western Cengage Learning.

de Haan, A. (1998). Social exclusion: An alternative concept for the study of deprivation. *IDS Bulletin, 29*(1), 10–19. doi: 10.1111/j.1759–5436.1998.mp29001002.x

Deloitte. (2009, August). *Agency amalgamation: Our point of view.* New South Wales: Service Delivery.

Department of Broadband, Communication and the Digital Economy (2009). *ICT and the nonprofit sector.* Canberra: Department of Broadband, Communication and the Digital Economy.

Dorling, D., Vickers, D., Thomas, B., Pritchard, J., & Ballas, D. (2008). *Changing UK: The way we live now.* Retrieved from http://sasi.group.shef.ac.uk/research/changingUK.html (Accessed 28th May 2015)

Edgar, D. (2001). *The patchwork nation: Rethinking government – Re-building community.* Pymple, New South Wales: Harper Collins.

Edler, J., & Uyarra, E. (2013). Public procurement of innovation. In S. P. Osborne, & L. Brown (Eds.), *Handbook of innovation in public services* (pp. 224–237). Cheltenham, UK: Routledge.

Elliott, L. (2013, August 19). Ashes to economy: Why Australia may be on the brink of a new collapse. *The Guardian.* Retrieved from www.theguardian.com/world/economics-blog/ 2013/aug/18/ashes-economy-australia-facing-new-collapse (Accessed 28th May 2015)

Erridge, A. (2007). Public procurement, public value and the Northern Ireland unemployment pilot project. *Public Administration, 85*(4), 1023–1043. doi: 10.1111/j.1467–9299.2007.00674.x

European Commission. (1992). *Towards a Europe of solidarity: Intensifying the fight against social exclusion, fostering integration.* Brussels: European Commission.

Fletcher, M. & Guttmann, B. (2013). Income inequality in Australia. *Economic Round-up, 2,* 35–54.

Friendly, M., & Lero, D. S. (2002). *Social inclusion through early childhood education and care.* (Working Paper Series: Perspectives on Social Inclusion).Toronto:The Laidlaw Foundation.

Gottlieb, A (1999). The great disruption: Human nature and the reconstruction of social order. New York: Free Press.

Gerber, E. R. (1999). *The populist paradox: Interest group influence and the promise of direct legislation.* Princeton, New Jersey: Princeton University Press.

Geyer, R. (1999). Can EU social policy save the social exclusion unit and vice versa? *Politics, 19*(3), 159–164. doi: 10.1111/1467–9256.00100

Goldsmith, S., & Eggers, W.D. (2004). *Governing by network: The new shape of the public sector.* Washington, D.C.: Brookings Institution Press.

Hall, P. D. (2011). Historical perspectives on nonprofit organizations in the United States. In R. D. Herman, & Associates (Eds.), *The Jossey-Bass handbook of non-profit leadership and management* (2nd ed., pp. 3–38). San Francisco, CA: Jossey-Bass.

Ham, C. (2012). Competition and integration in health care reform. *International Journal of Integrated Care, 12*(15), e126. Retrieved from www.ncbi.nlm.nih.gov/pmc/articles/PMC3440245/ (Accessed 28th May 2015)

Hardy, C. (1998). *The hungry spirit: Beyond capitalism: A quest for purpose in the modern world.* London: Random House.

Hayes, A., Gray, M., & Edwards, B. (2008). *Social inclusion: Origins, concepts and key themes.* Canberra: Australian Government.

Heathcote, J., Perri, F., & Violante, G.L. (2010). Unequal we stand: An empirical analysis of economic inequality in the United States, 1967–2006. *Review of Economic Dynamics, 13*(1), 15–51. http://doi.org/10.1016/j.red.2009.10.010

Held, D., McGrew, A., Goldblatt, D., & Perraton, J. (1999). *Global transformations: Politics, economics and culture.* Stanford, CA: Stanford University Press.

HM Treasury (2010). *HM Treasury Annual Report and Accounts 2010–2011.* Retrieved from www.gov.uk/government/uploads/system/uploads/attachment_data/file/221559/annual_report_accounts140711.pdf (Accessed 28th May 2015)

Homeshaw, J. (1995). Policy community, policy networks and science policy in Australia. *Australian Journal of Public Administration, 54*(4), 520–532. doi: 10.1111/j.1467–8500.1995.tb01165.x

Islam, M., & Siwar, C. (2013). A comparative study of public sector sustainable procurement practices, opportunities and barriers. *International Review of Business Research Papers, 9*(3), 62–84.

Jackson, E.T. (2013). Evaluating social impact bonds: Questions, challenges, innovations, and possibilities in measuring outcomes in impact investing. *Community Development, 44*(5), 608–616. doi:10.1080/15575330.2013.854258

Joy, M., & Shields, J. (2013). Social impact bonds: The next phase of third sector marketization? *Canadian Journal of Nonprofit and Social Economy Research, 4*(2), 39–55.

Joyce, P., Bryson, J., & Holzer, M. (Eds.) (2014). Introduction. In *Developments in strategic and public management: Studies in the US and Europe* (pp. 1–17). New York: Palgrave Macmillan.

Kalubanga, M. (2012). Sustainable procurement: Concept and practical implications for the procurement process. *International Journal of Economics and Management Sciences, 1*(7), 1–7.

Kanter, R. M. (2003). Thriving locally in the global economy. Harvard Business Review, 81(8), 119–128.

Kazi, T.B. (2011). Superbrands, globalization, and neoliberalism: Exploring causes and consequences of the *Nike* superbrand. *Student Pulse, 3*(12). Retrieved from www.studentpulse.com/articles/604/superbrands-globalization-and-neoliberalism-exploring-causes-and-consequences-of-the-nike-superbrand (Accessed 28th May 2015)

Keast, R.L. (2011). Joined-up governance in Australia: How the past can inform the future. *International Journal of Public Administration, 34*(4), 221–231. doi:10.1080/01900692.2010.549799

Keast, R., Waterhouse, J., Brown, K., & Mandell, M. (2005, August). Hard hats and soft hearts: Relationships and contracts in construction and human services. In *EGPA Conference*.

Keast, R., Waterhouse, J., Murphy, G., & Brown, K. (2011). *Putting it altogether: Design considerations for an integrated homeless services system*. Canberra, Australia: Department of Families, Housing, Community Services and Indigenous Affairs.

Kendall, J., & Knapp, M. (1993). *Defining the nonprofit sector: The United Kingdom*. (Working Paper No. 5). Baltimore, Maryland: The Johns Hopkins Institute of Policy Studies.

Kickert, W. J. M., Klijn, E-H., & Koppenjan, J. F. M. (1997). *Managing complex networks: Strategies for the public sector*. London: Sage Publications.

Kisby, B. (2010). The Big Society: Power to the people? *The Political Quarterly, 81*(4), 484–491. http://doi.org/10.1111/j.1467–923X.2010.02133.x

Koppenjan, J. F. M. (2012). *The new public governance in public service delivery: Reconciling efficiency and quality*. The Hague, Netherlands: Eleven International Publishing.

Labonte, R. N. (2004). Social inclusion/exclusion: Dancing the dialectic. *Health Promotion International, 19*(1), 115–121. doi: 10.1093/heapro/dah112

Labonte, R. N., Hadi, A, & Kauffmann, X. E. (2011). *Indicators of social exclusion and inclusion: A critical and comparative analysis of the literature*. Globalization and Health Equity Research Unit, Institute of Population Health, University of Ottawa EiE Change Working Paper No.2 Vol. 8, November 2011

Lund-Thomsen, P., & Costa, N. (2011). Sustainable procurement in the united nations. *Journal of Corporate Citizenship, 42*(19), 54–72. doi:10.9774/GLEAF. 4700.2011.su.00006

Lyons, M. (2001). *The third sector: The contribution of non-profit and cooperative enterprises in Australia*. Sydney: Allen & Unwin.

MacDermott, K., & Stone, C. (2013). *Death by a thousand cuts: How governments undermine their own productivity*. (Occasional Paper 30). Retrieved from https://cpd.org.au/wp-content/uploads/2013/08/CPD_OP30_Death-by-1000-cuts.pdf (Accessed 28th May 2015)

Mackay, H., & Conn, B. (1993). Reinventing Australia: The mind and mood of Australia in the 90's. Sydney: Angus & Robinson.

Madanipour, A. (1998). Social exclusion and space. In A. Madanipour, G. Car, & J. Allen, (Eds.), *Social exclusion in European cities: Processes, experiences and responses*. London: The Stationary Office.

Matten, D., & Moon, J.A. (2008). 'Implicit' and 'explicit' CSR: A conceptual framework for a comparative understanding of corporate social responsibility. *Academy of Management Review, 33*(2), 404–424. doi:10.5465/AMR.2008.31193458

McBratney, A., & McGregor-Lowndes, M. (2012). 'Fair' government contracts: Time to curb unfettered executive freedom? *Australian Journal of Administrative Law, 19*(1), 19–33.

McCrudden, C. (2004). Using public procurement to achieve social outcomes. *Natural Resources Forum, 28*(4), 257–267. doi: 10.1111/j.1477–8947.2004.00099.x

McCrudden, C. (2007). *Buying social justice: Equality, government and legal change*. Oxford, UK: Oxford University Press.

McCue, C., & Gianakis, G. (2001). Public purchasing: Who is minding the store? *Journal of Public Procurement, 1*(1), 71–95.

McDonald, C. (2006). *Challenging social work: The institutional context of practice*. Houndmills, UK: Palgrave Macmillan.

McHugh, N., Sinclair, S., Roy, M., Huckfield, L., & Donaldson, C. (2013). Social impact bonds: A wolf in sheep's clothing? *Journal of Poverty and Social Justice, 21*(3), 247–257. doi: 10.1332/204674313X13812372137921

McWilliams, A., Siegel, D. S., & Wright, P. M. (2006). *Corporate social responsibility: International perspectives*. (Working paper 0604). Troy, New York: Department of Economics, Rensselaer Polytechnic Institute.

Meehan, J., & Bryde, D. (2011). Sustainable procurement practice. *Business Strategy and the Environment, 20*(2), 94–106. doi: 10.1002/bse.678

OECD. (1996). *Building policy coherence: Tools and tensions*. (Occasional Paper No. 12), Paris: OECD.

OECD. (2007). *Broadband and the economy: Ministerial background report*. (Report DSTI/ICCP/IE(2007)3/FINAL). Retrieved from www.oecd.org/internet/ieconomy/40781696.pdf (Accessed 28th May 2015)

O'Flynn, J. (2009). The cult of collaboration in public policy. *Australian Journal of Public Administration, 68*(1), 112–116. doi: 10.1111/j.1467–8500.2009.00616.x

Olson, S. (2011). *Toward an integrated science of research on families: Workshop report*. Washington, DC: National Academies Press.

Osborne, S. P. (2006). The new public governance. *Public Management Review, 8*(3), 377–387. doi:10.1080/14719030600853022

Osborne, S. P. (2010). *The new public governance: Emerging perspectives on the theory and practice of public governance*. London: Routledge

Oster, S. M. (2003). Executive compensation in the nonprofit sector. *Nonprofit, Management & Leadership, 8*(3), 207–221. doi:10.1002/nml.8301

Ozanne, E., & Rose, D. (2013). *The organisational context of human services practice*. South Yarra, Victoria: Palgrave Macmillan.

Parker-Oliver, D., & Demiris, G. (2006). Social work informatics: A new speciality. *Social Work, 51*(2), 127–134. doi: 10.1093/sw/51.2.127

Parkinson, M. (1998). *Combating social exclusion: Lessons from area-based programmes in Europe*. Bristol, UK: The Policy Press.

Pearson, N. (1999). Positive and negative welfare and Australia's indigenous communities. *Family Matters, 54*(Spring/Summer), 30–35.

Percy-Smith, J. (2000). *Policy responses to social exclusion: Towards inclusion?* Maidenhead, UK: Open University Press.

Pestoff, V., Brandsen, T., & Verschuere, B. (2012). *New public governance: The third sector and co-production*. London: Routledge

Petrella, R. (1996). Globalisation and internationalisation. In R. Boyer, & D. Drache, (Eds.), *States against markets: The limits of globalization* (pp. 776–777). London: Routledge.

Phillips, R. (2007). Tamed or trained? The co-option and capture of 'favoured' NGOs. *Third Sector Review, 13*(2), 27–48.

Plunkett Foundation and Carnegie UK Trust (2012). *Rural broadband: Reframing the debate*. Retrieved from http://www.carnegieuktrust.org.uk/publications/2012/rural-broadband-reframing-the-debate (Accessed 28th May 2015)

Queensland Government (2007). *Sparse state: The death of distance*. Queensland Smart State Council Report, Office of the Chief Scientist November, Brisbane Queensland.

Retrieved from www.chiefscientist.qld.gov.au/images/documents/chiefscientist/reports/sparse-state.pdf (Accessed 28th May 2015)

Rhodes, R. A. W. (1996). The new governance: Governing without government. *Political Studies, 44*(4), 652–667. doi: 10.1111/j.1467–9248.1996.tb01747.x

Rittel, H. W. J., & Webber, M. M. (1973). Dilemmas in a general theory of planning. *Policy Science, 4*(2), 155–169. doi:10.1007/bf01405730

Rolfstam, M., Hommen, L., Edler, J., Tsipouri, L., & Rigby, J. (2005). *Literature review: Innovation and public procurement: Review of issues.* Retrieved from ftp://ftp.cordis.europa.eu/pub/innovation-policy/studies/chapter2_literature_review.pdf (Accessed 28th May 2015)

Rolfstam, M., Phillips, W., & Bakker, E. (2011). Public procurement and the diffusion of innovations: Exploring the role of institutions and institutional coordination. *International Journal of Public Sector Management, 24*(5), 452–468. doi:10.1108/09513551111147178

Rose, N. (1999). *Powers of freedom: Reframing political thought.* Cambridge, NY: Cambridge University Press.

Roy, M.J., Donaldson, C., Baker, R., & Kay, A. (2013). Social enterprise: New pathways to health and well-being? *Journal of Public Health Policy, 34*(1), 55–68. http://doi.org/http://dx.doi.org.ezp01.library.qut.edu.au/10.1057/jphp.2012.61

Ryan, N. (2001). Reconstructing citizens as consumers: Implications for new modes of governance. *Australian Journal of Public Administration, 60*(3), 104–109. doi: 10.1111/1467–8500.00229

Ryan, W. (1999). The new landscape for nonprofits. *Harvard Business Review, 77*(1), 127–136.

Ryan, W. (Ed.). (2003). *Intervention Logic Policy Network Conference,* Wellington, New Zealand, 30–31 January.

Sen, A. (2000). *Social exclusion: Concept, application and scrutiny.* (Social Development Papers No. 1). Manila: Asian Development Bank.

Schui, F. (2014). *Austerity: The great failure.* New Haven, CT: Yale University Press.

Scott, M. (2011). Reflections on the Big Society. *Community Development Journal, 46*(1), 132–137. http://doi.org/10.1093/cdj/bsq057

Shucksmith, M. (2012). *Future directions in rural development?* Report prepared for Carnegie UK Trust. Retrieved from www.ruralnetworkni.org.uk/download/files/pub_Future%20directions%20in%20RD%20Carnegie%20UK%20Report.pdf (Accessed 28th May 2015)

Silver, H. (1994). Social exclusion and social solidarity: Three paradigms. *International Labour Review, 133,* 531–578.

Silver, H. (2010). Understanding social inclusion and its meaning for Australia, *Australian Journal of Social Issues, 45*(2), 183–211.

Sommerville, P. (1998). Explanations of social exclusion: Where does housing fit in? *Housing Studies, 13*(6), 761–780. doi:10.1080/02673039883056

Stewart, J. (2002). Horizontal coordination: How far have we gone and how far can we go? The Australian View. *The Public Interest,* 21–26.

Stoker, G. (1998). Governance as theory: Five propositions. *International Social Sciences Journal, 50*(155), 17–28. doi: 10.1111/1468–2451.00106

Thompson, J. (2011). Reflections on social enterprise and the Big Society. *Social Enterprise Journal, 7*(3), 219–223. http://doi.org/10.1108/17508611111182377

Tierney, L. (1970). Social policy. In A. F. Davis, & S. Encel, (Eds.), *Australian Society* (2nd ed., pp. 200–223). Melbourne: Cheshire.

United Nations. (1995, March 6–12). *Report on the World Summit for Social Development.* Copenhagen, Denmark. Retrieved from www.un.org/documents/ga/conf166/aconf166–9.htm (Accessed 28th May 2015)

Van Dijk, J., & Hacker, K. (2003). The digital divide as a complex and dynamic phenomenon. *The Information Society, 19*(4), 315–326. doi:10.1080/01972240309487

Van Lange, P. A. M., De Cremer, D., Van Dijk, E., & Van Vugt, M. (2007). Self-interest and beyond: Basic principles of social interaction. In A. Kruglanski, & E. Higgins, (Eds.), *Social psychology: Handbook of basic principles* (2nd ed.) (pp. 540–561). New York: Guilford.

Walker, D., & Hampson, K. (2008). *Procurement strategies: A relationship-based approach*. Oxford, UK: Blackwell Publishing.

Walsh, P. (1993). Welfare policy. In B. Stevens, & J. Wanna (Eds.), *Goss government: Promise and performance of labor in Queensland* (pp. 215–225). South Melbourne: Maccmillan.

Williams, Z. (2012). *Social enterprise UK: The shadow state*. Report prepared for Social Enterprise United Kingdom.

3 Historical and contemporary developments in social procurement[1]

Introduction

As discussed in the introduction to this volume, social procurement is not new, but it is receiving renewed attention, resulting in emerging practices in the context of new public governance (NPG). Developments in policy and practice are, of course, underpinned by wider socio-economic and political drivers, as discussed in some detail in Chapter 2. In this chapter, we trace the history of social procurement in more specific terms and provide an overview of contemporary approaches. The purpose of this discussion is to outline the diversity of practices consistent with social procurement and their underpinning logics and to consider, where possible, the effects of emerging approaches on the production of social value.

Early history of procuring for social outcomes: differential approaches

Throughout history there have always been those who are less able, disadvantaged, and disconnected or needy; along with them came the associated societal actions to ameliorate barriers to their social or economic participation. Early responsibility for the care of the disadvantaged fell to families, feudal-lords, local communities or local parish churches. Between the 12th to 16th centuries a range of social upheavals occurred, such as land foreclosures, wars and the Industrial Revolution, which were clearly outside the capacity of individual philanthropy or local charities and stimulated some nation states to develop more organised systems of poverty relief, commencing with the British Poor Laws (1573), which focused on addressing the needs of the "worthy poor" (Fraser, 1973; Ware, 1989). To address the needs of the poor not accommodated by the state, a range of charitable and philanthropic movements gradually emerged across much of the Western world (Kendall & Knapp, 1993), including mutual-aid bodies such as Friendly Societies and cooperatives. While retaining many of the characteristics core to philanthropy and communitarianism, unsurprisingly the dissimilar political and social contexts generated differentiation in the models adopted (Tierney, 1970; Epsing-Andersen, 1990; Kendall & Knapp,

1993). These voluntary bodies provided direct services to people in need of social support and were largely autonomous in their operation, with very limited, if any, government financial sponsorship (Graycar, 1979; Kendall & Knapp, 1993; Brown & Keast, 2005; Hall, 2005).

From the mid-19th to 20th centuries a stronger and more deliberate use was made of public procurement as a mechanism to address growing social policy objectives, particularly unemployment and poor workplace conditions, which were seen as major threats to social cohesion. McCrudden (2004) observes that public works provided through government contracts were used to address the increased levels of unemployment at this time. Notably, these initiatives were focused predominantly on national issues of employment protection for working men, and generally overlooked the needs of more marginalised groups such as women, children and the disadvantaged, who were seen to be the responsibility of "the community" (Martin, 1996; McCrudden, 2004; Schulten, Alsos, Burgess & Pedersen, 2012). Over time, the application of public procurement to social objectives became more widespread; moving beyond working conditions to include broader employment and social issues and increasingly being used to stimulate local and regional development (McCrudden, 2004, 2007; Schulten et al., 2012). In addition, government procurement was extended to the purchase of a range of social support commodities provided by the growing not-for-profit sector and this contributed to the foundations for the so-called welfare state (Tierney, 1970; Fraser, 1973; Kendall & Knapp, 1993).

The rise of new social movements (Habermas, 1981) in the 1960s played a defining role in advancing affirmative action policies linked to new approaches to social procurement. In the United States, the civil rights movement in particular galvanised legislative developments that supported the establishment of affirmative action policies, including set-asides for so-called minority businesses in government contracting (McCrudden, 2004, 2007). The linking of government contracting to socio-economic participation goals of affirmative action gained ground in other jurisdictions, such as Canada, where the Federal Contractors Programme, which came into effect in 1986, made employment equity commitments binding upon government contractors at both the federal and provincial levels (McCrudden, 2004). The association between affirmative action and public procurement policies was not immediately taken up in jurisdictions outside North America, with supplier diversity initiatives a relatively new phenomenon in places such as the UK, Australia and South Africa (Ram & Smallbone, 2003; Rogerson, 2012; Theodorakopoulos, Ram, Shah & Boyal, 2005). Concurrent with advances in supplier diversity initiatives was the rise of the fair trade movement, which focused less on the state and more on improving the social conditions of economic production across increasingly globalised markets (Jaffee, 2012). As we will see in Chapter 5, civil society and the private for-profit sector have played substantial roles in transferring both policy and practice related to supplier diversity initiatives from North America to other parts of the world, while ethical consumption movements have been significant in influencing corporate citizenship.

The ongoing expansion of the welfare state and the third sector, coupled with their perceived failure to resolve social issues and global economic constraints, led to a growing consensus during the 1970s and 1980s on both sides of the political spectrum that the welfare state model was no longer economically or morally viable (Emy, 1993). Informed by the emergent new public management (NPM) ethos, grants-based procurement approaches gave way to privatisation, contracting and deregulation. For many, the application of competition to social service provision was problematic: fragmenting both service delivery and sectorial relationships, eroding the social fabric of the community (Funnel, 2001), undermining the ethos of public duty and service (Denhardt & Denhardt, 2000) and delivering few perceivable benefits to the social sector (6, Leat, Seltzer & Stoker, 1999). Nonetheless, contracting has become a cornerstone of current government procurements, while at the same time policy makers seek to draw upon the "integrative" benefits of collaborative and relational contracting mechanisms to mitigate the negative impacts of competition (O'Flynn, 2009; Pestoff, 2006).

Over the next 20 years, the incorporation of socio-economic and increasingly environmental goals into public procurement processes was commonplace at the local, national and international levels (McCrudden, 2004, 2007; Brammer & Walker, 2007). In addition to direct social service delivery and affirmative action imperatives, the scope of these initiatives has expanded to cover international development, the rise of social enterprises and regional development initiatives.

The early 1990s saw the advance of so-called green procurement strategies. Recognising that environmental risks transcend nation-state boundaries (Beck, 1992), environmental sustainability commitments have been legitimised and enabled through transnational institutions, such as the United Nations, with the 1992 Agenda 21 action plan for sustainable development becoming a key stimulus. Green procurement centres on identifying and procuring environmentally preferable products that make an appreciable contribution to environmental protection and that support environmental sustainability (Kunzlik, 2003). Many governments have subsequently introduced related procurement policies (Murray, 2000; Chave, 2003). Although green procurement has manifest as a policy commitment at all levels of government, practise has been particularly prevalent amongst local governments, explicitly linked to supporting the fulfilment of Agenda 21 commitments at the local level. Recent interest in social procurement has raised questions about potential conflict between social and environmental objectives (McCrudden, 2004), suggesting further complexity for governments seeking to balance regulatory, commercial and socio-economic procurement objectives (Erridge, 2007).

Towards the end of the 1990s, efforts to address the need for integration of fiscal management as well as social, environmental, and economic development objectives led to interest in sustainable development and its procurement mechanisms (Meehan & Bryde, 2010; Lund-Thomsen & Costa, 2011; Islam & Siwar, 2013). Brammer and Walker (2007, p. 4) identified that the purpose of sustainable procurement was to direct equal attention to social, economic and environmental aspects to ". . . secure a strong, healthy and just society, living within environmental limits". The first sustainable procurement standard – BS8903 – was established by the UK national standards body in 2010 and provides guidance on procurement approaches that consider the environmental, social and economic consequences of design, manufacture, logistics, delivery and disposal and suppliers' capacities in relation to these at all stages in the supply chain (ECO-buy, 2012). In addition to environmental objectives, sustainable procurement codes of practice have given rise to early emphases – particularly by local governments – on local economic development through purchasing from local businesses, as well as promoting ethical supply chains through fair trade purchasing where allowable under existing legislation (Preuss, 2009). In the UK, these developments also included the introduction of community benefit clauses, whereby socio-economic criteria are inserted into supply contracts and/or preferred purchasing from third-sector organisations or social enterprises (Preuss, 2009).

Social procurement objectives are clearly embedded within sustainable procurement frameworks. However, the influence of governance approaches that are concerned with reclaiming "the social" through networked activity, combined with challenges of contemporary social service delivery and strong advocacy from third-sector and social enterprise providers in some jurisdictions have given rise to a discourse on social procurement as a distinct domain of policy and practice. Each of these developments has informed the use of procurement approaches and instruments that sit alongside and supplement traditional models. In the following section, we consider some of these approaches and instruments, recognising – in keeping with our historical overview just presented – that some of these approaches are not new but are being reclaimed as part of a new discourse of social procurement.

Approaches to social procurement

There is a range of approaches to social procurement within the public sector and by private actors. These approaches vary in their levels of formality and reach. In 2007, Erridge (2007, p. 1027) noted that there had been relatively few formally structured public procurement projects that sought to fulfil socio-economic goals within the bounds of regulatory and commercial requirements, and limited documentation and dissemination of those projects that had been attempted. More recent literature suggests growth in practice – see, for example, Preuss, (2009) – although its documentation remains limited. Here, we provide an overview of some of the better-documented examples of purposeful approaches to social procurement, providing case study material and examples. This overview is not exhaustive, given the diversity of jurisdictional environments in which social procurement operates and the recent rapid growth of practice across world regions. Our purpose here is to provide some concrete examples that ground our discussion of social procurement and illuminate practical and conceptual issues to which we return in greater depth in subsequent chapters.

Bovaird (2006) identifies that emerging models of governance have influenced public procurement processes, stimulating new approaches that seek to resolve tensions between market-based service provision and the increasing need to add public value through both the process and outputs of public service delivery. He suggests that these approaches are stimulated by moves towards more collaborative work within public agencies and between public commissioners and private providers, combined with increasing complexity of multi-actor arrangements within procurement processes. In addition to acknowledging traditional transactional contracting arrangements, Bovaird (2006) proposes a typology of three new types of market relationships within the public procurement repertoire. These include: relational contracting, based on longer-term partnership arrangements embedded in contracts; partnership procurement, involving multiple providers and widening the distribution of risk; and, distributed commissioning, where a public-sector purchaser enables smaller agencies to determine service priorities that will be provided to them through the purchaser's budget (Bovaird, 2006, p. 85). While Bovaird's typology focuses on public procurement and is not confined to social value creation, it is useful as a starting point for classifying established and emerging approaches to social procurement. We have thus adapted it for our discussion, which follows. We note, however, that traditional contracting, characterised by ". . . a single commissioner of a service placing contracts with a range of providers for its services . . . based on an explicit specification of the service and performance criteria" (Bovaird, 2006, p. 83) remains a feature of social procurement and is thus incorporated into our discussion. We also note that a complement to developing new procurement processes and instruments is the cultural development required to legitimise new practices. We thus commence our review of emerging and established practice with a brief discussion of norm development.

Development of standards, guidelines and norms

As intimated in our historical review presented earlier in this chapter, the development of standards and norms – through legislation or legitimation of "best practice" – plays a considerable role in the adoption of social procurement across all sectors. This is discussed in some detail in relation to institutionalisation of social procurement in Chapter 4 and with regard to measuring social value in Chapter 7.

Supranational governmental and transnational civil society organisations, including the United Nations, the European Commission, and the International Standards Organisation (ISO) play an important function in the adoption of social procurement agendas. At the national level, the UK has been purposefully active in establishing leadership first in sustainable procurement and then in social procurement since the late 1990s (Preuss, 2007; Preuss, 2009). In the mid-2000s, the UK's Office of the Third Sector commissioned research into the barriers to including community benefit clauses into procurement contracts, as part of their Partnership in Public Services action plan for third-sector involvement. In 2008, the Social Clauses Project was established to "consolidate knowledge on the existing use and best practice of social clauses, provide clarity on the merits of using social clauses, and support good commissioning and procurement by producing user friendly materials to help decision makers" (Office of the Third Sector, 2008, p. 3).

The Scottish Procurement Directorate has produced a guidance note for public procurement professionals that provides concise advice to procurement officers on the "how to", "when" and "why" behind incorporating social issues into procurement practice (see Scottish Procurement Directorate 2007). These guidelines have been adapted to or have informed publications in a variety of jurisdictions, including being adapted transnationally by the European Commission (2010), and domestically by Australian state governments in New South Wales, Victoria and Western Australia. In terms of legislation, the UK Public Services (Social Value) Act 2012 has played a leading role in legislating social procurement standards, although these are largely discretionary in nature (Cabinet Office, 2015).

In a globalised environment where the reach of corporate practice exceeds national regulation, civil society networks play a substantial role in regulating and certifying practice related to social procurement and ethical purchasing standards (Jaffee, 2012; Ram, Theodorakopoulos, & Worthington, 2007). At the domestic level, the growth of hybrid social benefit providers – such as social enterprises and profit-for-purpose social businesses, which may be difficult to distinguish because they operate under a variety of legal forms – has also generated new imperatives for certification and quality assurance of their social value credentials. As discussed in Chapters 4, 5 and 7, these trends have given rise to civil society intermediaries and certification initiatives such as the National Minority Supplier Development Council in the United States, Supply Nation in Australia, and the Social Enterprise Mark in the UK, that play a substantial role in legitimising corporate practice and/or social-benefit providers whose roles are central to social procurement practices, discussed later. National and regional initiatives led by third-sector intermediaries, such as Buy Social Canada (http://buysocialcanada.ca/) and Social Procurement Australasia (http://socialprocurementaustralasia.com/), seek to promote practice by providing information resources and links to social procurement opportunities. Local civil society initiatives also play a role, quite literally, in mediating social procurement by connecting demand and supply through navigator functions. One such example is the Winnipeg Social Purchasing Portal in Canada (www.sppwinnipeg.org/), which provides an online directory and network that links prospective social procurers with social benefit suppliers in the local area.

Using traditional contracting to procure social value

As previously described, traditional contracting processes are characterised by a single purchaser competitively securing services from one or more providers based on pre-specified criteria. Early approaches to the new wave of social procurement sought to adapt traditional contracting processes and instruments so as to generate social value through the inclusion of public or community benefit clauses alongside core purposes of contracts, particularly in the development of public works. This approach to social procurement is typically positioned discursively within orthodox legal frameworks of providing greatest value for money, with social value simply a weighted criterion in the procurement process. Community benefit clauses may include criteria related to particular socio-economic outcomes, such as increased employment opportunities for people disadvantaged in the labour market, as well as social supplier diversity objectives that seek to ensure that social benefit providers, such as social enterprises, have increased participation in the delivery of public contracts. The use of public or community benefit clauses has been popularised in the UK since the early 2000s (Preuss, 2009). It has also become common in recent procurement activities of major public events, including the 2010 Vancouver Olympic Games, the 2014 Commonwealth Games in Glasgow and the 2015 Pan AM and Parapan AM Games in Toronto (LePage, 2014). However, preferred purchasing from excluded social groups and stimulation of supplier diversity through set-aside clauses in public contracts has a substantially longer history in North America, as noted in our historical overview presented earlier (McCrudden, 2004).

The Northern Ireland Unemployment Pilot Project, which formed part of a wider initiative to advance local social and economic objectives through public procurement, incorporated a contractual requirement that suppliers include within their bid an employment plan for including registered unemployed people to work on the contract. The initiative involved 15 government contracts from seven departments ranging in value from £700 000 to £8.5 million (Erridge, 2007). In an analysis of the pilot outcomes, Erridge (2007) found that it produced net job growth of 51 new positions – with 90% of participants remaining in employment at the time of the research – while adhering to standards of propriety and transparency in the letting of contracts and achieving economic efficiencies compared with other public contracts in similar industries.

In the Australian state of Victoria, The Public Tenant Employment Program (PTEP) "provides public housing tenants with opportunities such as accredited training to develop skills, confidence and qualifications and connects people to vacancies that lead to full and/or part time employment" (State Government of Victoria, 2009). The Victorian Office of Housing has developed a public housing tenant employment target, which requires that a proportion of the workforce delivering some public housing contracts are public housing tenants. The clause forms part of the award criteria of $100 million worth of public housing contracts in the areas of cleaning, security and property maintenance. Since 2003, this clause has created sustainable employment opportunities for hundreds of public housing tenants to obtain ongoing work (Social Traders, n.d., p. 2).

These are just two examples of embedding socio-economic goals in traditional contracts, both in the context of public procurement. As already noted, traditional contracting instruments have also been adapted to expand socio-economic benefits of procurement by stimulating both organisational and socio-cultural diversity within supply chains.

Relational and partnership commissioning approaches

While Bovaird (2006) treats relational and partnership approaches to commissioning as distinct categories, we find in the context of social procurement that these are often indivisible or operate along a continuum. As such, we elect here to discuss these two approaches together.

Beyond embedding community benefit clauses in traditional contracts, emerging approaches to social procurement have extended to relational purchasing from specified providers through preferred purchasing, social tendering, and related joint venture models. Preferred purchasing arrangements may be embedded in (private or public sector) organisational policy and relate to purposefully providing preference to particular providers in routine purchasing decisions. Depending on the social value that the purchaser seeks to generate, these providers may include local micro and small businesses, minority- or women-owned suppliers, social enterprises or privately certified socially responsible businesses, such as B Corporations.

Social tendering describes negotiated tendering with social benefit providers, and involves tailoring procurement opportunities to the competencies of these providers. This can involve: co-design of contracts with prospective social benefit suppliers; disaggregation of large contracts to make available smaller components to social benefit providers; and exclusive letting of larger contracts to specified providers, such as social enterprises (Burkett, 2010). Social tendering is used to stimulate markets for diverse providers by generating reliable income streams and establishing track record in supplying government purchasers. As Burkett & Langdon (2005) note, social tendering can be used to fulfil service obligations where particular tasks required by government purchasers are not economical for large-scale enterprises to provide. The use of social tendering varies across jurisdictions, partly because of legal constraints arising from national and regional competition policies. These are discussed in some detail in Chapter 4.

In some cases, social tendering arrangements may extend to more embedded partnership models, including joint venture approaches to respond to complex social challenges. One such documented example from Australia (see Burkett, 2010) is a joint venture between a Victorian local government, Yarra City Council (YCC), and a large charitable organisation, the Brotherhood of St Laurence (BSL). Faced with three seemingly unrelated challenges – social problems on the local housing estates, an ageing workforce and lack of demand for jobs for social council jobs, and quality problems with a large-scale cleaning contract that was coming to an end – YCC and BSL co-developed a response by creating a joint venture to establish a street sweeping enterprise that met quality needs of the council and provided pathways to employment for disadvantaged local residents. This approach involved several discrete elements related to the procurement process, including introducing variations to existing contracts, applying for an exemption to local government tendering requirements and establishing a memorandum of understanding between the parties that specified and provided conditions for monitoring the commercial and social outcomes of the initiative (Burkett, 2010). Early evaluative research of this case found that outcomes of the initiative included innovation within the council's own service delivery, as they integrated some aspects of the employment creation approach into other aspects of their work (Archer & Barraket, 2009), improved employment opportunities and pathways to employment for local residents, and increased commercial service quality arising from a more diverse supplier market (Burkett, 2010). While this case illuminates the possibilities of such partnership approaches, a dearth of documented evidence of either the practice or its effects makes it challenging to evaluate its reach or effectiveness.

Relational and partnership approaches have also given rise to new commissioning instruments, such as social impact bonds (also referred to as "pay for success" and "social benefit" bonds), that seek to maximise social innovation and/or distribute financial risk through cross-sector partnership responses to service delivery. In brief, social impact bonds are used to leverage up-front capital investments by ". . . private [for profit], philanthropic and/or public investors to . . . support project-oriented service delivery by public, private, or nonprofit actors, or a combination of these actors" (Joy & Shields, 2013, p. 40). Based on an outcomes-based payment model, social impact bonds rely on an intermediary that brokers the arrangement through which investors can recoup their capital investment (which typically resides with the third-sector service provider), as well as an additional financial return – which may vary from an agreed maximum percentage through to nothing – based on achievement of agreed results (McHugh, Sinclair, Roy, Huckfield & Donaldson, 2013). Initiated in 2010 in England, a small number of social impact bonds have now been executed in the United States, Canada, the Netherlands, Germany, Belgium and Australia (Bridges Impact+, 2014) They have been used to finance a variety of preventative and remedial interventions, including those focused on (re)offending and impacts of incarceration rates, economic participation of people highly disadvantaged in the labour market, public health management responses, and family strength and related impacts on foster care systems. Still in their early stages of implementation, social impact bonds have to date returned no or low returns to investors, based on social outcomes achieved. Early literature on the rise of social impact bonds warns that possible negative impacts on social value creation include the erosion of diversity and innovative capacity within the third sector as smaller organisations become less viable in the face of instruments that favour professionalised and large-scale providers (Joy & Shields, 2013), and the possible lost opportunities for community engagement and service co-design of financing models that concentrate on private capital markets (McHugh et al.,

2013). While the social impact bond is a novel financial instrument, the extent to which it advances (or erodes) social value creation remains largely unknown.

Distributed commissioning approaches

Distributed commissioning through local agencies has been a hallmark characteristic of rural area–based initiatives (ABIs) in the UK for many years (Bovaird, 2006). Under the Blair Government in the late 1990s, this approach gained greater prominence as part of the New Deal for Communities in metropolitan and metropolitan fringe locales, with the establishment of local governance arrangements to administer devolved funding in pursuit of social policy goals. There is an extensive literature on the outcomes and limitations of distributed procurement associated with ABIs in the UK during this period (see, for example, Raco, Parker & Doak, 2006; McCulloch, 2004; Geddes, 2006; Lawless, 2006; Davies, 2007). In one case study of the Caterham Barracks Community Trust, Bovaird (2006, p. 91) found that the Trust played a major role in the co-production of higher quality of life, both in its own neighbourhood and the wider district. However, two regularly cited concerns about distributed procurement within the UK ABI context are: the non-democratic nature and lack of public accountability of local partnerships empowered with decision-making over the allocation of public monies (Geddes, 2006; McCulloch, 2004; Raco, et al. 2006), and the limited potential for strong socio-economic outcomes where local decisions are bound by centrally determined performance indicators (Lawless, 2006; Geddes, 2006).

Distributed or partnership-based commissioning has taken a new turn in the UK with the advent of the Public Services (Social Value) Act 2012. This legislation has provided impetus for the development of joint social value strategies involving place-based cross-sector partnerships working in discussion with local residents to determine priority goals for socio-economic development. Similar developments are occurring in Australia. These approaches are considered in further detail in Chapter 7.

Another distributed commissioning approach is the lead agency model, which involves one organisation serving as a principal contractor and one or more other organisations functioning as subcontractors. The underpinning logic is that socio-economic objectives will be more effectively fulfilled where service delivery and inter-agency coordination are decentralised (Lawther & Martin, 2005, p. 218). In an example of the application of the lead agency in family services provision in the US counties of Orange and Osceola documented by Lawther & Martin (2005), it was found that socio-economic outcomes were better achieved because smaller agencies acting as subcontractors were relieved of some of their administrative functions and thus able to concentrate on high-quality service delivery. This study also found that the lead agency acted not just as a head contractor, but also became a change agent that brought more local partners and resources to the table to develop effective responses to child welfare in the region (Lawther & Martin, 2005, p. 219). Although this case demonstrates the potential benefits of the lead agency approach, it should be noted that, in some cases, the lead agency model has been found to reduce social innovation where large organisations become dominant at the expense of a diversity of providers in service delivery, and where network closure arises from preferred subcontracting (Productivity Commission, 2010).

New approaches to social procurement: benefits and limitations

Two presumed benefits of emerging emphases on social procurement are articulated in the available policy and practitioner literature. The first is the potential of procurement to stimulate social innovation; that is, new ideas with the potential to improve either the quality or the quantity of life (Pol & Ville, 2009, p. 881). The second presumed benefit is that social procurement can produce greater value for public spend by simultaneously fulfilling commercial and socio-economic procurement objectives. With regard to stimulating social innovation, Edler and Georghiou (2007, p. 949) suggest that "Public demand, when oriented towards innovative solutions and products, has the potential to improve delivery of public policy and services, often generating improved innovative dynamics and benefits from the associated spillovers". They particularly explore the demand-side as a driver to fuel innovation. Edler and Georghiou (2007, p. 956) suggest that public procurement has the advantage of achieving critical mass, which diminishes market risk for suppliers, enabling early economies of scale and learning. They also argue that public procurement can lower the transaction costs of adapting to new products, by implementing or demonstrating the use of an innovation and signalling its functionalities to the private market. This can build trust and interest in innovative products and establish meaningful standards for their use (Edler and Georghiou, 2007, p. 957).

Barlow and Köberle-Gaiser (2008), however, argue that not all relational models of public procurement offer innovation and efficiency benefits. They dispute Edler and Georghiou's (2007) premise based on an analysis of six cases within a private finance initiative (PFI) to operate and procure new National Health Service (NHS) hospitals in the UK, which have the stated purpose of stimulating service innovation through public procurement. They found that innovation was constrained in the cases they studied in two ways. First, risk allocation by commissioning authorities resulted in highly prescriptive project specifications from the outset, which minimised the flexibility required to negotiate innovative responses to hospital design and construction. Second, they found that strict separation between the project delivery (of hospital infrastructure) and the clinical operational side limited interactions between designers and end users (Barlow & Köberle-Gaiser, 2008, p. 1400). This research also found that the scale of the initiatives, which involved one-off hospital infrastructure development in a series of locales, led to limited diffusion of innovation through inter-project learning, with only one project in six conducting a detailed post-project evaluation. Finally, this study found that differences in organisational culture between private and public sectors limited innovation, with research respondents particularly identifying risk averseness and lack of creative thinking within the public sector as an inhibitor (Barlow & Köberle-Gaiser, 2008, p. 1398).

Barlow and Köberle-Gaiser's (2008) research suggests that the potential of a PFI to stimulate social innovation is in part contingent upon the approach to contract design. This finding is reinforced by Bovaird's (2006) case study analysis of the use of a PFI to administer revenues and benefits within a local authority. Reflecting on the apparent success of this case, he notes that:

> The explicit design of the contract to ensure that both parties would commit fully to the co-production – at both planning and implementation phases – of a new service configuration, was rewarded with a much more innovative set of behaviours than is typical in such collaborations between public and private sectors.
>
> (Bovaird 2006, p. 88)

These examples focused on the possible impacts of public procurement on social innovation in general terms. The available empirical literature on procurement relations between social enterprise and governments has noted threats to innovation where social enterprises' revenue streams are heavily reliant on government contracts (Aiken, 2006; Spear & Bidet, 2005). As these studies suggest, over-reliance on sources of revenue arising from monopsony (single purchaser) clients can inhibit the potential of social enterprises to be socially innovative where it leaves them economically vulnerable or subject to capture by governmental agendas not consistent with their own missions.

Beyond stimulating social innovation, the presumption that new approaches to social procurement can achieve relatively greater socio-economic outcomes than more traditional models remains constrained by lack of evidence. This in part reflects the newness of practice, with sufficient scale of measurable outcomes yet to be produced. It also reflects the amorphous nature of social value itself and the measurability challenges of assessing intangible value. This subject is discussed in detail in Chapter 7.

Conclusion

In this chapter, we have presented an overview of historical and contemporary developments in social procurement. We have observed that various approaches to social procurement have their origins in collective actions of civil society, alongside the establishment of the welfare state and subsequent advances in governance and public management frameworks that nominally seek to generate social value through public purchasing. Recent approaches to social procurement reflect wider trends in NPG, including imperatives to improve social innovation through more relational approaches to governing, and to distribute risk and leverage non-governmental resources through cross-sector activity. An observable tension in the available evidence of new approaches lies between efforts to improve effectiveness through improving social outcomes and achieving efficiencies of social spending that may, in some cases, decrease overall effectiveness. We have also noted that civil society and supranational governance actors play a significant role in navigating and legitimising new approaches to social value creation through procurement in a complex environment where hybrid models of provision are gaining ascendancy and regulation associated with global economic production exceeds domestic frameworks. Legitimacy formation plays a substantial role in developing new areas of practice or emerging institutional fields. We now turn in more detail to the institutional and resource enablers that inform such developments in social procurement.

Note

1   Parts of this chapter are drawn from Barraket & Weissman (2009).

References

6. P., Leat, D, Seltzer, K., & Stoker, G. (1999). *Governing in the round: Strategies for holistic government*. London: Demos.

Aiken, M. (2006). Towards market or state?: Tensions and opportunities in the evolutionary path of three UK social enterprises. In M. Nyssens, (Ed.), *Social enterprise: At the crossroads of market, public policies and civil society* (pp. 259–271). London: Routledge.

Archer, V., & Barraket, J. (2009). *Economic participation for health: an information and resource guide for local governments working with community enterprise*. Melbourne: Centre for Public Policy.

Barlow, J., & Köberle-Gaiser, M. (2008). The private finance initiative, project form and design innovation: The UK's hospitals programme. *Research Policy, 37*(8), 1392–1402. doi:10.1016/j.respol.2008.04.027

Barraket, J., & Weissman, J. (2009). *Social procurement and its implications for social enterprise: A literature review*. (Working Paper No: CPNS 48). Brisbane, Queensland: Queensland University of Technology.

Beck, U. (1992). *Risk society: Towards a new modernity*. London: Sage Publications.

Bovaird, T. (2006). Developing new forms of partnership with the "market" in the procurement of public services. *Public Administration, 84*(1), 81–102. doi: 10.1111/j.0033-3298.2006.00494.x

Brammer, S., & Walker, H. (2007). *Sustainable procurement practice in the public sector: An international comparative study*, School of Management Working Paper Series, University of Bath, United Kingdom.

Bridges Impact+. (2014). *Choosing social impact bonds: A practitioner's guide*. Bridges Ventures LLP. Retrieved from www.bridgesventures.com/wp-content/uploads/2014/10/ChoosingSocialImpactBonds_APractitionersGuide.pdf (Accessed 28th May 2015)

Brown, K., & Keast, R. (2005). Social services policy and delivery in Australia: Centre-periphery mixes. *Policy and Politics, 33*(3), 505–518. doi:http://dx.doi.org/10.1332/0305573054325774

Burkett, I. (2010). *Social procurement in Australia: A compendium of case studies*. Centre for Social Impact, Foresters Community Finance, Social Traders, Parramatta City Council, Victoria State Government, and Brisbane City. Retrieved from www.parracity.nsw.gov.au/__data/assets/pdf_file/0019/80128/SocialProcurementinAustralia-CaseStudyCompendium.pdf (Accessed 28th May 2015)

Burkett, I., & Langdon, D. (2005). *Social enterprise & social tendering: A guide for government departments, large social welfare organisations and corporations*. Palmwoods, Queensland: New Mutualism Group.

Cabinet Office. (2015). *Social value act review*. Retrieved from www.gov.uk/government/uploads/system/uploads/attachment_data/file/403748/Social_Value_Act_review_report_150212.pdf (Accessed 28th May 2015)

Chave, J. (2003). EU public procurement takes on a greener hue: Developments in the Application of Social and Environmental Factors in Public Procurement. *Business Law Review, 24*(1), 2–4.

Davies, J.S. (2007). The limits of partnership: An exit-action strategy for local democratic inclusion. *Political Studies, 55*(4), 779–800. doi: 10.1111/j.1467-9248.2007.00677.x

Denhardt, R.B., & Denhardt, J.V. (2000). The new public service: serving rather than steering. *Public Administration Review, 60*(6), 549–559. doi: 10.1111/0033-3352.00117

ECO-buy. (2012). *The quick guide to bs 8903 for procuring sustainably*. Retrieved from http://static1.squarespace.com/static/5212c4fae4b088f3b6718038/t/52aa9090e4b03e36e0bee7a2/1386909840060/Quick_Guide_to_BS8903.pdf (Accessed 28th May 2015)

Edler, J., & Georghiou, L. (2007). Public procurement and innovation: Resurrecting the demand side. *Research Policy, 36*(2007), 949–963. doi:10.1016/j.respol.2007.03.003

Emy, H. (1993). *Remaking Australia: The state, the market and Australia's future*. St Leonards, NSW: Allen & Unwin.

Epsing-Andersen, G. (1990). *The three worlds of welfare capitalism*. Cambridge: Polity Press & Princeton: Princeton University Press.

Erridge, A. (2007). Public procurement, public value and the Northern Ireland unemployment pilot project. *Public Administration, 85*(4), 1023–1043. doi: 10.1111/j.1467-9299.2007.00674.x

European Commission. (2010). Buying social: A guide to taking account of social considerations in public procurement. Luxemburg, European Union. doi:10.2767/18977.

Fraser, D. (1973). *The evolution of the British welfare state: A history of social policy since the Industrial Revolution*. The Macmillan Press: London, UK.

Funnel, W. (2001). *Government by fiat*. Sydney: University of New South Wales Press.

Geddes, M. (2006). Partnership and the limits to local governance in England: Institutionalist analysis and neoliberalism. *International Journal of Urban and Regional Research, 30*(1), 76–97. doi: 10.1111/j.1468-2427.2006.00645.x

Graycar, A. (1979). *Welfare politics in Australia: A study in policy analysis*. Melbourne: Macmillan.

Habermas, J. (1981). New social movements. *Telos, 1981*(49), 33–37. http://doi.org/10.3817/0981049033

Hall, P. (2005). *Historical perspectives on nonprofits in the United States*. www.hks.harvard.edu/fs/phall/Herman-CH1.pdf (Accessed 28th May 2015)

Islam, M., & Siwar, C. (2013). A comparative study of public sector sustainable procurement practices: Opportunities and barriers. *International Review of Business Research Papers, 9*(3), 62–84. Retrieved from www.irbrp.com/previous_issue/March/2013

Jaffee, D. (2012). Weak coffee: Certification and co-optation in the fair trade movement. *Social Problems, 59*(1), 94–116. doi: 10.1525/sp.2012.59.1.94

Joy, M., & Shields, J. (2013). Social impact bonds: The next phase of third sector marketization? *Canadian Journal of Nonprofit and Social Economy Research, 4*(2), 39–55.

Kendall, J., & Knapp, M. (1993). *Defining the nonprofit sector: The United Kingdom*. Working Papers of the John Hopkins Comparative Nonprofit Sector Project, Baltimore, Maryland, USA.

Kunzlik, P. (2003). Making the market work for the environment: Acceptance of (some) "green" contract award criteria in public procurement. *Journal of Environmental Law, 15*(2), 175–201

Lawless, P. (2006). Area-based urban interventions: Rationale and outcomes: The New Deal for Communities Programme in England. *Urban Studies, 43*(11), 1991–2011. doi: 10.1080/00420980600897859

Lawther, W.C., & Martin, L.L. (2005). Innovative practices in public procurement partnerships: The case of the United States. *Journal of Purchasing and Supply Management, 11*(5–6), 212–220. doi: 10.1016/j.pursup.2005.12.003

LePage, D. (2014). *Exploring social procurement*. Accelerating Social Impact CCC, Ltd. Retrieved from http://buysocialcanada.ca/files/2014/05/Exploring-Social-Procurement_ASI-CCC-Report.pdf (Accessed 28th May 2015)

Lund-Thomsen, P., & Costa, N. (2011). Sustainable procurement in the United Nations. *Journal of Corporate Citizenship, 42*(19), 54–72. doi:10.9774/GLEAF.4700.2011.su.00006

Martin, J.F. (1996). *The EC public procurement rules: A critical analysis*. Oxford: Clarendon Press.

McCrudden, C. (2004). Using public procurement to achieve social outcomes. *Natural Resources Forum, 28*(4), 257–267. doi: 10.1111/j.1477-8947.2004.00099.x

McCrudden, C. (2007). *Buying social justice: Equality, government procurement, & legal change.* Oxford: Oxford University Press.

McCulloch, A. (2004). Localism and its neoliberal application: a case study of West Gate New Deal for Communities in Newcastle Upon Tyne, UK. *Capital & Class, 28(2)*, 133–165. doi: 10.1177/030981680408300106

McHugh, N., Sinclair, S., Roy, M., Huckfield, L., & Donaldson, C. (2013). Social impact bonds: a wolf in sheep's clothing? *Journal of Poverty and Social Justice, 21*(3), 247–257. doi: http://doi.org/10.1332/204674313X13812372137921

Meehan, J, & Bryde, D. (2010) Sustainable procurement practice. *Business Strategy and the Environment, 20(2)*, 94–106. doi: 10.1002/bse.678

Murray, J. (2000). Effects of green purchasing strategy: The case of Belfast City Council. *Supply Chain Management, 5*(1): 37–44. doi: http://dx.doi.org/10.1108/13598540010312954

Office of the Third Sector, (2008). Social clauses project: Report of the social clauses project 2008. Retrieved from www.cabinetoffice.gov.uk/media/107238/social%20clauses%20report%20final.pdf (Accessed 20th November 2009).

O'Flynn, J. (2009). The cult of collaboration in public policy. *Australian Journal of Public Administration, 68*(1), 112–116. doi: 10.1111/j.1467-8500.2009.00616.x

Pestoff, V. (2006). Citizens as co-producers of welfare services: Preschool services in eight European countries. *Public Management Review, 8*(4), 503–520. doi:10.1080/14719030601022882

Pol, E., & Ville, S. (2009). Social innovation: Buzz word or enduring term? *Journal of Socio-Economics, 38*(6), 878–885.

Preuss, L. (2007). Buying into our future: sustainability initiatives in local government procurement. *Business Strategy and the Environment, 16*(5), 354–365. doi: 10.1002/bse.578

Preuss, L. (2009). Addressing sustainable development through public procurement: the case of local government. *Supply Chain Management: An International Journal, 14*(3), 213–223. doi: http://dx.doi.org/10.1108/13598540910954557

Productivity Commission, (2010). *Contribution of the not-for-profit sector: Research report*. Retrieved from www.pc.gov.au/inquiries/completed/not-for-profit/report (Accessed 28th May 2015)

Raco, M., Parker, G. & Doak, J. (2006). Reshaping spaces of local governance? Community strategies and the modernisation of local government in England. *Environment and Planning C: Government and Policy, 24*(4), 475–496. doi: 10.1068/c51m

Ram, M., & Smallbone, D. (2003). Supplier diversity initiatives and the diversification of ethnic minority businesses in the UK. *Policy Studies, 24*(4), 187–204. doi: 10.1080/0144287042000216117

Ram, M., Theodorakopoulos, N., & Worthington, I. (2007). Policy transfer in practice: Implementing supplier diversity in the UK. *Public Administration, 85*(3), 779–803. doi: 10.1111/j.1467-9299.2007.00671.x

Rogerson, C.M. (2012). Supplier diversity: A new phenomenon in private sector procurement in South Africa. *Urban Forum, 23*(3), 279–297. doi: 10.1007/s12132-012-9148-y

Schulten, T., Alsos, K., Burgess, P. & Pedersen, K. (2012). *Pay and other Social clauses in European public procurement: An overview on regulation and practices with a focus on Denmark, Germany, Norway, Switzerland and the United Kingdom.* Study on behalf of the European Federation of Public Service Unions (EPSU) Düsseldorf, December

Scottish Procurement Directorate, (2007). *Social issues in public procurement: A guidance note by the Scottish Procurement Directorate.* Available at www.scotland.gov.uk/Resource/Doc/116601/0053331.pdf (Accessed 5th November 2009)

Social Traders. (n.d.). *Building social enterprise through social procurement.* Retrieved from www.socialtraders.com.au/sites/www.socialtraders.com.au/files/Building%20Social%20Enterprise%20through%20Social%20Procurement.doc.pdf (Accessed 16th November 2009)

Spear, R., & Bidet, E. (2005). Social enterprise for work integration in 12 European countries: A descriptive analysis. *Annals of Public and Cooperative Economics, 76*(2), 195–231. doi: 10.1111/j.1370–4788.2005.00276.x

State Government of Victoria. (2009). Public Tenant Employment Program: Text and video. Available at www.housing.vic.gov.au/community-and-housing-partnerships/ptep [Accessed 1 September 2009].

Theodorakopoulos, N., Ram, M., Shah, M., & Boyal, H. (2005). Experimenting with Supply Chain Learning (SCL): Supplier diversity and ethnic minority businesses. *The International Entrepreneurship and Management Journal, 1*(4), 461–478. Oxford, UK: doi: 10.1007/s11365-005-4773-8

Tierney, L. (1970). Social policy. In A.F. Davis & S. Encel (Eds.), *Australian society* (2nd ed.). (pp. 200–223) Melbourne: Cheshire.

Ware, A. (1989) Introduction: the changing relations between charities and the state. In A. Ware (Ed.) *Charities and government.* (pp. 1–28.) Manchester: Manchester University Press.

4   Institutional and resource enablers of social procurement

> Innovations can grow wild, springing up weed-like despite unfavour-
> able circumstances, but they can also be cultivated, blossoming in greater
> abundance under favourable conditions . . . we can see why some
> macro-conditions are better for their cultivation.
>
> (Kanter, 1996, p. 93)

Different institutional contexts for social procurement produce different behaviours and outcomes. Just as certain crops grow better in some natural environments than others, so some business and regulatory environments are more
conducive to the effective implementation of social procurement than others. This chapter examines key institutional elements that enable or constrain
social procurement, with a particular focus on rules, actors in relationships and
resources (Scott, 2008). These institutional elements influence the widespread
adoption of social procurement, what institutional and innovation theorists
refer to as "diffusion" (Scott, 1995; Rogers, 2003).

Institutional perspectives on social procurement

At its simplest, social procurement is an idea. Contemporary approaches to
social procurement seek to innovate in response to complex needs and changing resource environments. As with any innovation, an idea like social procurement can flourish and grow, or be stifled and opposed. Ideas can be dangerous,
wonderful or even subversive as they challenge the established order. In short,
ideas have consequences (Sproul, 2000). The central idea of social procurement
is that any organisation can seek to achieve social good, directly or indirectly,
through its purchasing practices. However, some institutional environments
may be more or less amenable to such practices.

The institutional perspective is a very influential and prevalent view of the
behaviour of organisations, and what shapes that behaviour. An institution can
be defined as a durable social structure, which comprises symbolic elements
(such as rules, norms and beliefs), social activities (such as the relationships
between actors) and material resources (Scott, 2008). Essentially, institutions
provide ways of solving problems involving collective action (Moe, 1990). It

can be said that goals or procedures have become institutionalised when they achieve an established, "value-impregnated status" (Selznick, 1949, as cited in Scott, 2008, p. 22).

From an institutional perspective, organisations are constituted in and through social contexts, which produce norms and assumptions regarding what constitutes "acceptable behaviour" (Scott, 1993). While we have canvassed in the preceding chapter that activities consistent with social procurement are not new, contemporary interest in social procurement as a distinct domain of practice is indicative of an emerging institutional field (Scott, 2001; Scott, 2013), informed by sometimes competing institutional logics constitutive of new public governance (NPG) (Christensen & Lægreid, 2011). In these emergent conditions, where there is limited institutional support for or legitimation of newer social procurement practices, it can be difficult for an organisation to "break the mould" and purposefully pursue social goals through purchasing practices. This is because institutional structures can create inertia towards change (Hannan & Freeman, 1984), generating considerable pressure to homogenise practice in organisations. Such homogenisation of practice, or isomorphism (DiMaggio & Powell, 1983), has three sources: regulatory pressure (coercive isomorphism); the desire to imitate apparently successful organisations (mimetic isomorphism); or norms established by the influential actors such as various professions and universities (normative isomorphism). As Scott (1995) suggests: "The underlying logic is one of orthodoxy: we seek to behave in conventional ways, in ways that will not cause us to stand out or be noticed as different . . . We tend to imitate others whom we regarded as superior, as more successful" (p. 45). Indeed, conforming to such an external environment increases the legitimacy of an organisation and, potentially, its access to resources (Zucker, 1987).

However, institutional fields are not fixed; new organisational entrants bring new ideas, and shifting the priorities and institutional circumstances to which organisations must respond (Greenwood, Raynard, Kodeih, Micelotta & Lounsbury, 2011). Change can be facilitated by the provision of new templates, regulation, incentives and financial support (Klerkx, Aarts & Leeuwis, 2010), as well as via organisational "champions" pushing for the adoption of certain practices.

In this chapter, we explore some of the key institutional enablers for emergent practices of social procurement and their diffusion (Scott 1995). First, a discussion is presented as to what institutional conditions are needed to enable social procurement to stabilise as an institutional field. While there are different approaches to the conceptualisation of institutions (cf. Jepperson [1991] for an extended discussion), this chapter will focus particularly on the constructs of rules, resources and relationships. Institutions are an organised procedure which can be seen to consist of a set of rules (Jepperson, 1991) which, by specifying acceptable behaviour, act to constrain or enable actions (Scott, 2008). A second element of institutions is that of the actors and relationships between them – particularly in those works which emphasise networks as a special form of institutional arrangement (Owen-Smith & Powell, 2008; Beckert, 2010; North, 1990). In essence, institutions are socially constructed. The third element relates to the resources which are available (Scott, 2008), such as knowledge (Beckert, 2010). In this chapter, each of these enablers is discussed in detail in relation to social procurement. We suggest that, in an emergent institutional field such as contemporary social procurement, where rules are relatively open and contestable, relationships between actors and resources play a particularly significant role in legitimacy formation.

Conceptualising institutional enablers of social procurement

As previously outlined, the key elements of an institutional environment are what we have termed rules, relationships and resources.

Rules

Institutional rules enable certain types of behaviour, and also constrain other forms of behaviour (Scott, 2008). "Rules are shared understandings among those involved that refer to enforced prescriptions about what actions. . . are required, prohibited, or permitted" (Ostrom 2011, p. 17). To make this notion more accessible, North (1990) used the analogy of a game in which institutions provide the rules of the game while organisations are the players of the game. The "rules of the game" are important in understanding institutions (Fligstein 2001, pp. 112). For social procurement this means that the rules of the game around social procurement are fundamental to the way in which organisations

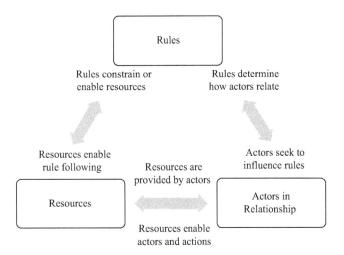

Figure 4.1 Institutional elements of a social procurement environment

Note: *Each of these elements informs the adoption of social procurement practice. A theoretical outline of each institutional enabler for social procurement is provided in the next section.*

"play the game" of social procurement, including, for example, the processes of decision-making and membership composition.

Beckert (2010) and Blom-Hansen (1997) both note that these rules can be formal in the sense of acts and regulations, or they can be more broadly sets of social norms, and codes of conduct which provide broad and agreed ways of acting in social contexts. Ostrom (2009) has referred to the former as "the rule of law" and the latter as the "rules in use", suggesting that each informs normative behaviours in policy settings (pp. 36–37). Rules in this sense include both formal (regulatory) as well as more informal rules (guides, templates, and "know how"), with their central importance being ". . . that they structure social interaction" (Blom-Hansen, 1997, p. 675). Social procurement is usefully examined from this perspective as it involves sets of activities, such as planning, tendering, contracting, delivering, reporting and, of course, rules and norms around these sets of activities. Organisations which adhere to "the rules" may be conferred a degree of legitimacy by their publics, both in terms of means as well as ends (Scott, 1991). In the context of social procurement, rules are emergent and sometimes prescribed by competing logics represented in the layering of practices of NPG, as well as normative demands of commercial behaviour. As Pache and Santos (2010) note, competing institutional demands may differ with regard to the goals they seek to legitimate or the means by which these are achieved, leading to negotiated and/or conflicting practices and outcomes. Next we consider some of the rules and norms around social procurement, their points of contradiction and their enabling and constraining effects on practice.

Actors in relationships

Any institutional environment involves actors whose actions are interrelated. Institutional rules both enable actions and constrain behaviours (Scott, 2008). Following a social constructionist approach, actors are viewed in institutional theory as being part of, rather than distinct from, their institutional environment (Scott 2008). Indeed the rules and actions which were noted earlier do not arrive *ex nihilo* [out of nothing]. Ostrom (2009) notes in relation to rules ". . . human agents must formulate them, apply them in particular situations, and attempt to enforce performance consistent with them" (p. 37). Rules are thus maintained through relationships (Scott, 2008, p.49).

Typically, institutional rules are seen to be relatively fixed and one of the main drivers of conformity in institutional settings (DiMaggio & Powell, 1983). However, other authors are not as convinced as to the fixed nature of rules and therefore institutions (Jepperson, 1991), noting that organisational actors can be involved in attempts to construct, change and enforce the rules by which they play (Beckert 2010; Scott 2008). These authors see more of a dynamic relationship between actors and the rules in institutional environments. Research in emergent institutional fields, where widely shared norms do not yet exist, suggest that some actors – particularly institutional entrepreneurs – play a significant role in co-producing the rules in use (Greenwood et al., 2011). This is consistent with Bovaird's (2006) analysis of the new kinds of market relationships emerging in public procurement practice, which was discussed in Chapter 2. A description of the sorts of actors and their roles in social procurement environments is presented later in this chapter. Institutional actors not only seek to influence the institutional rules, particularly policy rules, but also exchange resources through their network of relationships (Börzel, 1998).

Resources

For rules to be effective, some form of power, often in the form of access to resources, is needed (Scott, 2008). Similarly, those with excess resources seek some form of sanction from the institutional rules for their use (Scott, 2008). Indeed, many forms of analysis of formal and informal relationships note that these networks enable the mobilisation of resources for a particular task – whether to achieve policy outcomes (Börzel, 1998) or for entrepreneurial outcomes (e.g., Burt, 1992). As Börzel (1998) notes "Actors, who take an interest in the making of a certain policy and who dispose of resources (material and immaterial) required for the formation, decision or implementation of the policy, form linkages to exchange these resources" (p. 259). Social procurement is very useful to examine in this context because the use and creation of material resources (including people, finance and assets) are intrinsically involved, as is the generation of intangible resources such as social and cultural value. Some of the resources which might be involved are discussed later in this chapter.

As arenas of action, it should be evident that these three elements of institutions are not mutually exclusive, as rules enable action, and yet are influenced by the actors whose action they affect. Similarly, actors interested in a particular policy or rule develop and deploy resources in order to implement specific policy (Börzel, 1998). Hence the dynamics between each of these elements is depicted in Figure 4.1 as a set of interrelationships.

Social procurement rules

Understanding institutional rules involves conceptualising what is valued and important, as well as the proper way that things should be done (Klijn & Koppenjan, 2006). The regulatory and policy elements that seek to proscribe and prescribe social procurement activity are emblematic of the spoken rules of this emergent institutional field, particularly in the context of public sector-led procurement. Industry standards and related emerging norms also inform the rules in use amongst commercial and third-sector organisations seeking to purchase against a social bottom line. As has been discussed in Chapter 1 and will be returned to in Chapter 6, NPG is informed by the co-presence of competing and merging organising logics of hierarchies, markets and networks. This complexity is mirrored in sometimes divergent conceptualisations of the nature and purpose of social procurement, which has led to rather diffuse practices.

Recent work has set out in more detail approaches to social procurement, with a number of different approaches identifiable in the academic and policy literature. As is noted in Chapter 1, social procurement is the intentional procurement of social outcomes. However, there are at least four identifiable approaches to social procurement (Table 4.1).

The first type of social procurement (Type 1 in Table 4.1) involves the direct purchasing of social outcomes. The second type of social procurement (Type 2 in Table 4.1) seeks to deliver social outcomes as an indirect aspect of a procurement contract; for instance, employment generation on a highway project (for example, see Erridge, 2007). This approach is reflected in the sentiment embodied in guidelines for social procurement published by the Victorian state government in Australia, "Social procurement involves using procurement processes and purchasing power to generate positive social outcomes *in addition* to the delivery of efficient goods, services and works" (Department of Planning and Community Development, 2011, p. 2 *[emphasis added]*). Another example of this approach published by the Scottish Government (2008), states "The priority for all public procurement is to achieve Value for Money (VfM). Value for money does not, however, mean 'lowest price'". (p. 3). It is defined in the Scottish Public Finance Manual as "the optimum combination of whole life cost and quality to meet the end user's requirement" (Scottish Government, 2014, p. 7). The aim of the community benefits inclusion initiative is ". . . to examine the inclusion of community benefits clauses in contracts in a way which also achieved value for money" (Scottish Government, 2008, p. 3).

A third approach (Type 3 in Table 4.1) is to allocate a percentage of work to social benefit organisations. One of the key reasons for allocating a specific percentage or a project to social benefit organisations (often, social enterprises) is to make the size of the project manageable for a small organisation. One of the challenges of social benefit organisations tendering for government works

Table 4.1 Typology of social procurement

		Outcomes	
		Direct	*Indirect*
FOCUS	Procurement of social outcomes *(Focus on the contract)*	**Type 1** Procurement of social services	**Type 2** Procurement of social outcomes embedded in public goods, such as capital works
	Procurement from civil society organisations *(Focus on the tender)*	**Type 3** Procurement of services from social benefit organisations	**Type 4** Ethical supply chain management

Note: *This section draws heavily on Furneaux and Barraket (2014).*

is that they often lack capacity to deliver large contracts. Consequently, one way of developing their capacity is to tender smaller contracts specifically to these groups, and exclude larger groups from tendering. An alternative is to require lead contractors to engage social benefit organisations as subcontractors (Australian Capital Territory, 2014).

With regard to the constraining effects of institutional rules, this approach is difficult to implement in certain jurisdictions, where it may involve breach of competition guidelines (e.g., European Commission, 2010). As noted, government regulation can drive conformity and isomorphism in organisations (DiMaggio & Powell, 1983), or can prohibit specific actions (Ostrom, 2011). Thus, current legislation in some regions makes it difficult to implement this particular type of social procurement as it is prohibited under legislation. This example brings the coercive nature of regulation to the fore, as the institutional rules either enable or constrain action (Scott, 2008). Some policy bodies (e.g., European Commission, 2010) have sought to reframe regulatory constraints, suggesting that governments can, for example, maximise opportunities for small to medium enterprises (SMEs) and social enterprises to participate in social procurement activities by ". . . limiting the size of the contracts", thus making them accessible to smaller organisations, and ". . . making subcontracting opportunities more visible" (p. 9). This retains the competition element, but still increases opportunities for engagement. Thus the rules provide not just barriers to action, but may also stimulate new calls to action, or new approaches to action.

The fourth approach (Type 4 in Table 4.1) by which social outcomes can be included in procurement processes is via corporate social responsibility considerations in the supply chain (European Commission, 2014). By evaluating the procurement of a range of services rather than just direct purchasing of outcomes, governments, third-sector organisations and commercial firms can extend the range and scope of their social procurement outcomes. A classic example of this might be in the purchasing of coffee. Coffee in and of itself is not a social outcome. However, a supply chain consideration might consider buying fair trade coffee, to ensure that there is a social benefit further up the supply chain. By embedding social considerations in the supply chain purchasing arrangements, considerable extension of the consideration and appreciation of the importance of social outcomes in the procurement process can be acheived. In this context, the governance (and associated rules) of social procurement is manifested "horizontally", through organisation to organisation practices and transnational norms, rather than "vertically", through top-down policy prescriptions by national and supranational bodies (Arrowsmith, 2010; Boström & Karlsson, 2013). Supply chain considerations and corporate social responsibility are considered in more detail in Chapter 5.

We have suggested here that we can conceptualise the effects of the regulatory environment on social procurement in a number of ways. First, top-down or vertical policy directives can have coercive isomorphic effects (DiMaggio & Powell, 1983); yet, these may also provide the basis for deliberation and adaptation leading to normative change as policy bodies seek to accommodate new practices. Coercive forces may lead to wider adoption of social procurement practice where they direct organisations to explicitly consider social outcomes, either as "upstream" purchasers or "downstream" providers of services to other procurement actors. Yet, emerging prescriptions for social procurement must also function within pre-established institutional rules that may counter their purpose. For example, the well-established norms of competition policy consistent with market models of governance privilege best price over best value and preclude preferential purchasing from particular organisations in many jurisdictions. As well as top-down imperatives, horizontal pressures of increasingly globalised markets and shifts towards user-centredness are also stimulating new norms for social procurement, particularly with regard to embedding social purpose purchasing in supply chains.

The rules considered in this discussion variously constrain and enable social procurement activity, and require delicate navigation as they intersect with pre-established rules in relation to what constitutes appropriate practice with regard to procurement in the public sphere. These rules both inform and are informed by the roles and relationships of actors.

Organisational roles and relationships between actors

One of the ways in which institutional norms and values are crystallised is around the idea of "roles". In any given organisational field, organisations may take on a variety of roles (Beckert, 2010). Society has a set of expectations about the roles which various organisations should undertake. As Berger and Luckmann (1967) argue, ". . . all institutionalized conduct involves roles. Thus, roles share in the controlling character of institutionalization. As soon as actors are typified as role performers, their conduct is *ipso facto* susceptible to enforcement" (p. 74). These rules by which organisations carry out their roles tend to get set out as standard operating procedures (March & Olsen, 1989). Moreover, "Rules define relationships among roles in terms of what an incumbent of one role owes to incumbents of other roles" (Burns & Flam, 1987, cited by March & Olsen, 1989, pp. 36–37). Thus, it is important to acknowledge, as highlighted in Figure 4.1, that the institutional rules specify not just what can be done, but also the roles that actors can play.

Within procurement, there are a number of key organisational types. These types of organisations include government, non-profit, for-profit, and hybrid entities such as social enterprises, as well as intermediary groups which function to create connection and mutual understanding between different sectors. It is important to note that, while there are a number of different types of organisations, each organisation may in fact undertake a number of different roles.

Government tends to have the roles of financial stakeholder (funder and tax collector), regulator and contractor (Kearns, 1994). Non-profits typically are engaged in direct social service provision as well as advocating for the poor (Lyons, 1993, 1998). Commercial organisations are typically engaged in service provision in the pursuit of generating profits, while also acting as procurement agents in their own supply chain development. SMEs are sometimes explicitly positioned as producers of social value – in terms of local economic diversity and affirmative action – in social procurement frameworks. Social enterprises seek to engage in market activity in order to achieve social outcomes (Barraket, Collyer, O'Connor & Anderson, 2010). The hybridity of social enterprises creates challenges to their legitimacy, as they pursue roles typically undertaken by two different organisational types (Battilana & Lee, 2014; Dart, 2004). Intermediaries are primarily focused on networking, advocacy and disseminating information and thus play a significant role in navigating institutional boundaries; this topic is explored further later in this chapter. Chapter 6 expands on the growing condition of hybridity in contemporary society, highlighting the shifting configurations of roles, rules and resources that are increasingly characteristic of NPG as well as the managerial adjustments required.

Thus, different organisations take on different roles in social procurement contexts, which is another form of hybridity. This situation is made clearer visually, in Table 4.2, which sets out the range of roles against contexts and functions.

Of course, each of these roles is something similar to an "ideal type" in the Weberian sense (Weber, 1947, p.92) whereas in reality an organisation may function simultaneously in a number of different roles. Organisational actors may also act and be acted upon in divergent ways depending on the nature and direction of the relationships in play; for example, while micro and small enterprises are private for-profit firms, they are also constructed as social value creators in some approaches to social procurement that seek to stimulate local economic diversity and/or give priority to businesses owned by marginalised groups (McCrudden, 2004; Yoon, 2006). The net effect of multiple organisational actors all working towards a common objective of embedding social outcomes in procurement tends to be normative. Once a practice becomes established as "normal" or "standard" then considerable social pressure can be brought to bear as being the odd organisation out can be both materially and symbolically costly (Scott, 1995).

In an emerging institutional field, however, the structural roles of organisational actors may become contested as new roles overlay traditional roles arising from pre-existing institutional rules. It has been observed in relation to green procurement that this can lead to "ontological anxiety" (Meehan & Bryde, 2011) of organisational actors, as they seek to navigate conflicting roles arising from competing institutional agendas driven by command and control logics of hierarchical decision-making versus integrated and relational approaches consistent with network governance. Emerging institutional frameworks also give rise to negotiation and reification of roles, particularly for those that are peripheral to the field. In this context, the role of intermediaries as inscribers of norms and navigators of intersecting fields is very important for understanding the diffusion and uptake of social procurement.

Intermediaries, such as industry and sector representative organisations and networks, fulfil a number of important roles in relation to emerging iterations

Table 4.2 Social procurement actors and the roles they typically undertake

Organisational actor	Examples	Roles									
		Disseminate information	Regulator	Tax collector	Contractor	Service provision	Pursuit of profit	Pursuit of social outcomes	Capacity development	Advocate	Creating networks
Government	Local government authorities, state/regional governments, national government	✓	✓	✓	✓	Some		✓	✓		
Third sector	Non-profits, cooperatives				✓	✓		✓		✓	
Private for-profit	Companies, partnerships, corporations				✓	✓	✓				
	SMEs/minority-owned businesses				✓		✓	✓			
Hybrid (social enterprise)	Low-profit limited liability companies (L3C, CIC)				✓	✓	✓	✓		✓	
Intermediary	Advocacy groups, civil society networks, brokers	✓								✓	✓
Financial organisations	Banks, community finance organisations	✓							✓		

of social procurement. First, as representatives of collective interests, they play *advocacy roles* in shaping public policy. In the UK, for example, third-sector advocacy driven particularly by social enterprise, played a substantial role in placing discussions of social procurement on the public agenda (see, for example, Nicholls, Sacks & Walsham, 2006). Social Enterprise UK was instrumental in the formation of pro-social enterprise legislation in England, particularly the Public Services (Social Value) Act 2012 (Social Enterprise UK, 2013). At supranational and regional levels, the *Network for Sustainable Development in Public Procurement* (ENSIE, n.d.) is a network of trade union and non-government organisations (NGOs) which have a similar objective of promoting social and environmental considerations in EU legislation and policies, while Social Procurement Australasia seeks to advance social procurement as a tool for change in its region. Second, intermediaries play *legitimising roles* as sources of expert knowledge on best practice with regard to social procurement practice. This is discussed further in this chapter in relation to resources and with regard to measuring social value in social procurement in Chapter 7. Third, intermediaries *shape practice* by building demand-side interest and supply-side capacity to deliver social value through social procurement. Intermediaries fulfilling this role have recently grown in number across countries, with a particular concentration on social enterprise as a social value provider. Scotland has a number of intermediary groups. For example, *The Social Enterprise Networks [SENs]* (SENSCOT, n.d.) provides a "collective voice" peer support and resource sharing for social enterprises, while *Social Firms Scotland* (Social Firms Scotland, n.d.). provides support and training for developing social firms, as well as mapping the sector and seeking to influence policy and research. *Community Enterprise in Scotland* (CEIS, n.d.) provides finance and support for organisations seeking to gain access to government contracts in Scotland. In Australia, examples include *Social Ventures Australia* (SVA, n.d.), which provides consulting services in relation to business models, funding strategies, organisational change, measurement and evaluation, governance and collaborations, as well as providing some funding. *Social Traders* (Social Traders, n.d.) is another example of an intermediary whose core mission is to promote social enterprises in Australia, via developmental activities, resource development, consulting and research. In Canada, Social Enterprise Canada (Social Enterprise Canada, n.d.*a*) seeks to build strong non-profit organisations and healthier communities by developing and supporting social enterprises.

While each of these roles is different, they illuminate the functions of intermediaries as both translators and carriers of institutional logics within the emergent field of social procurement. By actively promoting social procurement practices, such organisations encourage work with other actors to promote social procurement as the "norm" and thus encourage the uptake of the practice more widely. Again this reinforces the institutional nature of social procurement (cf. Figure 4.1) as the actors are both constrained by, and also seek to encourage procurers – both public and private – to amend rules and practices so that they are more pro-social in nature. While rules, roles and relationships are important, so too are resources, both tangible and intangible (Scott, 2008). The role of resources as an institutional enabler of social procurement is discussed next.

Resources

Resources can either be tangible, including finance, physical assets, and human resources, or intangible (Börzel, 1998), including knowledge, information and social capital (Table 4.3). Resource access and use may be prescribed by rules, and resources flow through relationships and structuration of roles between actors.

Knowledge and information play particularly significant roles in the construction of emergent practice. For a wider set of actors to adopt a specific set of practices, some form of objectification of the practice is needed (Berger & Luckman, 1967). As Scott (2008) puts it, there needs to be a shift away from "this is the way we do this" to "this is how these things are done" (p. 125). This typically involves the creation of artefacts, templates and exemplars which set the overall tone and pattern of action for the behaviours sought (Keast, 2011, 2013). In other words, objectification is an institutional mechanism which enables the activity or practice to move beyond a couple of key organisations, and spread to a wide array of organisations. This is because, for an innovation to gain widespread support, the provision of resources, templates and exemplars enable understanding and adoption (Klerkx, Aarts, & Leeuwis, 2010). Examples of this objectification process might be the development of best practice guidelines, and resources, and demonstration projects, which produce common language and provide referents to common experience. Importantly this aspect of institutionalising practice involves more than just imitating the practices of others, although this is a first step.

More than just the creation of artefacts, objectification also involves developing arguments around why certain practices are undertaken. Here, researchers, professionals and lead agencies have a key role in providing rationales and justifications around specific practices, as do the lobbying activities of interest groups. In the absence of highly institutionalised rules, knowledge resources play a particularly significant role in instating and legitimising practice. This is apparent in the emergence of recent discourses of social procurement, where practice tools have preceded (or accompanied) policy developments in a number of jurisdictions. In Canada, for example, a tool kit was developed by Enterprising Nonprofits, and is now hosted by Social Enterprise Canada (n.d.*a*; n.d.*b*), which provides rationales for social value creation through procurement; frameworks for including social enterprises in procurement; and a resource library. Similarly, the European Commission (2010) has released a guide on socially responsible public procurement (SRPP) with the stated purpose to "(a)... raise contracting authorities' awareness of the potential benefits of SRPP and (b) explain in a practical way the opportunities offered by the existing EU legal framework for public authorities to take into account social considerations in their public procurement, thus paying attention not only to price but also to the best value for money" (European Commission 2010, p. 5). In Australia, there has been consolidation and distribution of knowledge resources, particularly at the local and state government levels, related to implementation of social procurement guidelines, with a particular focus on procurement through social enterprises. These resources provide a step by step process for developing social procurement policy and practice, including considerations on legal issues, building a business case, developing policies and plans which support social procurement, communications plans, identifying suppliers, and monitoring and evaluation.

Apart from tools for implementation, reports and exemplars of how other organisations have undertaken social procurement are also important. The European Union has released six case studies of social procurement outcomes from its member states (International Training Centre, 2009). Some regional governments have also released case studies of their own, such as in Scotland (Social Investment Scotland, n.d.) where a number of cases are highlighted, and the *First Port* ditto program (Firstport, n.d.) also provides a range of business models which are billed as ready for use. Additionally, case studies pertinent to state and local government procurement have been developed in Australia in New South Wales (Social Procurement Action Group, n.d.), Parramatta (Burkett, 2010), and Brisbane (Brisbane City Council, 2014), as well as cases developed and promoted by intermediary organisations such as Social Traders (n.d.).

From an institutional perspective, these exemplars are resources, which can assist other organisations to implement social procurement practice – part of the diffusion of institutional arrangements (Scott, 1995). They can assist networks of organisations to shift from normative assertions about what ought to happen to more practical application, showing ways that social procurement can be done (Scott, 2008). The creation of guides, templates and cases makes it possible for organisations to imitate practices in other organisations, reducing the costs involved in developing in-house or adopting new and innovative practices. The adoption of any of these resources, however, may not be well integrated with the local context and existing resources of the organisation seeking to adopt. Careful consideration needs to be made as to the suitability and adaptability of a solution from one context to another.

While knowledge-based resources play a significant role in inscribing practice in an emerging institutional field, the flow of financial resources is also important. Recent developments in social procurement have both informed and been informed by wider shifts in the financing of social value creation, both within governmental programs and the wider public sphere. The emergence of social impact bonds and related trends in outcomes-based funding (Jackson, 2013; Joy & Shields, 2013) are emblematic of the development of new instruments that seek to distribute the risks and benefits of social spending across sectors, mobilising non-traditional sources of finance in the fulfilment of social objectives. At the same time, growth in impact investing (Puttick & Ludlow, 2012) and community development financial institutions (Appleyard, 2011) potentially stimulate the supply-side possibilities of social procurement by supporting the capacity of social benefit organisations – particularly non-profits and social enterprises – to engage in new quasi-markets and supply opportunities. While the effectiveness of emergent approaches remains an open question, there is little doubt that they are contributing to recalibrating the landscape of the public sphere (Carmel & Harlock, 2008). A number of writers have observed that new instruments consolidate prevailing institutional norms – for example, in relation to neoliberal imperatives of market governance (Dart, 2004; Joy & Shields, 2013; McHugh, Sinclair, Roy, Huckfield, & Donaldson, 2013) – rather than produce new opportunities.

Beyond financial capital, human capital – particularly, human resources within organisations – is substantially affected by the emergence of new institutional fields and has a significant effect on the adoption of practice. Professional logic constitutes an intersecting institutional frame that guides behaviour amongst staff in both procurer and provider organisations. At the same time, substantial changes to top-down institutional rules typically require new workforce competencies (Keast & Mandell, 2013). The available literature on social and green procurement consistently identifies workforce structure and staff competencies – particularly within procuring organisations – as a key enabler or constraint on adoption of new purchasing activity (Erridge & Greer, 2002; Munoz, 2009; Munoz & Tinsley, 2008). The relationship between workforce competencies and NPG broadly and social procurement specifically, is considered in further detail in Chapters 6 and 8.

Social capital or network characteristics play a substantial role in facilitating organizational receptiveness to new rules, with the strength of ties between actors positively related to acceptance of institutional logics. These ties – manifested through conference attendance, professional associations and industry training, for example – link organisations to ". . . field-level institutional infrastructure" (Greenwood et al., 2011, p. 342). In distributed governance systems, bridging ties also play a significant role in enabling diverse actors – for example, organisations from different sectors – to develop new rules and practices that accommodate diverse organizational cultures (López-Gunn, 2012; Pelling, High, Dearing & Smith, 2008). Growing prominence of social procurement – stimulated in part by new legislation and policy frameworks in the UK and European Union – has given rise to a variety of professional forums that seek to raise procurement and commissioning staff knowledge of current and potential practice. Intermediary organisations such as Social Procurement Australasia are also active in facilitating events aimed at improving exposure to and knowledge between for-benefit providers and public procurers.

While rules might encourage or endorse social procurement, and relationships might provide access to information, resources are critical to enabling the establishment of social procurement practices. Particularly accessing policies might enable specific government departments or jurisdictions to contemplate enacting specific regulatory or policy vehicles to promote such activities. Availability of procedures and materials which help governments work through the

Table 4.3 Resource types and their functions in the emergence of social procurement

Resource type	Exemplars related to social procurement	Function(s) in an emerging institutional field
Knowledge and information	Guidelines, case studies	Reification and application of new practice
Financial capital	New financing instruments for social investment	Redirecting practice through capital flows
Human capital	Professional logics and practices	Strong influence on organisational culture and adoption of practice
Social capital	Professional networks and activities	Link to institutional field infrastructure through formation of social infrastructure

process for establishing social procurement practices in their organisation is also important. However, providing advice, finance, support, training and networking opportunities by funding organisations and intermediary groups is also important. These institutional enablers play a significant role in sustaining social procurement practice.

Conclusion

This chapter has outlined the way in which institutional environments shape social procurement. We have suggested that the widespread adoption of innovations such as social procurement is contingent on three institutional factors in interaction with each other. Rules either proscribe (prohibit) or prescribe (require) specific actions. In the case of social procurement this ranges from being silent on the issue, to requiring specific pro-social actions (such as reserving a percentage of contracts to social enterprises) or explicitly prohibiting such action with reference to pre-existing institutional rules. Other mid-range positions are possible, such as encouraging lead agencies to subcontract to social enterprises. Providing legal and policy frameworks that specifically require organisations to consider social and environmental considerations in their procurement practice plays a significant role in stimulating widespread adoption of social procurement, particularly amongst those organisations centrally positioned within the institutional field. However, such coercive approaches may lack significance to organisations structurally peripheral to the field (Greenwood et al., 2011), where mimetic isomorphism – through horizontal governance and reliance on reputational capital – plays a more significant role in practice adoption.

In emerging institutional fields, roles and relationships between actors are in formation. Relationships, often based on specific roles, can become key institutional enablers of social procurement, although these may also be subject to change as norms and related roles are negotiated over time. Actors share information with each other, and are carriers of knowledge in institutional networks. Actors can even seek to influence the rules which constrain and enable action, as these rules are socially constructed. Contemporary approaches to social procurement simultaneously demand adherence to established institutional frames while casting some actors in new, and sometimes conflicting, roles. In such liminal space, intermediaries serve bridging functions, with important roles in shaping and legitimising both policy and practice.

Finally, resources enable social procurement by providing exemplars and templates which can be copied in other jurisdictions and enable the vicarious learning by both institutional and organisational actors about what worked in what contexts and why, enabling diffusion of approaches. Additionally, in a more direct way, organisations which provide finance, guidance, support and networking opportunities enable social enterprises and other social businesses and non-profit organisations to engage with the policy process. Pro-social actors can leverage knowledge, finance and contacts in order to participate and deliver social outcomes via procurement. The emergence of new institutions and frameworks for action, which are reflective of the positioning of social procurement within new public governance, is discussed in detail in Chapter 6. The role and importance of such institutional factors in shaping a conducive environment for social procurement will be increasingly pertinent in the NPG context. This chapter therefore both outlines how roles, relationships and resources combine to inhibit or facilitate the growth of alternative approaches to procurement, and forecasts the challenges to be faced in the increasingly hybrid NPG context explicated in Chapter 6.

References

Appleyard, L. (2011). Community Development Finance Institutions (CDFIs): Geographies of financial inclusion in the US and UK. *Geoforum, 42*(2), 250–258. doi:10.1016/j. geoforum.2010.09.004

Arrowsmith, S. (2010). Horizontal policies in public procurement: A taxonomy. *Journal of Public Procurement, 10*(2), 149–186. doi:10.1017/cbo9780511576041.006

Australian Capital Territory. (2014). *Procurement Circular PC02: Social procurement.* Retrieved from www.procurement.act.gov.au/__data/assets/pdf_file/0007/276784/PC02-Social-Procurement-v3-Jul-2014.pdf (Accessed 28th May 2015)

Barraket, J., Collyer, N., O'Connor, M., & Anderson, H. (2010). *Finding Australia's social enterprise sector: Final report.* Retrieved from www.socialtraders.com.au/_uploads/rsfil/000263_bcda.pdf (Accessed 28th May 2015)

Battilana, J., & Lee, M. (2014). Advancing research on hybrid organizing: Insights from the study of social enterprises. *The Academy of Management Annals, 8*(1), 397–441. doi:10.1080/19416520.2014.893615

Beckert, J. (2010). How do fields change? The interrelations of institutions, networks and cognition in the dynamics of markets. *Organization Studies, 31*(5), 605–627. doi:10.1177/0170840610372184

Berger, P.L., & Luckmann, T. (1967). *The social construction of reality: A treatise in the sociology of knowledge*. London: Penguin.

Blom-Hansen, J. (1997). A new institutional perspective on policy networks. *Public Administration, 75*(4), 669–693. doi: 10.1111/1467–9299.00080

Börzel, T.A. (1998). Organizing Babylon: On the different conceptions of policy networks. *Public Administration, 76*(2), 253–273. doi: 10.1111/1467–9299.00100

Boström, M., & Karlsson, M. (2013). Responsible procurement, complex product chains and the integration of vertical and horizontal governance. *Environmental Policy and Governance, 23*(6), 381–394. doi:10.1002/eet.1626

Bovaird, T. (2006). Developing new forms of partnership with the 'market' in the procurement of public services. *Public Administration. 84*(1), 81–102. doi: 10.1111/j.0033-3298.2006.00494.x

Brisbane City Council. (2014). *Brisbane City Council Annual Procurement Policy and Contracting Plan 2014–2015*. Retrieved from www.brisbane.qld.gov.au/sites/default/files/20140819_-_appcp_14_15.docx (Accessed 28th May 2015)

Burkett, I. (2010). Social procurement in Australia: A compendium of case studies. In I. Burkett (Eds.), *Social procurement in Australia*. Retrieved from www.parracity.nsw.gov.au/__data/assets/pdf_file/0019/80128/SocialProcurementinAustralia-CaseStudyCompendium.pdf (Accessed 28th May 2015)

Burt, R.S. 1992. *Structural holes: The social structure of competition*. Cambridge, MA: Harvard University Press.

Carmel, E., & Harlock, J. (2008). Instituting the third sector as a governable terrain: Partnership, procurement and performance in the UK. *Policy & Politics, 36*(2), 155–171. doi:10.1332/030557308783995017

Christensen, T., & Lægreid, P. (2011). Complexity and hybrid public administration: theoretical and empirical challenges. *Public Organization Review, 11*(4), 407–423. doi:10.1007/s11115–010–0141–4

Community Enterprise in Scotland (CEIS). (n.d.) *CEIS*. Retrieved from www.ceis.org.uk/about-ceis/ (Accessed 28th May 2015)

Dart, R. (2004). The legitimacy of social enterprise. *Nonprofit management and leadership*, 14(4), 411–424. doi: 10.1002/nml.43

Department of Planning and Community Development. (2011). *Procurement for social and economic development outcomes in local communities: Mapping and analysis methodology*. Retrieved from www.dtpli.vic.gov.au/__data/assets/pdf_file/0003/224859/DPCD-Social-Procurement-Mapping-Analysis-Methodology-Final.pdf (Accessed 28th May 2015)

DiMaggio, P.J., & Powell, W.W. (1983). The iron cage revisited: Institutional isomorphism and collective rationality in organizational fields. *American Sociological Review, 48*(2), 147–160. doi:10.2307/2095101

Erridge, A. (2007). Public procurement, public value and the Northern Ireland Unemployment Pilot Project. *Public Administration, 85*(4), 1023–1043. doi:10.1111/j.1467–9299.2007.00674.x

Erridge, A., & Greer, J. (2002). Partnerships and public procurement: Building social capital through supply relations. *Public Administration, 80*(3), 503–522. doi: 10.1111/1467–9299.00315

European Commission (2010). *Buying social: A guide to taking account of social considerations in public procurement*. Retrieved from http://ec.europa.eu/social/BlobServlet?docId=6457&langId=en (Accessed 28th May 2015)

European Commission (2014). *Corporate social responsibility: National public policies in the European Union compendium*. Retrieved from http://ec.europa.eu/information_society/newsroom/cf/dae/document.cfm?doc_id=7377 (Accessed 28th May 2015)

European Network of Social Integration Enterprises (ENSIE). (n.d.). *ENSIE*. Retrieved from www.ensie.org/

Firstport (n.d.). *Ditto*. Retrieved from www.firstport.org.uk/projects/ditto

Fligstein, N. (2001). Social skill and the theory of fields. *Sociological Theory*, *19*(2), 105–125. doi: 10.1111/0735-2751.00132

Furneaux, C., & Barraket, J. (2014). Purchasing social good(s): A definition and typology of social procurement. *Public Money & Management*, *34*(4), 265–272. doi:10.1080/09540962.2014.920199

Greenwood, R., Raynard, M., Kodeih, F., Micelotta, E.R., & Lounsbury, M. (2011). Institutional complexity and organizational responses. *The Academy of Management Annals*, *5*(1), 317–371. doi:10.1080/19416520.2011.590299

Hannan, M.T., & Freeman, J. (1984). Structural inertia and organizational change. *American Sociological Review*, *49*(2), 149–164. Retrieved from www.jstor.org/stable/2095567 (Accessed 28th May 2015)

International Training Centre. (2009). *Study contract: Social considerations in public procurement*. Retrieved from http://ec.europa.eu/social/BlobServlet?docId=695&langId=en (Accessed 28th May 2015)

Jackson, E.T. (2013). Evaluating social impact bonds: Questions, challenges, innovations, and possibilities in measuring outcomes in impact investing. *Community Development, 44*(5), 608–616. doi:10.1080/15575330.2013.854258

Jepperson, R.L. (1991). Institutions, institutional effects, and institutionalism. In W.W. Powell, & P.J. DiMaggio, (Eds.), *The new institutionalism in organizational analysis* (pp. 143–163). Chicago, IL: University of Chicago Press.

Joy, M., & Shields, J. (2013). Social impact bonds: The next phase of third sector marketization? *Canadian Journal of Nonprofit and Social Economy Research*, *4*(2), 39–55. Retrieved from www.anserj.ca/anser/index.php/cjnser/article/view/148/94 (Accessed 28th May 2015)

Kanter, R. (1996). When a thousand flowers bloom: Structural, collective, and social conditions for innovation in organizations. In P. Meyers (Ed.), *Knowledge management and organisational design* (pp. 93–131). Newton, MA: Butterworth-Heinemann.

Kearns, K.P. (1994). The strategic management of accountability in nonprofit organizations: An analytical framework. *Public Administration Review*, *54*(2), 185–192. Retrieved from www.jstor.org/stable/976528 (Accessed 28th May 2015)

Keast, R. (2011). Joined-up governance in Australia: How the past can inform the future. *International Journal of Public Administration*, *34*(4), 221–231. doi: 10.1080/01900692.2010.549799

Keast, R. (2013). *Contemporary airport governance and management and hyper-hybridity*. World Congress on Engineering Asset Management.

Keast, R., & Mandell, M.P. (2013). Network performance: A complex interplay of form and action. *International Review of Public Administration*, *18*(2), 27–45. doi:10.1080/12294659.2013.10805251

Klerkx, L., Aarts, N., & Leeuwis, C. (2010). Adaptive management in agricultural innovation systems: The interactions between innovation networks and their environment. *Agricultural Systems*, *103*(6): 390–400. http://dx.doi.org/10.1016/j.agsy.2010.03.012

Klijn, E.H., & Koppenjan, J.F. (2006). Institutional design: Changing institutional features of networks. *Public Management Review*, *8*(1), 141–160. doi: 10.1080/14719030500518915

López-Gunn, E. (2012). Groundwater governance and social capital. *Geoforum*, *43*(6), 1140–1151. doi:10.1016/j.geoforum.2012.06.013

Lyons, M. (1993). The history of nonprofit organisations in Australia as a test of some recent nonprofit theory. *Voluntas*, *4*(3) 301–325. doi: 10.1007/BF01398151

Lyons, M. (1998). Defining the nonprofit sector: Australia. In L.M. Salamon, H.K. Anheier, (Eds.), *Working papers of The Johns Hopkins Comparative Nonprofit Sector Project: Comparative Nonprofit Sector Project*. Baltimore: John Hopkins Institute for Policy Studies.

March, J., & Olsen, J. (1989). *Rediscovering institutions*. Ebook edition retrieved from https:// play.google.com/store/books/details?id=PptVLvIoSWwC, March, New York: Free Press.

McCrudden, C. (2004). Using public procurement to achieve social outcomes. *Natural Resources Forum, 28*(4), 257–267. doi:10.1111/j.1477–8947.2004.00099.x

McHugh, N., Sinclair, S., Roy, M., Huckfield, L., & Donaldson, C. (2013). Social impact bonds: A wolf in sheep's clothing? *Journal of Poverty and Social Justice, 21*(3), 247–257. doi: 10.1332/204674313X13812372137921

Meehan, J., & Bryde, D. (2011). Sustainable procurement practice. *Business Strategy and the Environment, 20*(2), 94–106. doi:10.1002/bse.678

Moe, T.M. (1990). Political institutions: The neglected side of the story. *Journal of Law, Economics, & Organization, 6* (SPEISS), 213–253. doi:10.1093/jleo/6.special_issue.213

Munoz, S.A. (2009). Social enterprise and public sector voices on procurement. *Social Enterprise Journal, 5*(1), 69–82. doi:10.1108/17508610910956417

Munoz, S.A., & Tinsley, S. (2008). Selling to the public sector: Prospects and problems for social enterprise in the UK. *The Journal of Corporate Citizenship*, *32*. 43–62. Retrieved from www.socialenterprisecanada.ca/en/learn/nav/resourcelibrary.html?page=resourceDetail. tpt&iddoc=321145 (Accessed 28th May 2015)

Nicholls, J., Sacks, J., & Walsham, M. (2006). *More for your money: a guide to procuring from social enterprises*. Retrieved from www.socialenterprise.org.uk/data/files/publications/sec_pro curement_guide_final_06.pdf

North, D.C. (1990). *Institutions, institutional change, and economic performance*. Cambridge, NY: Cambridge University Press.

Ostrom, E. (2009). Institutional rational choice: An assessment of the Institutional Analysis and Development Framework. In Sabatier, Paul A. (Eds.), *Theories of the policy process* (pp. 21–64). Retrieved from http://libcat.library.qut.edu.au/search~S8?/asabatier/ asabatier/1%2C6%2C12%2CB/frameset&FF=asabatier+paul+a&5%2C%2C6/index-sort=- New York: Westview Press:. (Accessed 28th May 2015)

Ostrom, E. (2011). Background on the Institutional Analysis and Development Framework. *Policy Studies Journal, 39*(1), 7–27. doi: 10.1111/j.1541-0072.2010.00394.x

Owen-Smith, J., & Powell, W.W. (2008). Networks and institutions. In R. Greenwood, C. Oliver, R. Suddaby, & K. Sahlin-Andersson (Eds.), *The sage handbook of organizational institutionalism* (pp. 594–621). New York, NY: Sage Publications.

Pache, A.-C., & Santos, F. (2010). When worlds collide: The internal dynamics of organizational responses to conflicting institutional demands. *Academy of Management Review, 35*(3), 455–476. doi: 10.5465/AMR.2010.51142368

Pelling, M., High, C., Dearing, J., & Smith, D. (2008). Shadow spaces for social learning: A relational understanding of adaptive capacity to climate change within organisations. *Environment and Planning A, 40*(4), 867–884. doi: 10.1068/a39148

Puttick, R., & Ludlow, J. (2012). *Standards of evidence for impact investing*. Retrieved from http:// apsocialfinance.com/wp-content/uploads/2013/02/2012-nesta_standardsofevidence forimpactinvesting1.pdf (Accessed 28th May 2015)

Rogers, E. (2003). *Diffusion of innovations* (5th ed.). New York, NY: Free Press.

Scott, W.R. (1991). Unpacking institutional arguments. In W. Powell, & P.J. DiMaggio, (Eds.), *The new institutionalism in organizational analysis* (pp. 164–182). Chicago: University of Chicago Press.

Scott, W.R. (1993). Recent developments in organizational sociology. *Acta Sociologica, 36*(1), 63–68. doi:10.1177/000169939303600105

Scott, W.R. (1995). *Institutions and organizations.* Thousand Oaks, CA: Sage Publications.

Scott, W.R. (2001). *Institutions and organizations: Ideas, interests, and identities.* Thousand Oaks, CA: Sage Publications.

Scott, W.R. (2008). *Institutions and organizations: Ideas, interests, and identities* (3rd ed.). Los Angeles: Sage Publications.

Scott, W.R. (2013). *Institutions and organizations: Ideas, interests, and identities* (4th ed.). Los Angeles: Sage Publications.

Scottish Government. (2008). *Community benefits in public procurement guidance note.* Retrieved from www.scotland.gov.uk/Publications/2008/02/12145623/1 (Accessed 28th May 2015)

Scottish Government. (2014). *Procurement policy manual version 8.0.* Retrieved from www.gov.scot/Resource/0045/00459290.pdf (Accessed 28th May 2015)

Social Enterprise Canada (n.d.*a*). *enp: Enterprising non-profits.* Retrieved from www.socialenterprisecanada.ca/en (Accessed 28th May 2015)

Social Enterprise Canada (n.d.*b*). *Introduction: Purchasing from social enterprises blends business and social values.* Retrieved from www.socialenterprisecanada.ca/en/toolkits/purchasingtoolkit/#sthash.gv9kYsxh.dpuf (Accessed 28th May 2015)

Social Enterprise Networks Scotland (SENSCOT). (n.d.) *The SENs: Connecting social enterprise across Scotland.* Retrieved from www.se-networks.net/ (Accessed 28th May 2015)

Social Enterprise UK. (2013). *Social Value Act.* Retrieved from www.socialenterprise.org.uk/policy-campaigns/latest-campaigns/social-value-act (Accessed 28th May 2015)

Social Firms Scotland (n.d.). *Social firms Scotland.* Retrieved from www.socialfirms.org.uk/whoweare/ourhistory.asp (Accessed 28th May 2015)

Social Investment Scotland (SIS). (n.d.) *Social investment Scotland: Connecting capital with communities.* Retrieved from www.socialinvestmentscotland.com/looking-for-investment/case-studies/

Social Procurement Action Group (SPAG). (n.d.). *Social procurement in NSW: A guide to achieving social value through public sector procurement.* Retrieved from www.wollongong.nsw.gov.au/services/community/Documents/Social%20Procurement%20in%20NSW%20-%20Full%20Guide1%20at%2015%20October%202012.pdf (Accessed 28th May 2015)

Social Traders (n.d.). *Social procurement.* Retrieved from www.socialtraders.com.au/social-procurement (Accessed 28th May 2015)

Social Ventures Australia (SVA). (n.d.). *Social Ventures Australia works with innovative partners to invest in social change.* Retrieved from http://socialventures.com.au/who-we-are/ (Accessed 28th May 2015)

Sproul, R.C. (2000). *The consequences of ideas.* Wheaton, IL: Crossway Books.

Weber, M. (1947). *The theory of social and economic organization.* (A.M. Henderson, & T. Parsons, Trans.). New York, NY: Free Press.

Yoon, K. (2006). Bid preference in license auctions: Affirmative action can achieve economic efficiency. *International Journal of Industrial Organization, 24*(3), 593–604. doi:10.1016/j.ijindorg.2005.09.002

Zucker, L. (1987). *Institutional theories of organization, Annual Review of Sociology, 13*(1), 443–464. doi: 10.1146/annurev.so.13.080187.002303

5 Social procurement and the corporate sector

In the previous chapter, we considered how institutions shape social procurement practice. We noted that, as an emerging institutional field, social procurement presents particular openings for private actors to negotiate and contribute to norm-setting and legitimacy formation. We observed particular roles for corporate actors in developing supply chains consistent with social procurement objectives. In this chapter, we provide a more in-depth analysis of the functions of private for-profit actors – particularly corporate firms – in social procurement and their relationship to concurrent developments in corporate social responsibility.

Organisational concerns for environmental, financial and social outcomes have manifested in initiatives such as corporate social responsibility (CSR) and triple bottom line reporting. With regard to social procurement, these concerns are addressed through ethical purchasing arrangements, principally by taking into account social and environmental considerations as part of CSR, but also increasingly when making supply chain decisions. Initially, corporate practices were driven by consumer demand for goods and services that had been produced in a manner that did not harm ecological and social systems. More recently, demand from both individual consumers and governmental commissioners has increased for the active generation of social and environmental benefits through the social value chain.

One of the difficulties in studying supply chains is that there are many differing definitions (Ritchie & Brindley, 2007). For our discussion, we understand supply chains to be both networks of firms and the flow of information, materials and funds within and between network members (Ahi & Searcy, 2013). CSR is understood here to be "decisions and actions taken for reasons at least partially beyond the firm's direct economic or technical interest" (David, 1960, p. 70). While this definition captures a variety of inflections of CSR, it is important to note that the academic literature identifies a variety of approaches and underlying motivations of CSR; these are detailed later in this chapter.

Corporate social responsibility and its evolution

The fundamental idea in CSR is that businesses have an obligation to work to improve society (Frederick, 1994). According to an early proponent, "the substance of social responsibility arises from concern for the ethical conse-quences of one's acts as they might affect the interests of others" (Davies, 1967, p. 46). The earliest actual report of CSR dates from the 1930s, with such works as "Measurement of the Social Performance of Business" (Kreps, 1940). The single most significant publication which authors often credit as bringing CSR into mainstream thought (e.g., Falck & Heblich, 2006) is "Social Responsibili-ties of the Businessman"[1] (Bowen, 1953). Like many other fields under study, there are differing academic views on what CSR is. Four main perspectives can be identified in terms of how organisations might approach CSR (Garriga & Melé, 2004); these are outlined in Table 5.1.

The framework provided by Garriga and Melé (2004) will be used to analyse the field of CSR in more detail, and extend into the next section an under-standing of social procurement in supply chains.

Instrumental CSR approaches

Instrumental approaches to CSR see that businesses exist to make a profit; however, CSR has a place provided that it does not interfere with the pursuit of profit (Garriga & Melé, 2004). Porter and Kramer (2006) summarise this approach by arguing "companies should operate in ways that secure long term economic performance by avoiding short term behaviour that is socially det-rimental or environmentally wasteful" (p. 81). So the focus here is to pursue CSR in order to avoid negative outcomes for the firm. As David (1960) argued, the "avoidance of social responsibility leads to gradual erosion of social power" (p. 73). Negative examples of this are the Exxon Valdez oil spill and the disas-trous impact this had on pristine wilderness (Du & Vieira Jr, 2012).

Another variation on the instrumental approach is to note that investment in CSR practices can lead to an increase in profits for shareholders (Garriga & Melé, 2004). Rather than attending to CSR in order not to negatively affect the bottom line, this approach seeks to use CSR to actively improve the bottom line. CSR can create a competitive advantage for firms, by addressing internal factors such as employee skills, safety and health; together with external factors

Table 5.1 Main approaches to CSR

Approach	Perspective of business	Role of CSR
Instrumental	Businesses exist for profit	CSR is valid as a means to profits
Political	Businesses exist in a society	CSR is a social obligation
Integrative	Businesses depend on society for existence	CSR is essential for a business to operate
Ethical	Businesses have an ethical obligation	CSR is a moral duty

Adapted from Garriga & Melé, 2004.

of water use, energy use, environmental impact, and supplier access and viability (Porter & Kramer, 2011). The important issue here is that organisations can seek to do good, but see this as a means to an end.

The third instrumental variation is to see CSR as a form of reputation management, where the goal is to improve the image of the organisation, and to insure against future potential negative feedback (Porter & Kramer, 2006). Here CSR reporting is implemented in such a way as to enhance the community's view of the organisation (Gray, Owen & Maunders, 1987), or to pursue legitimacy (Hatch & Cunliffe, 2006). Good reputation can lead to the attraction and retention of quality employees, as well as the external good will towards a company (Falck & Heblich, 2006). A good example of this sort of approach was the rapid response of Johnson and Johnson to the poisoning of its Tylenol product in the early 1980s. So swift and comprehensive was the recall of potentially lethal products that the organisation's code of conduct became celebrated, and is often held up as an example of how other organisations should behave (Burke & Logsdon, 1996).

The final instrumental CSR approach occurs when pursuit of CSR can lead to some form of competitive advantage (Garriga & Melé, 2004). As Ambec and Lanoie (2008) note, CSR may result in a direct improvement of the bottom line due to enhanced waste and safety management. From this perspective, CSR policies would seek to reuse materials, reduce waste, remanufacture goods, recycle waste and dispose of relatively fewer waste products (Sarkis, 2003), because this efficiency would likely lead to cost savings. It is possible that a decision to purchase products and services from social enterprises will deliver both positive financial and social outcomes for an organisation (Thompson, 2008), and that this will provide a competitive advantage to firms. A growing suite of tools is enabling these purchasing practices. Examples include buying guides, such as the UK Buy Social Guide (Social Enterprise UK, 2013a), which encourages companies to consider ways they can achieve CSR targets through the purchasing of services from social enterprises and online marketplaces, such as Good Spender (Good Spender, n.d.) in Australia, which seeks to link (corporate and individual) consumers with social enterprises for trading purposes. This topic is discussed further in relation to supply chains below.

Clearly, the public has a view on the sincerity of an organisation's response to a CSR issue (Sen & Bhattacharya, 2001). While the Johnson and Johnson example was viewed positively, a purely instrumental approach misses the opportunities which arise from long-term investment in communities and sustainable technologies (Du & Vieira Jr, 2012). The reason for this is that sincerity of intent is likely to be viewed far more positively than purely instrumental attempts to sway public perceptions (Fort, 2014).

Political CSR approaches

Political conceptions of CSR follow the logic that business has a social obligation, or must fulfil a "social contract" in order to be effective (Garriga & Melé, 2004). This social contract involves a set of obligations to society and operates from an understanding that businesses cannot exist apart from the societies in which they are located. From this perspective, the reporting of CSR involves an acquittal of accountability obligations. Carroll (1991) argued that corporate social responsibility could be viewed as a pyramid, with making money the bottom of the pyramid, moving up to obeying the law, being ethical and finally being a good corporate citizen.

New public governance arrangements explored in this volume blur previously well-demarcated boundaries between state and market functions. Businesses are increasingly cast both as "rule makers" in their roles as co-producers of societal good and navigators of globalised market arrangements, and as "rule takers" through traditional forms of state regulation and oversight (Pies, 2011). Corporate citizenship illuminates the increasing complexity of corporate performance as it involves a sense of commitment towards the community by businesses (Garriga & Melé, 2004). Porter and Kramer (2006) note that, while CSR is often framed in terms of moral absolutes, "most corporate social choices involve balancing competing values, interests and costs" (p. 81). While earlier discourses of CSR generally described a set of discrete and instrumental practices, notions of corporate citizenship speak more broadly to the function of private for-profit firms as political actors in setting societal rules (Pies, 2011). As discussed in Chapter 4, for example, individual corporations have been significant in the transfer of supplier diversity commitments across national and industry boundaries, in some cases preceding the establishment of public policy frameworks (Shah & Ram, 2006). This subject is discussed further in this chapter in relation to policy and regulation.

Integrative CSR approaches

Integrative approaches are different from the previous two approaches in that they view businesses as being dependent on their communities (Garriga & Melé, 2004). This view suggests that businesses are active members of all communities and therefore should be involved in policy making (Porter & Kramer, 2006). Businesses are in the community and engage with an array of stakeholders when enacting their work. Stakeholder salience theory is a particular derivative of this approach, which characterises organisations (or their managers) as seeking to navigate the expectations and influence of different stakeholders based on relative power and salience of these stakeholders (Agle, Mitchell & Sonnenfeld, 1999). When one is more focussed on what a stakeholder might do to stop a business practice, this conceptualisation of CSR has moved considerably away from the "concern for ethical consequences of one's actions" (Davies, 1967, p. 46). A useful way of examining this idea is to examine the notion of a "social license to operate".

The earliest reference to the notion of "social license to operate" was coined by Mitch Anderson, who argued that Chevron had nearly lost its "social license to operate" because of the multiple local government agencies boycotting their products (cited in the Solar Times, 2008, p. 7). The term appears to have entered the academic lexicon specifically in relation to mining via Moore (1996).

If one accepts that stakeholders have power over the corporation and can influence its success, a consideration of a "social license to operate" becomes feasible. Organisations that rely heavily on good relationships with specific communities, such as mines, developers and chemical factories, commonly use this approach (Porter & Kramer, 2006). A key driver for this is because there is a lack of public trust in these sorts of industries (Owen & Kemp, 2013), primarily because of historical economic and social failures.

Pragmatically, while mines have to obtain a formal license from the government they also need to obtain a social license to operate (Prno & Slocombe, 2012). While the former may be a one-off or time-bound process, the latter is an iterative and ongoing process of negotiation. As Nelson (2006) argued: "If a community does not support the development of a mine, commodity process, no matter how high, will not generate a positive production/development decision" (p. 161). So mining firms need to engage with their community and gain community support. Similarly, the use of community benefits agreements in the United States are one mechanism by which developers seek to establish a social license to operate through negotiation and commitment to additional socio-economic goals determined with the communities in which new developments are initiated (Been, 2010).

While a social license to operate reflects a relational process between corporations and the communities in which they are embedded, it has been noted that in some industries and jurisdictions, governments are becoming a third-party stakeholder. In the Australian mining industry, for example, state government initiatives such as Queensland's guidelines on developing social impact management plans reflect an increasing focus on regulating interactions between communities and firms (Lacey, 2013) in the interests of generating positive, or minimising negative, social consequences of corporate activities.

Ethical CSR approaches

The final approach to CSR is informed by ethical conceptions, which focus on the obligation of businesses to behave in an ethical manner, regardless of the context or consequences (Garriga & Melé, 2004). Donaldson and Preston (1995) note that, while there can be instrumental approaches to stakeholder management, an alternative is normative approach. As Wijnberg (2000) observes, Donaldson and Preston (1995) emphasise the obligation aspect of managers stating that they "should" behave in a specific manner. Normative approaches are often examined in relationship to public policies around social procurement – particularly requiring organisations to have some form of CSR policy in place.

Positioning CSR in the social procurement typology

Recall from Chapter 1 the introduction of a typology of social procurement, which enabled a comparison of different approaches (Table 5.2). It is instructive to position CSR in relation to this framework.

Table 5.2 Typology of social procurement

		Outcomes	
		Direct	*Indirect*
F O C U S	"Procurement of" social outcomes *(Focus on the contract)*	**Type 1** Procurement of social services from third-sector organisations	**Type 2** Procurement of social benefits embedded in capital works
	"Procurement from" social providers *(Focus on the tender)*	**Type 3** Procurement of non-traditional services from diverse suppliers	**Type 4** Ethical supply chain management

CSR and ethical supply chain management typically fall into Type 4 social procurement. This is because the procurement process achieves social outcomes indirectly, and these outcomes are the direct effect of the procurement event (Furneaux & Barraket, 2014). When considering how CSR fits in relation to other types of social procurement, it is worth considering typically how it would be implemented and assessed.

For social procurement, particularly Types 1 and 3, procurement involved the direct achievement of social outcomes. In other words, the outputs are specified in the procurement instrument as measurable deliverables – typically outputs but increasingly as outcomes.

For CSR, though, managing social impact through the supply chain does not in and of itself result in the procurement of social outcomes. Typically, CSR involves assessment against activities, while the outputs are different. For example, a coal mine would see the actual outputs around tonnes of coal produced, and the CSR activities are not the ends of the activity, but rather a means to an end. It is here that CSR crosses vectors in the Procurement Typology. To garner community support, mining companies, for example, can be engaged in the direct procurement of community infrastructure such as roads, education and training, community support, sports and recreation and health (KPMG, 2013). However, as previously outlined, the purchasing of such goods occurs as an activity on the way towards mining, which is the main activity. In effect, the legitimacy that the purchasing of these services has created is simply another necessary input (Hatch & Cunliffe, 2006) in the production process. Depending on your perspective, procurement of social outcomes by mines can either be direct or indirect social procurement.

Factors driving CSR

CSR is driven by a variety of factors. These include wider concerns about sustainable development discussed in Chapter 3 and demographic and technological influences canvassed in Chapter 2. The European Economic and Social

Committee (2001) identifies a range of factors informing CSR. These are sum-marised in Table 5.3.

As Table 5.3 shows, while CSR certainly applies to the internal dynamics of the firm, it also applies to external elements, and supply chain considerations apply to human rights, communities and the business partners of firms. One of the key drivers for CSR is, of course, government regulation and quasi-regulation in relation to CSR. This is discussed in some detail in the next section.

Government regulation and CSR

As noted in Chapter 4, the external environment of an organisation can act to enable or make difficult specific activities such as social procurement. In

Table 5.3 Internal and external aspects of CSR (summarised from European Commission 2001)

Internal	
Human resource management	Work-life balance, equity, job security, rehabilitation, responsible recruitment, training
Occupational health and safety	Beyond regulatory requirements, also involved in certification and pre-qualification schemes, whereby companies are certified as meeting occupational health and safety standards
Socially responsible restructuring	Involving all stakeholders (government, company, employee representatives)
Managing environmental impacts	Reducing consumption, emissions and waste

External	
Local communities	Providing jobs, wages, benefits, tax revenues, provision of vocational training; assisting charities; sponsoring sporting and cultural events; caring directly for environmental impact
Business partners, suppliers and consumers	Behaving ethically with suppliers, promoting entrepreneurs, mentoring start-ups, corporate venturing, providing quality goods and services to customers which are safe and reliable
Human rights[1]	There is an obligation to ensure that business partners are meeting international labour obligations, and are not involved in human rights abuses
Global environmental concerns	There is a growing consideration of the role of business in development, achieving social and environmental goals through their supply chains.

[1]See the ILO Tripartite Declaration of Principles concerning Multinational Enterprises and Social Policy (ILO, 2006) and the OECD Guidelines for Multinational Enterprises (OECD, 2011).

particular, government regulations are able to both prohibit certain actions (proscription), and mandate or require specific actions (prescription). A CSR example of this was recounted by English (1983) in relation to effective management of hazardous waste in water systems: "There is then double protection against contamination by hazardous wastes: the prescriptive new laws which impose management and operational requirements, and the proscriptive water pollution control laws which restrict discharges into water" (p. 234). Moreover, with regulation there are direct and indirect effects. Another example is provided by Bartel and Thomas (1985), who note that:

> The direct effects of the Occupational Health and Safety Act are improvements in safety for workers and increases in manufacturing costs that decrease wages and profits. Alongside these direct effects however, are the general equilibrium 'indirect effects'—the competitive advantages that arise from the asymmetrical impacts of regulation among different firms and workers. For example, if the cost burden of certain regulation falls heavily on one group, but lightly on another, then an indirect effect of these regulations is to provide a competitive advantage to the second group of firms.
>
> (p. 3)

Other indirect effects might also accrue, such as increased demand, or increased loyalty for products, from clients who desire triple bottom line outcomes, or because the organisation has an improved public image due to ethical procurement practice. As noted in relation to the Northern Ireland Unemployment Pilot Project discussed in Chapter 3, some commercial providers saw business value in being able to distinguish themselves as respondents to a public tender process that embedded welfare goals in public works (Erridge, 2007). In addition, the increased regulatory requirements may result in improved internal processes and considerable process innovation.

A good example of how the indirect benefits of certain legislation can lead to large-scale adoption is in relation to "green building" standards, which require environmental factors to be considered in the design of buildings (Kibert, 2012). Indeed, rather than causing loss of revenue, environmental regulation can create opportunities for companies to achieve strategic competitive advantage compared to non-environmentally friendly organisations (c.f. Azzone & Bertele, 1994; Porter & van der Linde, 1995). For example, by reducing the amount of electricity used (through timers and efficient lighting), and water usage (through timers and limiters), considerable economic benefits may be achieved by organisations, alongside environmental outcomes (Esty & Winston, 2009; Kats, 2003; Ries, Bilec, Gokhan & Needy, 2006). Some authors argue that it is only once this link between the economic and environmental performance of organisations has been clearly established, that environmental concerns will become widely adopted (Schaltegger & Synnestvedt, 2002; Stefan & Paul, 2008). Kibert (2012) notes that there has indeed been a significant increase in applications for green building certification with the U.S. Green

Buildings Council[2] since its inception in 1999. Thus, paying attention to environmental issues can lead to cost savings for organisations in the long term, and so makes economic as well as environmental sense. This is consistent with the instrumental approach to CSR discussed previously.

While regulatory regimes can result in indirect commercial benefits, they can also produce normative cultures, which transfer through commercial practice to jurisdictions in which compliance is not mandated. With their origins in the United States, policies related to increasing supplier diversity – linked to increased social diversity within the populace (Shah & Ram, 2006; Worthington, 2009; Worthington, Ram, Boyal & Shah, 2008) – are an early example of regulatory prescriptions that have substantially shaped commercial practices with regard to social procurement. With an early focus on increasing market opportunities for ethnic minority businesses (EMB) as part of a wider prescriptive affirmative action agenda in the United States and Canada, supplier diversity approaches – both mandatory and voluntary – have now been adopted in a variety of jurisdictions to grow market opportunities for Indigenous Australian-owned businesses, lesbian-, gay-, bisexual-, transgender- and intersex-owned businesses, businesses owned and led by women, and social enterprises. It is observed in the literature that, while the role of government should not be understated, transnational transfer of policy and practice has been enabled by civil society intermediaries, particularly the US National Minority Supplier Development Council and by prominent practice and the apparent positive business impacts for leading corporations of purposeful diversification of their supply chains (Shah & Ram, 2006; Ram, Theodorakopoulos & Worthington, 2007; Worthington, 2009). Thus, while regulatory compliance has been the impetus for the uptake of supplier diversity strategies, the normative effects of reputational benefits and mimetic isomorphism (DiMaggio & Powell, 1983) amongst private for-profit firms have been significant to their adoption beyond their originally targeted demographic groups and across jurisdictions.

The increasingly relational repertoire of public procurement strategies (Bovaird, 2006) appears to be generating new interdependencies – and related commitments to co-responsibility – between non-traditional partners in relation to social value creation. At the time of writing, high-profile actors in the UK construction industry are rallying in support of a funding campaign to save the Building Lives social enterprise, which supports disadvantaged young people into apprenticeships in the industry (Considerate Constructors Scheme, n.d.). In the face of a growing skills shortage, combined with a growing orthodoxy of procurers embedding socio-economic goals into public works projects, the mutual benefits of such arrangements are emphasised.

In summary, policy and regulation – as discussed in relation to the formation of rules that underpin practice rules in Chapter 4 – has a normative effect on organisations, through proscription and prescription. If advantages were demonstrated as being achieved through conformance with a particular legislative agenda, then the regulation may be imitated by other organisations or in other jurisdictions. This understanding is summarised in Table 5.4.

Table 5.4 Intent and impact of environmental (waste water) regulation on firms[1]

		Intent of legislation	
		Proscription	*Prescription*
Impact of legislation on firms	Direct impact	Firms are prohibited from the dumping of certain substances into waterways. Cleaner waterways are the outcome.	Firms are required to manage their operations in a specific way to minimise risks to the environment. Firms which handle their waste better is the outcome.
	Indirect impact	Organisations gain a competitive advantage by not dumping.	Firms which comply with regulations gain a competitive advantage over other firms

[1]Based on English, 1983 and Bartel & Thomas, 1985.

Thus, regulation can enable or prohibit the implementation of a range of activities, such as social procurement. Moreover, such regulation can have a direct impact – and a more indirect impact – on the organisations involved.

Over- and under-compliant responses

The range of approaches already presented has set a rather rosy view of CSR policy and practice. The fact is that organisations can take approaches to meeting CSR expectations either by under- or over-performing. This concept is summarised in Table 5.5.

Oliver (1991) outlined a set of responses an organisation might make to demands for compliance or conformance with a set of requirements. We have adapted this approach to account for responses to CSR legislation.

While there certainly can be under-compliant approaches, such as avoidance, the opposite can also be true and some organisations can elect to over comply, an example of which is the shared value movement. Porter and Kramer (2011) are key advocates for this approach and recently argued that, beyond being responsive or strategic, firms could aim to "enhance the competitiveness of a company while simultaneously advancing the economic and social conditions in the communities in which it operates" (p. 6). The intentional achievement of social good while also achieving financial benefit is an approach typically associated with social enterprises (Dart, 2004). However, Porter and Kramer (2011) extend this and argue that such an approach can be undertaken by any business.

An explicit example of the shared value approach is Landmarc (Social Enterprise UK, 2013b) in the UK, which partners with the Department of Defence to ensure safe working environments for training of army personnel, while also delivering value to the communities in which the services are delivered. This sort of activity would seem to best fit in the Type 1 social procurement, the deliberate achievement of social outcomes.

Table 5.5 Compliance responses and their effects[1]

Response	Description	Outcomes for Organisations	Examples
Advocate	Actively promote and advocate for CSR adoption	Long-term value creation (economic and social)	Intermediary groups, such as Social Enterprise UK
Acquiesce	Organisations can follow the rules in a number of ways, ranging from imitating the behaviour of other organisations to deliberately or incidentally following the rules.	Organisations which comply with institutional rules are elevated in terms of legitimacy. Some competitive advantage may accrue.	Mining companies may well enact CSR, but as the section previously noted, this can be for a variety of reasons.
Compromise	Sometimes organisations have to balance multiple institutional demands for their resources and so organisations may attempt to bargain with or try to placate stakeholders through bare-minimum compliance.	Compliance with norms is more partial in nature, and organisations are more concerned with their own interests.	This goes to the concerns raised about the public perception of the sincerity of CSR practices in organisations.
Avoid	When the costs of compliance are too high, organisations can try to avoid the expectations, a form of passive resistance. This may involve attempts to conceal actions and pretend that requirements have been complied with; reducing the ability of external organisations to examine activities; or simply trying to avoid the need to comply in the first place.	The outcome for the organisation is to avoid the need to comply in the first place.	An example is pharmaceutical companies in Bangladesh, 75% of whom made sweeping qualitative statements in order to meet reporting obligations (Azim & Azam, 2013).
Defy	This is a more active attempt to resist institutional pressures to conform. This can be in the form of dismissing the requirements, challenging the societal norms or attacking these norms.	The organisation rejects the norms imposed on it, and is likely to occur when the perceived consequences for non-compliance are low.	Proposals for mandatory reporting in Europe have been weakened due to lobbying, so as to be voluntary and not apply to most businesses (Bizzarri, 2013)

Response	Description	Outcomes for Organisations	Examples
Manipulate	This is the most active form of resistance, and involves attempts by organisations to put pressure on other actors, or the institutional pressures themselves.	The organisation uses whatever power it has to overturn the norms it does not wish to comply with.	

[1]Adapted from Oliver (1991) and Zadek (2004).

Having considered elements of CSR, which are often applied within a firm, the construct needs to be expanded to consider supply chain management issues. Carter and Easton (2011) note that, while CSR is a critical part of the supply chain research, much of this has occurred without recognising the relationship between environment, diversity, human rights, philanthropy and safety. As has been noted in the preceding paragraphs, organisations engage in CSR through their own activities and also via their supply chain (for example, the purchasing of sporting services by mines in order to achieve a social license to operate). This is discussed in detail next.

Supply chain management and social outcomes: core concepts

To understand the notion of supply chain management, one must start with the notion of a firm. Coase (1937), in his Nobel Prize–winning article, notes that one of the main reasons for the existence of firms in the first place is to reduce transaction costs in the marketplace. Whenever goods and services are purchased from the market, there are inevitably aspects of information asymmetry and uncertainty that create transaction costs for organisations (Vining & Globerman, 1999). Conversely, many organisations, including within governments, have undergone processes of determining whether, even with these transaction costs factored in, outsourcing certain operations or functions could be done more cheaply by another organisation. Consequently, a significant decision in the procurement process is deciding whether to deliver the service in house or whether to purchase the service from the market – the "make or buy" decision (McIvor, 2005; Vining & Globerman, 1999).

As briefly outlined in Chapter 1, a "purchasing" decision involves establishing how an action or project will deliver on outcomes and outputs, and focuses on the acquisition of the asset or service (Murray, 2009). *Procurement* can be defined as "the process of acquiring goods, works and services covering both acquisition from third parties, and from in house providers" (Local Government Authority, 2003, p. 17). Thus, procurement clearly involves assessment of a supply chain. Thinking of social procurement and purchasing in a supply chain sense may range in corporate practice from small-scale purchasing decisions to procure coffee supplies from fair trade sources, to substantive organisational policy commitments to supplier diversity, such as those established by the National Australia Bank to procure from Indigenous, women-owned and social enterprises.

Beyond supply chain social procurement, private for-profit firms are also engaging – both as initiators and partners – in new approaches to value chain development that recognise social value as a form of value realised through cross-sector arrangements.

Social value chain

In broad terms, *value chains* refer to commercial responses to the dynamics of global markets, through business models that are responsive to rapid market changes and generate new capabilities through less focus on resource ownership and acquisition and greater emphasis on unique combinations of relationships between suppliers, customers, shareholders, governments, workers, and sometimes, competitors (Walters, 2004). Value chain thinking includes consideration of elements across the operational life cycle, such as production, procurement, packaging distribution and logistics (see, for example, Sarkis, 2003).

Value chains are typically understood in terms of generating competitive advantage. Partnership and distributed procurement approaches outlined in Chapter 3, along with changing consumer sentiments with regard to ethical purchasing (Bucic, Harris & Arli, 2012) are stimulating value chain responses that focus on environmental or social value as a source of such advantage. Where corporate actors are value chain creators, this is typically organised around embedding social or environmental purchasing into supply chain relationships.

Again, the Landmarc case provides a good example of practice here. While government purchases services from Landmarc, Landmarc purchases through its supply chain numerous products and services. According to a recently commissioned report, social enterprises comprise at least 60% of the organisations in the supply chain, as well as some non-profit organisations in relation to wounded personnel (Social Enterprise UK, 2013*b*).

Social value chain development may also be initiated by social benefit providers in order to scale their social impacts through distribution opportunities afforded by partnership with large firms. In recent developments in Australia, for example, an award-winning social enterprise, Sprout Ventures, is working with a major property and infrastructure company to develop community infrastructure within master-planned estates in metropolitan fringe areas. Here, the social enterprise is the value chain creator, and there is bottom-line appeal for the collaborating companies in the marketing value and cost efficiencies of working with social enterprise in commercial and regulatory environments that are increasingly requiring developers to systematically demonstrate the social value added of their projects.

While value chain developments that have been adapted to social value creation stress the importance of flexibility and rapid response to market opportunities, trends in CSR have typically placed a somewhat competing procedural emphasis on disclosure of organisational practices as a necessary condition for transparency: "Consumers do not only want good and safe products, but they also want to know if they are produced in a socially responsible manner" (European Economic and Social Committee, 2001, p. 19). In the following section, we briefly consider regulatory and organisational developments in social performance reporting as they pertain to corporate social procurement.

Social responsibility reporting and auditing

Consistent with the conditions of the "audit society" (Power, 1997) which we discuss in Chapter 7, social procurement is generating new imperatives for CSR reporting and "auditable performance" (Power, 2000, p. 114). Examples of this include the European Economic and Social Committee recommendation on the recognition, measurement and disclosure of environmental issues in the annual accounts and reports of companies (European Commission, 2001). The Danish Ministry of Social Affairs has developed a Social Index which provides a way of measuring how a company performs in terms of corporate social responsibility, and large Danish companies are required to report on the CSR, or explain why they have not done so (Corporate Sustainability Reporting, n.d.). While the Danish law is targeted and provides guidance on CSR reporting, the recently introduced 2011 French law (Article 225) is prescriptive and requires mandatory reporting, and third-party assurance, against 42 economic, financial, social and governance categories (Morris, 2012). Article 225 thus goes far beyond CSR and is the earliest move towards sustainability reporting. According to Ernst and Young (2012), "Article 225 arguably represents the strongest stance yet taken by any country to require transparency from businesses on the environmental, social and governance front" (p. 2). The French law is mandated for listed companies and will increasingly be applied to unlisted companies, both those domiciled in France and those who do business with France. While undoubtedly coercive (DiMaggio & Powell, 1983), the fact that all listed and major unlisted companies are required by law to report on the same set of measures provides considerable impetus to the sustainability agenda.

While many multinational companies issue reports on health and safety, and environmental impact, reports on human rights and child labour are not so readily reported (European Economic and Social Committee, 2001). To move this reporting agenda forward, consensus is needed as to the content and structure of these sorts of reports. One way of advancing this agenda globally is via integrated reporting. "Integrated reporting is about integrating material financial and non-financial information to enable investors and other stakeholders to understand how an organisation is really performing" (Institute of Chartered Accountants, 2013, n.p.). It is important to note that the International Integrated Reporting Council (2013) has released an Integrated Reporting Framework, which provides a global approach to the reporting of multiple capitals by organisations: financial, manufactured, intellectual, human, social, relationship, natural. By acknowledging that all of these "capitals" contribute to the performance of an organisation, this global reporting initiative shifts the focus away from purely financial or manufactured assets. While currently being trialled by 100 companies initially, the framework is likely to be rolled out in OECD countries quite rapidly thereafter. We return to the nature and function of metrics in our discussion of social value creation and its measurement in Chapter 7.

Conclusion

In this chapter, we have considered the relationship between CSR and social procurement, and the ways in which different approaches to CSR drive procurement processes that have direct and indirect effects on social outcomes. We have observed that, while CSR typically originates at the level of the firm, networked approaches to governance and social value creation are placing a new emphasis on social impacts influenced through value chain dynamics. As both initiators and members of supply chains, corporations are playing changing CSR roles pertinent to social procurement. These include growing interdependence between private for-profit and third-sector providers, and navigation of increasing regulation of corporate-community relations historically relegated to private practice. The rise of corporate power is an undoubtable feature of new public governance (NPG). At the same time, this rise generates new responsibilities and new interdependencies, which suggest that this power must be understood as relational rather than absolute. In the next chapter, we return to a bigger picture analysis of the networks and interdependencies of NPG and their implications for practice across sectors.

Notes

1   Carroll (1999) wryly notes that this title suggests there where "no businesswomen during this period, or at least they were not acknowledged in formal writings" (p. 269).
2   Similar organisations and systems are prevalent in most OECD countries.

References

Agle, B.R., Mitchell, R.K., & Sonnenfeld, J.A. (1999). Who matters to CEOs? An investigation of stakeholder attributes and salience, corporate performance, and CEO values. *The Academy of Management Journal, 42*(5), 507–525. doi: 10.2307/256973
Ahi, P., & Searcy, C. (2013). A comparative literature analysis of definitions for green and sustainable supply chain management. *Journal of Cleaner Production, 52*, 329–341. doi: 10.1016/j.jclepro.2013.02.018
Ambec, S., & Lanoie, P. (2008). Does it pay to be green? A systematic overview. *The Academy of Management Perspectives, 22*(4), 45–62. doi:10.5465/AMP.2008.35590353
Azim, M.I., & Azam, M.S. (2013). Corporate sustainability reporting by pharmaceutical companies: Is it what it seems to be? *Corporate Ownership and Control, 11*(1), 754–764.
Azzone, G., & Bertele, U. (1994). Exploiting green strategies for competitive advantage. *Long Range Planning, 27*(6), 69–81. doi:10.1016/0024–6301(94)90165–1

Bartel, A.P., & Thomas, L.G. (1985). Direct and indirect effects of regulation: A new look at OSHA's impact. *Journal of Law and Economics*, *28*(1), 1–25.

Been, V. (2010). Community benefits agreements: A new local government tool or another variation on the exactions theme? *University of Chicago Law Review*, *77*(1), 5–35.

Bizzarri, K. (2013). *Refusing to be accountable: Business hollows out new EU corporate social responsibility rules*. Retrieved from Corporate Europe Observatory website: http://corporateeurope.org/eu-crisis/2013/04/refusing-be-accountable

Bovaird, T. (2006). Developing new forms of partnership with the 'market' in the procurement of public services. *Public Administration*, *84*(1), 81–102. doi: 10.1111/j.0033-3298.2006.00494.x

Bowen, H.R. (1953). Social responsibilities of the businessman. New York: Harper & Row.

Bucic, T., Harris, J., & Arli, D. (2012). Ethical consumers among the millennials: A cross-national study. *Journal of Business Ethics*, *110*(1), 113–131. http://doi.org/10.1007/s10551–011–1151-z

Burke, L., & Logsdon, J.M. (1996). How corporate social responsibility pays off. *Long Range Planning*, *29*(4), 495–502. doi: 10.1016/0024–6301(96)00041–6

Carroll, A.B. (1991). The pyramid of corporate social responsibility: Toward the moral management of organizational stakeholders. *Business Horizons*, *34*(4), 39–48. doi:10.1016/0007–6813(91)90005-G

Carroll, A.B. (1999) Corporate social responsibility: Evolution of a definitional construct. *Business and Society*, *38*(3), 268–295. doi: 10.1177/000765039903800303

Carter, C.R., & Easton, P.L. (2011). Sustainable supply chain management: Evolution and future directions. *International Journal of Physical Distribution and Logistics Management*, *41*(1), 46–62. doi: 10.1108/09600031111101420

Coase, R.H. (1937). The nature of the firm. *Economica*, *4*(16), 386–405. doi: 10.1111/j.1468–0335.1937.tb00002.x

Considerate Constructors Scheme. (n.d.) *Help save the Building Lives charity*. Retrieved from www.ccscheme.org.uk/index.php/help-save-the-building-lives-charity (Accessed 28th May 2015)

Corporate Sustainability Reporting. (n.d.). Corporate sustainability reporting: The website about CSR reporting of companies. Retrieved from www.reportingcsr.org/_denmark-p-46.html (Accessed 28th May 2015)

Dart, R. (2004). The legitimacy of social enterprise. *Nonprofit Management and Leadership*, *14*(4), 411–424. doi: 10.1002/nml.43

David, K. (1960). Can business afford to ignore social responsibilities? *Californian Management Review*, *2*(3) 70–76.

Davies, K. (1967). Understanding the social responsibility puzzle: What does the businessman owe to society? *Business Horizons*, *10*(4), 45–50.

DiMaggio, P.J., & Powell, W.W. (1983). The iron cage revisited: Institutional isomorphism and collective rationality in organizational fields. *American Sociological Review*, *48*(2), 147–160. doi:10.2307/2095101

Donaldson, T., & Preston, L.E. (1995). The stakeholder theory of the corporation: Concepts, evidence, and implications. *Academy of Management Review*, *20*(1), 65–91. doi:10.5465/AMR.1995.9503271992

Du, S., & Vieira Jr, E.T. (2012). Striving for legitimacy through corporate social responsibility: Insights from oil companies. *Journal of Business Ethics*, *110*(4), 413–427. doi:10.1007/s10551–012–1490–4

English, J.F. (1983) Hazardous waste regulation: A prescription for clean water. *Seton Hall Law Review*, *13(2)*:229–261.

Ernst & Young (2012). *How France's new sustainability reporting law impacts US companies.* Retrieved from www.ey.com/Publication/vwLUAssets/Frances_sustainability_law_to_impact_US_companies/$FILE/How_Frances_new_sustainability_reporting_law.pdf

Erridge, A. 2007 Public procurement, public value and the Northern Ireland Unemployment Pilot Project. *Public Administration, 85*(4):1023–1043. doi:10.1111/j.1467-9299.2007.00674.x

Esty, D., & Winston, A. (2009). *Green to gold: How smart companies use environmental strategy to innovate, create value, and build competitive advantage.* Hoboken: NJ, John Wiley & Sons.

European Commission (2001, June 11). Accounting: Commission issues recommendation on environmental issues in companies' annual accounts and reports. *European Commission.* Retrieved from http://europa.eu/rapid/press-release_IP-01–814_en.htm (Accessed 28th May 2015)

European Economic and Social Committee (2001). *Green paper: Promoting a European framework for corporate social responsibility.* (Report No. COM(2001) 366 final). Retrieved from http://eur-lex.europa.eu/legal-content/EN/TXT/?qid=1432823985747&uri=CELEX:52001DC0366 (Accessed 28th May 2015)

Falck, O., & Heblich, S. (2006). Corporate social responsibility: Doing well by doing good. *Business Horizons, 50*(3), 247–254. doi:10.1016/j.bushor.2006.12.002

Fort, T.L. (2014). The paradox of pharmaceutical CSR: The sincerity nexus. *Business Horizons, 57*(2), 151–160. doi:10.1016/j.bushor.2013.10.006

Frederick, W.C. (1994). From CSR1 to CSR2: The maturing of business-and-society thought. *Business and Society, 33*(2), 150–164. doi: 10.1177/000765039403300202

Furneaux, C., & Barraket, J. (2014). Purchasing social good(s): a definition and typology of social procurement. *Public Money & Management, 34*(4), 265–272. http://doi.org/10.1080/09540962.2014.920199

Garriga, E., & Melé, D. (2004). Corporate social responsibility theories: Mapping the territory. *Journal of Business Ethics, 53*(1–2): 51–71. doi:10.1023/B:BUSI.0000039399.90587.34

Good Spender (n.d.). *Good spender: Where you're shopping makes a difference.* Retrieved from www.goodspender.com.au/ (Accessed 28th May 2015)

Gray, R.H., Owen, D.L., and Maunders, K.T. (1987) *Corporate social reporting: Accounting and accountability.* London: Prentice-Hall International.

Hatch, M.J., and Cunliffe, A.L. (2006). *Organization theory: Modern, symbolic, and postmodern perspectives.* (2nd ed.). New York: Oxford University Press.

Institute of Chartered Accountants (2013). *Integrated reporting.* Retrieved from www.charteredaccountants.com.au/Industry-Topics/Sustainability/Integrated-reporting.aspx (Accessed 28th May 2015)

International Integrated Reporting Council (2013). *International integrated reporting framework.* Retrieved from www.theiirc.org/wp-content/uploads/2013/12/13–12–08-THE-INTERNATIONAL-IR-FRAMEWORK-2–1.pdf (Accessed 28th May 2015)

International Labour Office (2006). *Tripartite declaration of principles: Concerning multinational enterprises.* Retrieved from www.ilo.org/wcmsp5/groups/public/—-ed_emp/—-emp_ent/—-multi/documents/publication/wcms_094386.pdf (Accessed 28th May 2015)

Kats, G.H. (2003). *Green building costs and financial benefits.* Boston, MA: Massachusetts Technology Collaborative.

Kibert, C.J. (2012). *Sustainable construction: Green building design and delivery.* eBook. https://libcat.library.qut.edu.au/search~S8?/akibert/akibert/1%2C1%2C10%2CB/frameset&FF=akibert+charles+j&7%2C%2C10 (Accessed 28th May 2015)

KPMG (2013). *The community investment dividend: Measuring the value of community investment to support your social licence to operate.* Retrieved from www.kpmg.com/ID/en/IssuesAndInsights/ArticlesPublications/Documents/community-investment-dividend-social-licence-resources.pdf (Accessed 28th May 2015)

Kreps, T.J. (1940). Measurement of the social performance of business. In *An investigation of concentration of economic power for the temporary national economic committee* (Monograph No. 7). Washington, DC: U.S. Government Printing Office.

Lacey, J. (2013). Can you legislate a social licence to operate? Retrieved from https://theconversation.com/can-you-legislate-a-social-licence-to-operate-10948 (Accessed 28th May 2015)

Local Government Authority (2003). *National procurement strategy for local government.* London: Office of the Deputy Prime Minister.

McIvor, R. (2005). *The outsourcing process.* Cambridge, UK: Cambridge University Press.

Moore, W.H. (1996). The social license to operate. *PIMA magazine, 78*(10), 22–23.

Morris, J. (2012). *The five W's of France's CSR reporting law.* Retrieved from *www.bsr.org/en/our-insights/report-view/the-five-ws-of-frances-csr-reporting-law* (Accessed 28th May 2015)

Murray, J.G. (2009). Towards a common understanding of the differences between purchasing, procurement and commissioning in the UK public sector. *Journal of Purchasing and Supply Chain Management, 15*(3): 198–202. doi:10.1016/j.pursup.2009.03.003

National Australia Bank. (n.d.). *Supplier diversity.* Retrieved from http://cr.nab.com.au/what-we-do/supplier-diversity (Accessed 28th May 2015)

Nelson, J.L. (2006). Social license to operate. *International Journal of Mining, Reclamation and Environment, 20*(3), 161–162. doi: 10.1080/17480930600804182

OECD (2011). *OECD guidelines for multinational enterprise: 2011 addition.* Paris: OECD Publishing. doi: 10.1787/9789264115415-en

Oliver, C. (1991). Strategic responses to institutional processes. *Academy of Management Review, 16*(1), 145–179. doi: 10.5465/AMR.1991.4279002

Owen, J.R., & Kemp, D. (2013). Social licence and mining: A critical perspective. *Resources Policy, 38*(1), 29–35. doi: 10.1016/j.resourpol.2012.06.016

Pies, I. (2011). Corporate citizenship and new governance: The political role of corporations. In I. Pies, & P. Koslowski, (Eds.), *Corporate citizenship and new governance: The political role of corporations* (pp. 1–6). Dordrecht, Netherlands: Springer.

Porter, M.E., & Kramer, M.R. (2006). Strategy and society: The link between competitive advantage and corporate social responsibility. *Harvard Business Review, 84*(12) 78–92.

Porter, M.E., & Kramer, M.R. (2011). Creating shared value: How to reinvent capitalism—and unleash a wave of innovation and growth. *Harvard Business Review.* Retrieved from https://hbr.org/2011/01/the-big-idea-creating-shared-value (Accessed 28th May 2015)

Porter, M.E., & van der Linde, C. (1995). Toward a new conception of the environment-competitiveness relationship. *Journal of Economic Perspective, 9*(4), 97–118. doi:10.1257/jep.9.4.97

Power, M. (1997). *The audit society: Rituals of verification.* Oxford, New York: Oxford University Press.

Power, M. (2000). The audit society: Second thoughts. *International Journal of Auditing, 4*(1), 111–119. doi:10.1111/1099–1123.00306

Prno, J., & Slocombe, D.S. (2012). Exploring the origins of 'social license to operate' in the mining sector: Perspectives from governance and sustainability theories. *Resources Policy, 37*(3), 346–357. doi:10.1016/j.resourpol.2012.04.002

Ram, M., Theodorakopoulos, N., & Worthington, I. (2007). Policy transfer in practice: Implementing supplier diversity in the UK. *Public Administration, 85*(3), 779–803. doi:10.1111/j.1467–9299.2007.00671.x

Ries, R., Bilec, M.M., Gokhan, N.M., & Needy, K.L. (2006). The economic benefits of green buildings: A comprehensive case study. *The Engineering Economist, 51*(3), 259–295. doi:10.1080/00137910600865469

Ritchie, B., & Brindley, C. (2007). An emergent framework for supply chain risk management and performance measurement. *Journal of the Operational Research Society, 58*, 1398–1411. doi:10.1057/palgrave.jors.260241

Sarkis, J. (2003). A strategic decision framework for green supply chain management. *Journal of Cleaner Production, 11*(4), 397–409. doi:10.1016/S0959-6526(02)00062-8

Schaltegger, S., & Synnestvedt, T. (2002). The link between 'green' and economic success: Environmental management as the crucial trigger between environmental and economic performance. *Journal of Environmental Management, 65*(4), 339–346. doi:10.1006/jema.2002.0555

Sen, S., & Bhattacharya, C.B. (2001). Does doing good always lead to doing better? Consumer reactions to corporate social responsibility. *Journal of Marketing Research, 38*(2), 225–243. doi: 10.1509/jmkr.38.2.225.18838

Shah, M., & Ram, M. (2006). Supplier diversity and minority business enterprise development: Case study experience of three US multinationals. *Supply Chain Management: An International Journal, 11*(1), 75–81. doi:10.1108/13598540610642493

Social Enterprise UK. (2013*a*). *Do a great deal: Buy social: The social enterprise supply chain guide.* Retrieved from www.socialenterprise.org.uk/uploads/files/2013/11/buysocialguide.pdf (Accessed 28th May 2015)

Social Enterprise UK. (2013*b*). The landmarc difference. Retrieved from www.socialenterprise.org.uk/uploads/files/2013/09/suk08_landmarc_medressinglepg_r22.pdf (Accessed 28th May 2015)

Solar Times (2008, Third Quarter). SF board of supes condemns Chevron abuses worldwide. *Solar Times.* Retrieved from http://solartimes.org/pdf/qtr3_2008.pdf (Accessed 28th May 2015)

SproutHub (n.d.). *SproutHub.* Retrieved from www.sprouthub.com.au/ (Accessed 28th May 2015)

Stefan, A., & Paul, L. (2008). Does it pay to be green? A systematic overview. *The Academy of Management Perspectives, 22*(4), 45–62. doi:10.5465/AMP.2008.35590353

Thompson, J.L. (2008). Social enterprise and social entrepreneurship: Where have we reached? *Social Enterprise Journal, 4*(2), 149–161. doi:10.1108/17508610810902039

Urban Communities / AMES (2011). *Social enterprise: Making it work: A case for social procurement.* Department of Education, Employment and Workplace Relations. Canberra: Australian Government. Retrieved from www.socialtraders.com.au/_uploads/_ckpg/files/A%20Case%20for%20Social_Procurement_Full_FINALMarch19_2012.pdf (Accessed 28th May 2015)

Vining, A., & Globerman, S. (1999). A conceptual framework for understanding the outsourcing decision. *European Management Journal, 17*(6), 645–654. doi:10.1016/S0263-2373(99)00055-9

Walters, D. (2004). New economy – new business models – new approaches. *International Journal of Physical Distribution & Logistics Management, 34*(3/4), 219–229. doi:http://doi.org/10.1108/09600030410533556

Wijnberg, N.M. (2000). Normative stakeholder theory and Aristotle: The link between ethics and politics. *Journal of Business Ethics, 25*(4), 329–342. doi:10.1023/A:1006086226794

Worthington, I. (2009). Corporate perceptions of the business case for supplier diversity: How socially responsible purchasing can 'Pay'. *Journal of Business Ethics, 90*(1), 47–60. doi:10.1007/s10551-008-0025-5

Worthington, I., Ram, M., Boyal, H., & Shah, M. (2008). Researching the drivers of socially responsible purchasing: A cross-national study of supplier diversity initiatives. *Journal of Business Ethics, 79*(3), 319–331. doi:10.1007/s10551-007-9400-x

Zadek, S. (2004, December). The path to corporate responsibility. *Harvard Business Review,* Retrieved from www.foundationforeuropeanleadership.org/assets/downloads/infoItems/75.pdf (Accessed 28th May 2015)

6 Governing beyond government: third–sector and next–practice networks

Introduction: governance in transition

The provision of social services and value has historically occurred through a range of procurement processes and governance modes. In this chapter, we suggest that social value and its procurement has progressed through four design and delivery regimes that draw upon, and mix, elements from a suite of governance modes, transitioning from a strong community focus to public sector ascendance, new public management (NPM), networks and partnerships. Although new public governance (NPG) assembles elements of all modes, network governance is dominant, highlighting the complex hyper-hybrid reality of design, procurement and delivery of public goods and services in contemporary society. This has implications for the way in which social procurement is enacted and the actors involved.

Over the past few decades governance has become an important concept as society shapes and reshapes the way it functions. Broadly defined, *governance* signifies processes of social coordination (Kooiman, 1993), including the way in which decisions are made and resources are allocated to achieve stated outcomes (Wamsley, 1990). The literature often conceptualizes governance and governance arrangements as a linear progression from governance via government to governance by networks (Rhodes, 1997; Stoker, 1998). However, as several authors have noted, not only do these linear conceptualizations of transition not fully capture the various transformations that have taken place over time in relation to the provision of social services, but also they fail to account for the layering arising from the mix of new and residual governance processes, mechanisms and actors (Hartley, 2005; Keast, Brown & Mandell, 2006; Sullivan & Skelcher, 2002) as well as the inherent complexity of the interactions between actions and processes (Geyer & Rihani, 2010; Koppenjan & Klijn, 2004).

With the formal definition of governance covered, the chapter next identifies key governance modes and their differentiating characteristics.

Governance modes: prominent typologies

The public management literature identifies three dominant governance modes: state, market and community or network approaches (Frances, Levacic, Mitchell & Thompson, 1991). These modes are often described by the locations in which their respective activities occur: bureaucracy, market and community. Each mode is guided by a set of assumptions prescribing the way they enable coordination as well as pointing to the conditions in which they best operate. To expand, the state mode draws upon hierarchical structures, and uses legitimate authority as the vehicle to coordinate the actions of members in order that they perform as planned (Lowndes & Skelcher, 1998): this top-down approach also sets the direction for the design and delivery of public services. Comprised of individuals and firms operating through short-term, spontaneous price transactions based on supply and demand, the market mode relies predominantly on legal contractual arrangement and price signals to bring dispersed suppliers and purchasers together for short and highly specified exchanges (Frances et al., 1991). By contrast, network governance coordination is achieved through social or communal organizing principles (Kickert, Klijn & Koppenjan, 1997) in which the interpersonal facets such as trust, reciprocity and mutual benefit are the "glue that bind" (Powell, 1990, p. 325). Drawing from the extant governance literature Table 6.1 summarises and sets out the core elements of each of these governance modes and their associated integration mechanisms, management foci and procurement approach.

Table 6.1 Governance modes

Governance modes	Bureaucracy	Market	Network
Outcome focus	Certainty	Efficiency	Reflexivity
Relationships	Hierarchical	Contractual independent	Social/communal
Interdependency	Low—tending towards dependence	Low—tending towards independence	High
Integrating mechanisms	Legal authority, formal rules, regulations, mandates, policies, procedures	Arms-length contractual transactions, price, supply and demand	Social exchange, common vision, trust, reciprocity
Institutional arrangements	Departments, committees, taskforces	Partnerships, mergers, alliances, acquisitions	Compacts, accords, negotiation tables, informal networking
Issues complexity	Large scale, often unique, but not complex	Intermediate complexity	Complex

Governance modes	Bureaucracy	Market	Network
Accountability	To elites and the public	To self, boards, shareholders, members	To group – internal
Scope for opportunism	Low – limited by rules	High – encouraged through short-term arrangements	Medium – mediated by long-term relationships

Based on Powell (1990), and Keast, Brown and Mandell (2006).

While regularly presented as distinctive forms, the reality is that governance modes are often mixed, with the potential for the co-existence and overlap of various elements (Bardach & Eccles, 1991; Borys & Jemison, 1989; Evers, 1990; Rose, 1987). As an example, in Chapter 2 it was shown that welfare delivery has at various times been procured by the state, produced by private market actors and distributed with assistance from voluntary associations in civil society.

All the same, distinguishing the three modes and their underpinning logics is valuable for gaining an understanding of the different ways that society is organized. The framework set out in Table 6.1 will be used to tease out and make more apparent the governance modes and their mixes and to demonstrate the progression to next practice networks within the NPG mode.

Third-sector governance in transition

It has been established in previous chapters that, since its inception, the third sector has passed through a number of changes in terms of its role and function in the design, procurement and delivery of public and social services as well as the relationship with government. For some authors (Hartley, 2005; Osborne, 2006, 2010) the change in these governance regimes closely mirrors the three phases identified for public administration generally – early state phase, NPM and NPG – except that third-sector activity in social support and procurement preceded early state involvement. As the following section highlights, although mixed, each phase is characterised by a dominant governance emphasis leading to community-, state- and market-centric approaches.

Community centric

The history of the community sector has been argued to be characterised by steady secularisation, coupled with increasing formalisation of voluntary action (Kendall & Knapp, 1993). Initially, social support was provided by family, feudal lords, work guilds and the church (Chesterman, 1979). Building on this early personalised support, the 18th and 19th centuries saw the formation of philanthropic and charity organisations by members of the middle class. As Kendall & Knapp (1993) noted, these new approaches often combined innovation in service provision with an advocacy function to direct broader attention to new and persistent social issues. Also around this time, particularly in the latter part of the 19th century, mutual aid organisations such as friendly societies and cooperatives for working class people were beginning to be established. These entities were introduced to provide a safeguard against the effects of poverty and hardship for issues outside of government support (Kendall & Knapp, 1993; Tierney, 1970).

A key feature of these early efforts of social support and services was the mix of communitarian elements of philanthropy, mutual aid and collective action. The voluntary contribution of time and money was central to this process, with citizens giving help to construct many early social and physical infrastructures (McKinney, 1995; Tierney, 1970). Following this line, many of the emergent formalised support bodies were funded directly by citizen donations.

Given these arrangements, early social service provision was arguably dominated by a community-centric governance approach, characterised by traditions of philanthropy, mutual aid, interpersonal relationships and collective action. Gerlach and Palmer (1981) provide a rationale for the approach: "People give up personal independence to gain the support of others in mutual aid . . . as they negotiate settlements . . . they build yet other bonds of mutual obligation" (p. 326).

Under this community-centric model the procurement and provision of services was achieved mainly through local networks, voluntary action and philanthropic support. Growing levels of hardship and associated social unrest around the mid-19th century led to a greater appreciation by governments of the benefit of a more cohesive society and to the community or network mode eventually being supplemented by government subsidization of some selected services, and, eventually, some limited grant-giving to support "worthy" initiatives (Graycar, 1977; Brown & Keast, 2005, Knapp & Kendall, 1991).

Progressively from the late 19th to the early 20th centuries the state began to replace community models, voluntary organising and organisations as the principal actors and arenas for social service provision. This shift occurred partly in response to a growing awareness of the need for government mechanisms to generate social cohesion particularly following the social unrest caused by World War I, as well as to respond to what Salamon (cited in Powell & Steinberg, 2006), claimed as the "failures" of the community-centric, voluntary mode such as particularism, paternalism and amateurism. In response to these concerns, government attention and effort gradually expanded into fields where voluntary groups and agencies had previously been sole actors (Kendall & Knapp, 1993; Salamon, 1987). This broadening of the scope of government or statutory welfare commenced with more wide-reaching and extensive grant funding of the sector into the four main areas of concern – income support, healthcare, education, social support – that continue to underpin universal government social service provision.

Nonetheless, alongside the state system, a small but significant number of providers continued to operate, fully funded by private fees and contributions. Thus, community governance's role as a "statutory supplementer" (Kramer, 1981) was established (Graycar, 1977; Kendall & Knapp 1993; Tierney, 1970). Over the 1960s and 1970s, this limited safety-net role gradually expanded to include a range of initiatives previously outside of the scope of government such as community development and required a considerable investment of government funding. Supporting this expanded role was the growing recognition of the important role of intermediary bodies in ensuring a healthy and vibrant voluntary sector (Wolfenden, 1978). In a minor way, the market mode also became involved in the provision of some social, as well as physical infrastructures, particularly in the evolving colonial nations. This practice is referred to as the *mixed economy* (Quiggin, 1999) because it drew upon market funds to support government development and became the cornerstone to modern day public-private partnerships.

Following the management ethos of the time, a model of government organisation evolved that was predominantly hierarchical and bureaucratic and focused on the provision of universal services (Hasenfeld, 1983) and consisted of standardized tasks, processes and work arrangements (Hughes, 1998). Procurement practices emerged that were procedurally driven, professionally determined and implemented, with recipients largely dependent on state redistributive processes (Polanyi, 1957). Hence the emerging second phase constituted a largely state-centric model where hierarchy was the dominant integrating mechanism, with a focus on vertical line management to ensure accountability and top-down, administrative decision-making in relation to the purchasing and delivering of public services.

Market centric

By the 1980s and early 1990s, governments and hierarchical governance and procurement increasingly were understood to be the cause of, rather than the solution to, many of the new and intractable problems. During this period a consensus emerged, shaped at least in part by the pressure of global economic constraints (McCrudden, 2004) and the nascent neo-liberal ideology that was gaining ground globally (Davis & Wood, 1998), that the ". . .state had become too big, too costly, too rigid, too standardised and too insensitive to individual needs" (Considine, 2001, p. 5). With the bureaucratic mode of governance having been proclaimed as largely "obsolete" (Hughes, 1998), market-based governance principles and practices, such as competition, user-pays and individualism, were widely introduced to the public-sector environment. Broadly captured under the label of NPM (Hood, 1995), this largely economic agenda led to a number of broad-ranging reforms designed to enhance, reduce, supplement and, in some cases, replace bureaucracy and bureaucratic procurement of social services with the goal of greater efficiency, effectiveness and economy.

The market mode, with its managerial focus and arm's length approach to regulation, paved the way for more decentralized and entrepreneurial styles of operation (Bogason, 2000; Osborne & Gaebler, 1992). A number of timely, positive and necessary changes to the operation of the public sector resulted, including the shift from the former "one size fits all" approach to more flexible and responsive styles. While acknowledging that NPM did secure some real improvements in the quality of public sector management, particularly important changes in the measurement of costs and outcomes as well as generating some efficiency savings (6, Leat, Seltzer & Stoker, 1999; Kettl, 2000; Röber, 2000), many noted that these gains were frequently short-term and transient (Davis & Rhodes, 2000) or negligible in their impact (Pollitt, 2000; Pollitt & Bouckaert, 2004).

Furthermore, under the market-centric mode, it is hardly surprising that the dominant procurement approach drew from its central elements of competition, contestability and confrontation, underpinned by detailed contract specifications, the short-term or one-off contracts (Walker & Hampson, 2008) and, at least initially, the preference for economic (cheapest price) over social and environmental (best value) outcomes (Schulten, Alsos, Burgess & Pedersen, 2012). Implementation of the market model for social services was challenged by the complex nature of the problems and service solutions which often defied contract specifications, leading in some instances (the prisons as a good example) to the practice of "cherry-picking" the least problematic clients and inappropriate detention and intervention practices (Harding, 1997). Also, for many theorists, the market mode and its procurement practices were poor integrating instruments for the delivery of social services and, in fact, led to more fragmentation resulting from purchaser and provider splits and the growing competition between government and agencies which undermined the cooperative relationships that had previously characterized the sector (McCrudden, 2004; Milward & Provan, 2003). This was also the conclusion of Flynn, Williams and Pickard (1996) in the health-care arena, who argued that difficulties in specifying contracts led to assertive purchasers whose style "...engenders or exacerbates suspicious attitudes and feelings of mutual distrust" and who called for alternative mechanisms of exchange (p. 136).

Mixed modes

The task of bringing the fragmented elements of the service system back together was to be achieved through the introduction of network modes of governing and a stronger emphasis on interpersonal rather than contractual or authority relationships. Davis and Rhodes (2000) explain the rationale for the adoption of network governance: "Marketisation may have introduced the private sector and quality competition to delivering public services, but it also fragmented the institutional structure of the public sector. Networks put it back together again" (p. 95).

Networks and their relational emphasis thus became a moderating mechanism to ameliorate the hard edges of pure, adversarial contracting and reduce some of the associated problems (Newman, 2000) such as the higher transaction costs of establishing and monitoring ongoing short-term procurement practices as well as litigation tendencies caused by incomplete specifications (Macaulay, 1963; Ring & van de Ven, 1992). This process was facilitated by the growing use of relational contracting to replace competition, contention and adversarial behaviours, with an emphasis on trust, the pursuit of common benefits and longer-term contractual arrangements (Lazar, 2000; Thompson & Sanders, 1998). Such a network governance shift points to a re-thinking of purchasing and procurement patterns, as Flynn et al. (1996) highlight: "Their clan-like structure, and their promotion of the virtues of co-operation and interdependence, necessitates both a management approach and a purchasing strategy based on high trust, and soft or relational contracting" (p. 147).

Relational contracts also provide greater opportunities to clarify party roles and responsibilities as well as establish processes of reciprocity over competition. Such principles formed the basis of a growing number of inter-organisational arrangements emerging from this period, including alliance partnering, joint ventures, value chains and various other networked arrangements (Vincent-Jones, 2000; Walker & Hampson, 2008). At the same time, community as a service support site also came back into prominence as governments realized their financial and expertise limitations in effectively addressing ongoing intractable and emergent new social issues. Thus, alongside and commensurate with public sector networks as tools for service delivery was a revived interest in communitarianism approaches, particularly the return to earlier movements such as co-production (Alford, 1998; Bovaird, 2007; Ostrom, 1996; Brandsen & Pestoff, 2006), as well as the introduction of new inflections of community-focused governance, for example, community engagement (Adams & Hess, 2001). In these models, citizens are presented as active agents – rather than as passive recipients or customers – in the design and delivery of social services, with the dual objectives of providing more responsive, citizen-centric services as well as the development of improved cost efficiencies from user-informed innovations.

In this "relational era", although public institutions were no longer seen as the source of all power or the primary organising centre for policy and service, the state was by no means in full retreat (Osborne, 2006; Weiss, 1998). Rather, government power and roles were reconfigured, dispersed across new sites of interaction and augmented through new strategies and technologies (Kennett, 2008). Rhodes (1997) referred to this expansion as a "differentiated policy" which was divided and fragmented into a variety of interdependent public, semi-public and private agencies, coupled with an expansion of governance and procurement approaches. Following this line Osborne (2006, 2010) talked of the emergence of a plural state, where multiple, independent actors contribute to the delivery of public services and a pluralist state, where multiple processes inform the policy-making system. The focus on achieving mutual, rather than individual, goals shifts network actors from independent to interdependent relationships; that is, they rely on others to achieve goals (Kickert et al., 1997; Koppenjan & Klijn, 2004). Procurement in this context is achieved through multiple and often long chains of actors and resources needing to be brought together in new ways in order for collective value to be reached.

As discussed in Chapter 3, the growing hybridity of the social policy and service governance environment has been described by a number of public management authors as representing an emergent governance form: NPG (Koppenjan 2012; Osborne, 2006, 2010; Pestoff, Brandsen & Verschuere, 2012). It is argued by these researchers that NPG more realistically captures the plural and pluralist complexities of contemporary governance and acknowledges the multiple sets of people and processes that inform and shape service policy development and service provision. In this new governance reality the hybrid mixes are the norm, with networks combined with other modes in assorted ways to leverage the best aspects of particular governance modes, while minimalising the less functional aspects. As Koppenjan (2012) noted:

> Network governance does not function independently of hierarchical and NPM-like [new public management-like] arrangements. Rather, it acts in concert with these arrangements, as a necessary and decisive component of a more encompassing, hybrid assembly.
>
> (p. 32)

While hybrids have been an ongoing feature of the social and public service and its procurement, the current environment is arguably even more mixed and changing or, as Keast (2013) recently described it, one of an amplification of hybridity, reflecting Esmark's (2009) view of the growing oscillation between governance modes and their integrating apparatus. NPG therefore is about the judicious mixing of key elements from each of the governance modes in order to facilitate the requisite outcomes of effectiveness, transparency, quality and integration (Koppenjan, 2012). Koppenjan (2012) goes on to describe this process of unbundling and rebundling as creating "assemblies" of governance and organisational forms and stressed that many combinations would be necessary to meet diverse purposes. The challenge is to design these institutional and governance assemblies fit-for-purpose in order that they support the achievement of appropriate interactions and outcomes. Given the composite nature of NPG and its network/relationship ascendancy, design and management cannot be imposed unilaterally; instead, as Koppenjan (2012) prescribes, they must be ". . .defined, applied, monitored, enforced and adjusted in mutual consultation and interaction" (p. 31).

For some time now the management of networks has been a core organisational task and a specific set of network management functions has been developed, quite separate to the conventional management functions of planning, coordinating, staffing and controlling. Network management is focused on the "steering of interaction processes" (Kickert & Koppenjan, 1997, p. 47) and comprises the following elements: activating, mobilizing, framing and synthesizing

(Agranoff & McGuire, 2001; Klijn & Koppenjan, 2000; McGuire, 2002). Similarly the procurement approach within the NPG mode must be adjusted to fit hybridity with network dominance. Goldsmith and Eggers (2004) encapsulated this essential shift in procurement style:

> Traditionally the most important requirement for a procurement officer to succeed was to know all the rules and follow them without deviation. Not anymore. Acquisitions officers must now be more than mere purchasers or process managers... [they] Need to approach their work as a search for the right mix of components.
>
> (p. 166)

In essence, in the NPG era, with its differentiated polity, layered governance arrangements, extended service supply chains and shifting networks of providers, the procurement task now centres on being a network and relational manager, not just a contract manager (Goldsmith & Eggers, 2004).

This increasingly complex governance situation calls for new insights and approaches to assist those charged with the responsibility for governing, procuring and managing assets and services. It requires next-practice network management and procurement tasks and skills that are beyond the early set identified by Klijn and Koppenjan (2000) and, subsequently, Agranoff and McGuire (2001) and McGuire (2002), of which network navigation and negotiation are central functions (Keast & Waterhouse, 2014).

Next-practice networks: navigating and negotiating

It has been established previously that NPG is characterized by co-existing and layered hybrid mixes that are constantly being configured and reconfigured to achieve diverse and shifting outcomes (Hartley, 2005; Koppenjan, 2012). These hybrid arrangements are creating increasingly crowded policy domains (Lowndes & Skelcher, 1998; Keast et al., 2006) in which new and reconfigured governance arrangements sit alongside the existing tripartite model, with residual or legacy elements knocking up against each other, sometimes supporting processes and at other times producing confounding results.

Humans struggle to understand and manage complex social systems, especially when they are overlaid with uncertainty and change (Gunderson & Holling, 2002). The messiness of NPG network compositions, structures and processes can make it difficult for members to identify and leverage the system or relationships to achieve identified outcomes (Koppenjan & Klijn, 2004). The obvious, if not the only, consequence of the growing governance complexity is the dilemma of confusion and uncertainty for procurers, producers and users. Finding a way to navigate the system is not straightforward when there is no single point of contact. Questions of "who provides what for whom?" and "who is connected to whom?" and "under what conditions?" are difficult to determine, challenging the ability to craft useful assemblies. Furthermore, despite the rhetoric, NPG networks are rarely alliances of equals and are often faced with power inequalities that must be carefully navigated to enable effective working relationships (Klijn & Koppenjan, 2000).

To overcome these issues it is proposed that next-practice network architects, managers and members must function as their own learning systems capable of identifying, configuring and reconfiguring relevant component parts to design their optimal modes (Waterhouse, Keast & Brown, 2011). Increasingly this task involves the capacity to redefine presenting problems and, in so doing, redesign network governance relations and possibly in the course of this action discard some previous structures or members. Waterhouse et al. (2011) suggest that such measured action is aligned with the notions of reflective practice, which is defined by Moon (1999) as "...a set of abilities and skills, to indicate the taking of a critical stance, an orientation to problem solving or state of mind" (p. 63). In this context network members are actively engaged in reviewing their current governance arrangements to ascertain ongoing relevance and effectiveness. Unpacking the composition of the governance process and relationships and attaining a deeper understanding of the participants' positions and goals provides a useful basis for the negotiation processes that follow.

Network negotiation

Negotiation is a central network task. For, as Scharpf (1994) notes, networks rely on a "negotiation rationality" in which processes, policy and products as well as the structure and purpose of the networks themselves are moulded in and through recurrent negotiations between actors. Several authors (Anklam, 2007; Koppenjan & Klijn, 2004; Waterhouse et al., 2011) have identified that negotiation in networks comprises two distinct but interrelated stages. In the first stage network members focus on negotiating "the rules of the game"; that is, reaching agreement on how the presenting problem is defined and how members will work together.

Negotiating the rules of the game

Managing networks is a complex task, involving not only securing the alignment of effort but also the synchronisation of relationships, all to the common purpose. Particularly in relation to the latter, a preliminary task is getting consensus around how people will work together (Innes & Booher, 1999). Establishing what several authors (Kickert et al., 1997; Klijn & Koppenjan, 2000) have referred to as the rules of the game is key to network working. The rules of the game are established by agreeing on the set of norms, procedures and behaviours guiding interaction and behaviour between members. The agreements and their guiding principles, such as shared access to information and equal power to speak and challenge others (Healey, 1997; Innes & Booher, 1999) prepare the grounds for the deeper dialogue and knowledge exchange needed to create new ways of working, and new forms of service delivery and its procurement. Thus, several interrelated purposes and tasks are involved in this first stage of network negotiation. Watson (1982) expands on these functions as follows:

> . . . finding out or guessing intelligently what one power needs to know about another . . . sifting and collating the information received . . . and from other sources, and of producing a coherent picture of the issues and developments abroad on which decisions are needed . . . determining the options available to a government and submitting them for decision . . . communicating and explaining a government's decision to another government.
>
> (pp. 123–125)

Watson (1982) goes on to identify that the emphasis at this stage is not on imposing your own objectives onto another, but on finding out about the other, persuading others to contribute to the collective resolution. The main technique is "...the maintenance by continual persuasion of order in the midst of change" (Watson, 1982, p. 223). For Putnam (1988), negotiation involves both persuasion and argumentation as each party is focused on influencing the other and intends to justify one's claims. Marcussen and Torfing (2003) in their study of governance networks refer to this as "negotiation bargaining". For all these authors, networked-based or relational negotiation extends beyond persuasion because both parties try to deal with conflicting interests, make mutual adjustments and seek mutually satisfactory solutions (Roloff, Putnam & Anastasiou, 2003). There is resonance here for partnership models of social procurement discussed in earlier chapters.

Relational negotiation tasks align closely with the network management functions of activating and framing proposed by Agranoff and McGuire (2001), where effort is directed towards identifying who needs to be involved and getting members on the same page (Keast & Waterhouse, 2014). Dialogue is central to problem setting and solving efforts in networks (Cohen, 2008; Innes & Booher, 1999), and Taylor (2000) has suggested that establishing and implementing network rules requires the development of a sophisticated "relationship vocabulary" to help smooth over the conflicting interests that are present despite the interdependence that brings them together. It is important to note that consensus is not always the outcome of network negotiations. Despite their relational emphasis, or perhaps because of this, these entities are still subject to conflict between members as well as power inequalities (Koppenjan & Klijn, 2004). In these instances trust and obligation are not always sufficient to sustain the networks and keep negotiations open; thus, network management skills are required to reframe and refocus efforts.

Once these "ground rules" are established the negotiation task can turn to determining agreed solutions, goals and actions.

Negotiating goals and actions

Through the ongoing interactions just stated, members engage in sense making efforts that help them to synchronise their ideas and positions or, as Dewulf et al. (2009) terms it, to "create over-laps" that allow for mutually agreeable goals and processes to be reached. In view of this, as Marcussen and Torfing (2003) suggest, negotiation in networks combines elements of both bargaining and deliberation, such that actors may bargain over the distribution of resources to maximise their outcomes; however, to ensure the production of trust and obligation this bargaining takes place within a framework of deliberation that facilitates understanding, learning and joint action.

There are two main types of negotiation: distributive and integrative. Cohen (2008) and others (Keast & Waterhouse, 2014; Waterhouse et al, 2011) believe that the relational orientation of networks lends itself towards the integrative or interest-based negotiation approach. In this style the focus is on retaining a long-term relationship and achieving the best (win/win) outcomes for the groups as a whole (Fisher & Ury, 1981) rather than pushing short-term, self-interested or procedurally derived satisficing as in the market or hierarchy modes, respectively.

Conclusion

Networks in various forms have long been the cornerstone of social service delivery and the production of social value. NPG is also anchored in networks; however, these are next-practice networks that are deliberately combined with other governance modes and their associated apparatus (Esmark, 2009) to create institutional hybrids in order to best achieve public and social good.

The practice of configuring and reconfiguring hybrid NPG arrangements has led to a complex operating environment for those charged with the responsibility for procuring and delivering quality social services. This chapter has provided a basic framework to assist in the distillation of governance modes within current hybrids and the identification of core elements that can be mixed to achieve outcomes. This assemblage task involves choosing not only between governing structures but also the mix of structures and strategies for managing them. Changing governance modes also demand an extension of skill sets that the next-practice network managers and procurers will require to operate effectively. Several authors have begun to isolate different competencies necessary for working in complex, hybrid environments, including relationship building and management, capability for dispersed and collaborative leadership, negotiation and working with ambiguity (see, for example, Keast & Mandell, 2014; and Koliba, Meek & Zia, 2010). Despite their centrality to new governance, such skills are often not present, highly sought after or appreciated within organisations (Goldsmith & Eggers, 2004). Their deficit can seriously undermine effective social procurement practices and outcomes, particularly where high-level skills are required to facilitate adjustments from competitive to cooperative working relationships between bodies. For procurement officers the new approach can be particularly challenging as it moves them from the backroom comfort of technical compliance to managing networks. At a broader level, NPG and next practice networks are also likely to raise old debates about the democratic basis of decision-making and public value in relation to social procurement. These are pertinent to considerations regarding defining and assessing social value, which are considered in the next chapter.

References

6, P., Leat, D., Seltzer, K., & Stoker, G. (1999). *Governing in the round: Strategies for holistic government*. London: Demos.

Adams, D., & Hess, M. (2001). Community in public policy: Fad or foundation. *Australian Journal of Public Administration, 60*(2), 13–23. doi: 10.1111/1467–8500.00205

Agranoff, R., & McGuire, M. (2001). After the network is formed: Processes, power and performance. In M. Mandell (Ed.). *Getting results through collaboration: Networks and network structures for public policy and management* (pp. 11–29). Westport, CT: Quorum Books.

Alford, J. (1998). A public management road less traveled: Clients as co-producers of public services. *Australian Journal of Public Administration, 57*(4), 128–137. doi: 10.1111/j.1467–8500.1998.tb01568.x

Anklam, P. (2007). *Net work: A practical guide to creating and sustaining networks at work and in the world*. Burlington, MA: Elsevier.

Bardach, J., & Eccles, R.G. (1991). Price, authority and trust: From ideal types to plural forms. In G. Thompson, J. Frances, R. Levacic, & J. Mitchell (Eds.). *Markets, hierarchies and networks* (pp. 277–292). London, UK: Sage.

Bogason, P. (2000). *Public policy and local governance: Institutions in postmodern society*. Roskilde University, Denmark: Edward Elgar Publishing.

Borys, B., & Jemison, D. B. (1989). Hybrid arrangements as strategic alliances: Theoretical issues in organizational combinations. *Academy of Management Review, 14*(2), 234–249. doi: 10.5465/AMR.1989.4282106.

Bovaird, T. (2007). Beyond engagement and participation: User and community co-production of public services. *Public Administration Review, 67*(5), 846–860. doi: 10.1111/j.1540–621 0.2007.00773.x.

Brandsen, T. & Pestoff, V. (2006). Co-production, the third sector and the delivery of public services: An introduction. *Public Management Review* 8(4) 493–501. doi 10.1080/14719030601022874

Brown, K.A., & Keast, R.L. (2005). Social services policy and delivery in Australia: Centre-periphery mixes. *Policy and Politics, 33*(3), 505–518. doi: 10.1332/030557305 4325774.

Chesterman, M.M. (1979). *Charities, trusts and social welfare*. London: Weidenfeild and Nicolson.

Cohen, J. (2008). Negotiation, meet new governance: Interests, skills and selves. *Law and Social Enquiry, 33*(2), 501–562. doi: 10.1111/j.1747–4469.2008.00111.x

Considine, M. (2001). *Enterprising states: The public management of welfare-to-work*. Cambridge University, UK: Cambridge University Press.

Davis, G.C., & Rhodes, R.A.W. (2000). From hierarchy to contracts and back again: Reforming the Australian public service. In M. Keating, J. Wanna, & P. Weller (Eds.). *Institutions on the edge* (pp. 74–98). St Leonards, NSW: Allen & Unwin.

Davis, G., & Wood, T. (1998). Is there a future for contracting in the Australian public sector? *Australian Journal of Public Administration, 57*(4) 85–97. doi: 10.1111/j.1467–8500.1998. tb01564.x.

Dewulf, A., Gray, B., Putnam, L., Lewicki, R., Aarts, V., Bouwen, R., & van Woerkum, C. (2009). Disentangling approaches to framing in conflict and negotiation research: A meta-paradigmatic perspective. *Human Relations, 62*(2), 155–193. doi: 10.1177/0018726 708100356.

Eggers, W. D., & Goldsmith, S. (2004). *Governing by network: The new shape of the public sector.* Washington, DC: Brookings Institution Press.

Esmark, A. (2009). The functional differentiation of governance: Public governance beyond hierarchy, markets and networks. *Public Administration, 87*(2), 351–370. doi: 10.1111/ j.1467–9299.2009.01759.x.

Evers, A. (1990). Shifts in the welfare mix: Introducing a new approach for the study of transformations in welfare and social policy. In A. Evers, & H. Winterberg (Eds.). *Shifts in the welfare mix: Their impact on work, social services and welfare policies* (pp. 7–30). Frankfurst Am Main: Verlag.

Fisher, R., & Ury, W. (1981). *Getting to yes: Negotiating agreement without giving in.* Boston, MA: Houghton Mifflin.

Flynn, R., Williams, G., & Pickard, S. (1996). *Markets and networks: Contracting in community health services.* Buckingham, UK: Open University Press.

Frances, J., Levacic, R., Mitchell, J., & Thompson, G. (1991). Introduction. In G. Thompson, J. Frances, R. Levacic, & J. Mitchell (Eds.). *Markets, hierarchies and networks: The coordination of social life* (pp. 1–21). London, UK: Sage.

Gerlach, L., & Palmer, G. (1981). Adaptation through evolving interdependence. In P. C. Nystrom, & W. H. Strarbuck (Eds.). *Handbook of organizational design volume 1: Adapting organizations to their environments* (pp. 323–384). Oxford, UK: Oxford University Press.

Geyer, R., & Rihani, S. (2010). *Complexity and public policy: A new approach to 21st century politics, policy and society.* New York: Routledge.

Graycar, A. (1977). *Social policy: An Australian introduction,* Melbourne: Macmillan.

Gunderson, L. H., & Holling, C. S. (2002). *Panarchy: Understanding transformations in human and natural systems.* Washington, DC: Island Press.

Harding, R. (1997). *Private prisons and public accountability.* Buckingham UK: Open University Press.

Hartley, J. (2005). Innovation in governance and public services: Past and present. *Public Money & Management, 25*(1), 27–34. doi: 10.1111/j.1467–9302.2005.00447.x

Hasenfeld, Y. (1983). *Human service organizations.* Englewood Cliffs, NJ: Prentice-Hall.

Healey, P. (1997). *Collaborative planning: Shaping places in fragmented societies.* London, UK: Macmillan

Hood, C. (1995). The 'new public management' in the 1980s: Variations on a theme. *Accountancy, Organizations and Society, 20*(2/3), 93–109. doi:10.1016/0361–3682(93)E0001-W.

Hughes, O. (1998). *Public management and administration: An introduction* (2nd ed.). Basingstoke: Macmillan.

Innes, J., & Booher, D. (1999). Consensus building as role playing and bricolage: Toward a theory of collaborative planning. *Journal of the American Planning Association, 65*(1) 9–26.

Keast, R. L. (2013). *Contemporary airport governance: Hyper-hybridity and management.* World Congress on Engineering Asset Management, Hong Kong, 30 October—1 November.

Keast, R. L., Mandell, M., & Brown, K. A. (2006). Mixing state, market and network governance modes: The role of government in "crowded" policy domains. *International Journal of Organizational Theory and Behavior, 9*(1), 27–50.

Keast, R. L., & Mandell, M. (2014). The collaborative push: Moving beyond rhetoric and gaining evidence. *Journal of Management and Governance, 18*(1), 9–28. doi: 10.1007/s10997–012–9234–5

Keast, R. L., & Waterhouse, J. (2014). Collaborative networks and innovation: The negotiation-management nexus. In C. Ansell, & J. Torfing (Eds.). *Public innovation through collaboration and design* (pp. 148–167). UK: Routledge.

Kendall, J., & Knapp, M. (1993). *Defining the non-profit sector: The United Kingdom.* Working Papers of the John Hopkins Comparative Nonprofit Sector Project, University of Kent: Canterbury.

Kennett, P. (2008). *Governance, globalization and public policy.* Northampton: Edward-Elgar Press.

Kettl, D. F. (2000). *The global public management revolution.* Washington, DC: Brookings Institute.

Kickert, W. J. M., Klijn, E-H., & Koppenjan, J. F. M. (1997). *Managing complex networks: Strategies for the public sector.* London, UK: Sage.

Kickert, W. J. M., & Koppenjan, J. F. M. (1997). Public management and network management: An overview. In W. J. M. Kickert, E-H. Klijn, & J. F. M. Koppenjan (Eds.). *Managing complex networks: Strategies for the public sector* (pp. 35–61). London, UK: Sage.

Klijn, E-H., & Koppenjan, J. F. M. (2000). Public management and policy networks: Foundations of a network approach to governance. *Public Management 2*(2), 135–158. doi: 10.1080/14719030000000007

Knapp, M., & Kendall, J. (1991). Policy issues for the UK voluntary sector in the 1990s. *Annals of Public and Cooperative Economics, 62*(4), 711–732. doi: 10.1111/j.1467–8292.1991.tb01375.x.

Koliba, C., Meek, J. W. & Zia, A. (2010). *Governance networks in public administration and public policy.* Boca Raton, FL: CRC Press.

Koppenjan, J. F. M. (2012). *The new public governance in public service delivery: Reconciling efficiency and quality.* The Hague: Elven International Publishing.

Koppenjan, J. F. M. & Klijn, E-H. (2004). Managing uncertainties in networks: A network approach to problem solving and decision making. London: Routledge.

Kooiman, J. (1993). *Modern governance: New government-society interactions.* London: Sage.

Kramer, R. M. (1981). *Voluntary agencies in the welfare state.* Berkley, CA: University of California Press.

Lazar, F.D. (2000). Project partnering: Improving the likelihood of win/win outcomes. *Journal of Management in Engineering, 16*(2), 71–83. doi: 10.1061/(ASCE)0742–597X(2000)16:2(71).

Lowndes, V., & Skelcher, C. (1998). The dynamics of multi-organizational partnerships: An analysis of changing modes of governance. *Public Administration, 76*(2), 313–333. doi: 10.1111/1467–9299.00103.

Macaulay, S. (1963). Non-contractual relationships in business: A preliminary study. *American Sociological Review, 28*(1), 55–67. Retrieved from www.jstor.org/stable/2090458 (Accessed 28th May 2015)

Marcussen, M., & Torfing, J. (2003). *Grasping governance networks.* Working paper series number 5, centre for democratic network governance, Roskilde University: Denmark.

McCrudden, C. (2004). Using public procurement to achieve social outcomes. *Natural Resources Forum, 28*(4), 257–267. doi: 10.1111/j.1477–8947.2004.00099.x.

McGuire, M. (2002). Managing networks: Propositions on what managers do and why they do it. *Public Administration Review, 62*(5), 599–609. doi: 10.1111/1540–6210.00240.

McKinney, H. J. (1995). *The development of local public services, 1650–1860: Lessons from Middletown.* Connecticut Westport, Conn: Greenwood Press.

Milward, H. B., & Provan, K. (2003). Managing the hollow state: Collaboration and contracting. *Public Management Review, 5*(1), 1–18. doi: 10.1080/1461667022000028834.

Moon, J. A. (1999). *Reflection in learning and professional development: Theory and practice.* London, UK: Kogan Page.

Newman, J. (2000). Beyond the New Public Management? Modernising public services. In J. Clarke, J. Gewirtz, & E. McLauchlin (Eds.). *New managerialism: New welfare?* (pp. 45–61). London: Sage.

Osborne, D., & Gaebler, T. (1992). *Reinventing government: How the entrepreneurial spirit is transforming the public sector.* Reading, MA: Addison-Wesley.

Osborne, S. P. (2006). The new public governance. *Public Management Review, 8*(3), 377–387. doi: 10.1080/14719030600853022.

Osborne, S. P. (2010). *The new public governance? Emerging perspectives on the theory and practice of public governance.* London, UK: Routledge.

Ostrom, E. (1996). Crossing the great divide: Coproduction, synergy, and development. *World Development, 24*(6), 1073–1087. doi:10.1016/0305-750X(96)00023-X.

Pestoff, V., Brandsen, T., & Verschuere, B. (2012). *New public governance, the third sector and co-production.* London: Routledge.

Polanyi, K. (1957). *The great transformation: The political and economic origins of our time.* Boston, MA: Beacon Press.

Pollitt, C. (2000). Is the emperor in his underwear? An analysis of the impacts of public management reform. *Public Management: An international Journal of Research and Theory, 2*(2), 181–200. doi: 10.1080/14719030000000009

Pollitt, C., & Bouckaert, G. (2004). *Public management reform: A comparative analysis.* Oxford: Oxford University Press.

Powell, W. W. (1990). Neither market nor hierarchy: Network forms of organization. *Research in Organizational Behavior, 12*, 295–336. Retrieved from http://woodypowell.com/wp-content/uploads/2012/03/10_powell_neither.pdf (Accessed 28th May 2015)

Powell, W. W. & Steinberg, R. (2006). *The non profit sector: A research handbook.* New Haven, CT: Yale University Press

Putnam, R. D. (1988). Diplomacy and domestic politics: The logic of two-level games. *International Organization, 42*(3), 427–460. Retrieved from http://journals.cambridge.org/action/displayBackIssues?jid=INO (Accessed 28th May 2015)

Quiggin, J. (1999). The future of government: Mixed economy or minimal state. *Australian Journal of Public Administration, 58*(4), 39–53. doi: 10.1111/1467-8500.00126.

Rhodes, R. A. W. (1997). *Understanding governance: Policy networks, governance, reflexivity and accountability.* Buckingham: Open University Press.

Ring, P. S. & van de Ven, A. H. (1992). Structuring cooperative relationships between organizations. *Strategic Management Journal, 13*(7), 483–498. doi: 10.1002/smj.4250130702.

Röber, M. (2000). Competition: How far can you go? *Public Management: An international Journal of Research and Theory, 2*(3), 311–336. doi: 10.1080/14719030000000020

Roloff, M. E., Putnam, L. L., & Anastasiou, L. (2003). Negotiation skills. In J. O. Greene, & B. R. Burleson, (Eds.). *Handbook of communication and social interaction skill* (pp. 801–833). Mahwah, NJ: Lawrence Erlbaum.

Rose, R. 1987. Common goals but different roles: The state's contribution to the welfare mix. In R. Rose, & R. Shiratori, (Eds.). *The welfare state east and west* (pp. 13–39). New York: Oxford University Press.

Salamon, L. M. (1987). Partners in public service: The scope and theory of government-nonprofit relations. In W. W. Powell, (Ed.). *The nonprofit sector: A research handbook* (pp. 99–117). New Haven, CT: Yale University Press.

Scharpf, F. W. (1994) Games Real Actors Could Play: positive and negative coordination in embedded negotiations. Journal of Theoretical Politics, 6(1), 27–53. doi: 10.1177/0951692894006001002

Schulten, T., Alsos, K., Burgess, P., & Pedersen, K. (2012). *Pay and other social clauses in European public procurement: An overview on regulation and practices with a focus on Denmark, Germany,*

Norway, Switzerland and the United Kingdom. Study on behalf of the European Federation of Public Service Unions (EPSU), Düsseldorf.

Stoker, G. (1998). Governance as theory: Five propositions. *International Journal of Social Sciences, 50*(155), 17–28. doi: 10.1111/1468–2451.00106.

Sullivan, H.C., Skelcher, C., (2002). *Working across boundaries: Collaboration in public services*. Basingstoke: Palgrave Macmillan.

Taylor, J. (2000). So they are now going to measure empowerment, *INTRAC 4th International Workshop on the Evaluation of Social Development* Oxford, April.

Thompson, P.J. & Sanders, S.R. (1998). Peer-reviewed paper: Partnering Continuum. *Journal of Management in Engineering, 14*(5), 73–78. doi: 10.1061/(ASCE)0742-597X(1998)14:5(73).

Tierney, L. (1970). Social policy. In A.F. Davis, & S. Encel, (Eds.). *Australian society: A sociological introduction* (2nd ed., pp. 200–223). Melbourne: Cheshire.

Vincent-Jones, P. (2000). Contractual governance: Institutional and organizational analysis. *Oxford Journal of Legal Studies, 20*(3), 317–351. doi: 10.1093/ojls/20.3.317.

Walker, D., & Hampson, K. 2008. *Procurement strategies: A relationship-based approach*. Oxford, UK: Blackwell Publishing.

Wamsley, G. L. (1990). *Refounding public administration*. Newbury Park, CA: Sage Publications.

Waterhouse, J. M., Keast, R., & Brown, K. A. (2011). *Negotiating the business environment: Theory, practice for all governance styles*. Melbourne: Tilde Press.

Watson, A. (1982). *Diplomacy: The dialogue between states*. London: Eyre Methuen.

Weiss, L. (1998). *The myth of the powerless state: Governing the economy in a global era*. Cambridge: Polity Press.

Wolfenden, J. (1978). *The future of voluntary organizations: Report of the Wolfenden committee*. London: Croom Helm.

7 Assessing and measuring social value

Introduction

The nominal purpose of social procurement is to generate social value through purchasing processes. As we have discussed in previous chapters, new approaches to social procurement are driven by efficiency or accountability demands (for purchasers) and market development opportunities (for providers), informed by growing popular interest in the role of particular organisations and processes in delivering social impacts. Regardless of the impulses driving social procurement, social value creation is the presumed outcome. Yet, just what is social value? And how is it calculated and assessed in social procurement processes?

There has been an explosion of interest in measuring social value – or, social impacts – in recent years. Reminiscent of Power's (1997) observations of the "audit society" this interest is influenced by a number of factors consistent with new public governance (NPG) imperatives. Power (2000) noted that a systematic rise in interest in auditing, monitoring and evaluation was linked to the advent of new public management (NPM) (Hood, 1995) and associated shifts in regulatory regimes including indirect regulation from below, and the establishment of "control of control" regimes within distributed governance arrangements. He also observed that growing citizen demands for increased transparency was driving the institutionalisation of audit and evaluation practices (Power, 2000). Concurrent with the advancement of Power's conceptualisation of the audit society was the emergence of a discussion regarding the nature and role of public value creation. With its origins in public administration in the United States (see Moore, 1995), early discussions of public value focused on the work of public administrators and their potential to create new value through entrepreneurial processes (Williams & Shearer, 2011). Subsequent advancements in public value literature have focused on the nature and negotiation of public values (Bozeman & Johnson, 2015; Jørgensen & Bozeman, 2007), the relationship between public value aspirations and organisational structure and delivery (Bovaird, 2006), and the relationship between debates regarding public value and wider paradigmatic developments in new approaches to governance (Benington, 2009; Stoker, 2006). While key authors have given limited attention to the role and function of civil society in public value creation, there is a growing body of literature that recognises the wider public sphere as a domain in which public value is created (Bryson, Crosby & Bloomberg, 2014; Jacobs, 2014).

Recent interest in measuring social value is driven by imperatives consistent with both the logic of the audit society and paradigmatic questions regarding public value creation in an era of NPG. However, the distributed nature of this interest – amongst civil society organisations and funders, purchasers, and social investors from all sectors – means that popular discussion about measuring social value is characterised by a variety of inflections leading to fragmentation and diverse framing of the nature and purpose of social value. Differing normative agendas are thus at work in present conceptions of social value, the reasons it should be measured and the mechanisms by which this may be achieved.

In this chapter, we consider recent interest in the measurement of social value. Given our focus on social procurement in this volume, our primary focus here is on the construction and measurement of social value in relation to its place in purchasing processes. This aspect of identifying and evaluating social value creation is, as is explored later in the chapter, inextricably bound up with both technical and political questions regarding the nature and value of social goods. To locate our considerations within the broader debates regarding measuring social value, we commence with a discussion of recent drivers of the "measurement turn". We then go on to review current approaches to social impact measurement in broad terms and in relation to social procurement in particular. Extending this discussion, we consider the practical and political challenges associated with measuring social value in the context of social procurement. Our central argument is that the assessment of social value in social procurement is not simply an instrumental process, but a normative one that has potentially powerful consequences for establishing the symbolic legitimacy of particular outputs and outcomes, and for relocating strategic decision-making within organisations.

Drivers of interest in social value measurement

As outlined in Chapter 2, social procurement is not a new phenomenon, with various iterations of creating social value through purchasing practices identifiable within the public sector since the 19th century. Early examples of social procurement by the public sector utilised public purchasing to shape fair labour practices in the UK and to stimulate employment opportunities for people with a disability in the United States (McCrudden, 2004). In these contexts, as in contemporary examples, public purchasing is utilised as a lever to achieve specific social objectives in addition to the primary purchasing goals. These approaches were typically characterised by increasing government agencies' compliance with social progress agendas or stimulating activity that supported social outcomes amongst marginalised groups within the citizenry.

The rise of NPM (Hood, 1995) in the 1980s shifted attention in public spending from inputs to outputs (Considine, 2001) or the set of activities that prescribe "what has been done", while more recent iterations of network governance (Considine, 2005; Hajer & Wagenaar, 2003; Rhodes, 1997; Sørensen & Torfing, 2005) purportedly emphasise outcomes, or the "effects" of what has been done, as well as relying on more distributed modes of generating outcomes via a range of government and nongovernment actors. These more recent governance regimes have given rise to interest in social value creation as an outcome of public, private and cross-sectoral interventions. Accompanying this interest has been a growing debate about the ways by which the creation of social value can be "seen" and measured.

Alongside shifts in regimes of governing, developments in corporate social responsibility and new discourses of social entrepreneurship have placed a new spotlight on the socially progressive and regressive effects of market economics. In Chapter 5, we examined developments in corporate behaviour and its relationship to social procurement. It is salient here to revisit the observation that, concurrent with growing discussion of the nature and creation of public value, commentators on corporate behaviour were identifying new trends in both enacting and marketing social and environmental performance as part of corporate citizenship in an increasingly globalised market (Salzmann, Ionescu-Somers & Steger, 2005). Increasing permeability of boundaries between nation-states combined with the related rise of online and mobile technologies have generated market demands for social responsibility amongst private for-profit firms. These have both contributed to and been informed by transnational norm-setting (Mueckenberger & Jastram, 2010) through industry standards development and self-regulation, which are discussed further in this chapter in relation to social purchasing assessment practices.

The performance measurement demands generated by market logics of NPM and changing approaches to corporate performance have been mirrored in practices within the third sector (Barraket & Yousefpour, 2013). For not-for-profit organisations with direct funding relationships with governments, shifts towards outcomes-based funding (Julian, 2001; Julian & Clapp, 2000) have had both isomorphic effects (DiMaggio & Powell, 1983), which are resulting in an increased focus on evaluation and measurement of social performance in order to command legitimacy with government funders. Developments in strategic philanthropy have also influenced the link between funding regimes and social performance measurement, with a greater emphasis on the outcomes of funding rather than organisational activity purportedly guiding funding decisions (Katz, 2005)[1]. At the same time, increased proximity between citizens and third-sector organisations as a result of the growth of social networking technologies (Hopkins & Thomas, 2002; Vromen, 2014) have generated both new demands and new opportunities for citizen-centred thinking and communication between third-sector organisations and the communities they seek to serve.

The reification of social value and its measurement has proven particularly significant to market-oriented third-sector organisations in growing their activities to meet their missions. In the case of social enterprise, Jed Emerson's blended value proposition – or the nature of "value" as a combination of economic returns "with" social and environmental impacts – provided early influence, suggesting that the creation of blended value was both possible and measurable (Emerson, 2003). At the level of practice, social enterprise leaders in some jurisdictions – initially in the United States and then with growing significance, the UK – have been active in promoting the desirability of measuring social returns as part of an explicit effort to develop markets for the social enterprise sector (Nicholls, Sacks & Walsham, 2006). Measuring social value has been framed by some social enterprise advocates as an essential feature of social enterprise sustainability, predicated on the assumption that social value creation is a distinguishing feature of social enterprise and thus a discrete feature of these organisations' competitive advantages (Nicholls et al., 2006). Governmental moves towards quasi-market development that place service choice in the hands of the citizenry have resulted in new third-sector and private for-profit market entrants, creating further demands on third-sector organisations – particularly those in the social services domain – to both measure and communicate their social value to "downstream" service users and "upstream" service purchasers.

While changes within sectors have generated particular demands for the measurement of social value, these are also being stimulated by the emergence of hybrid models of social service delivery and social innovation (see Pol & Ville, 2009) that transcend sectoral boundaries. New financing instruments such as social impact bonds discussed in Chapters 2 and 3 create new demand for prescribing and measuring performance related to social value creation (Jackson, 2013), while emerging movements in social finance and impact investing more broadly require metrics for organisational performance that reliably measure both financial and social bottom lines (Brown, 2006; Burkett, 2010; Weber & Geobey, 2012). This has led to the development of metrics such as IRIS – a resource of the not-for-profit Global Impact Investing Network – which seek to provide standardised information to inform effective impact investment decisions.

Each of these developments positions the measurement of social value (or social impacts) at the centre of success of NPG arrangements that seek to produce social outcomes. Yet, each also demands different outputs of social value measurement to fulfil different knowledge conditions and serve diverse practical ends. The information needs regarding social performance of a prospective impact investor may be, for example, substantially different to those of a governmental purchaser within a specific service domain, or those of citizens who are users of specific services. While the importance of measuring social value creation and social performance of individual organisations seems to have gained widespread symbolic legitimacy (Suchman, 1995), the diversity of interests informing practice has created fragmentation and some anxiety as organisations and individual service professionals seek to navigate multiple stakeholder needs and divergent prescriptions arising from multiple institutional logics (Greenwood, Raynard, Kodeih, Micelotta & Lounsbury, 2011).

Our focus in this chapter is on the measurement of social value in relation to social procurement specifically. In this domain, as in others, decisions regarding the assessment and reward of social value creation are informed by trade-off factors between competing institutional imperatives, available knowledge and practices, and the ways in which social value is understood and operationalised in routine practices (Wilkinson & Kirkup, 2009).

Approaches to defining social value in social procurement

Proponents of social procurement make much of the value-added of purchasing against a social as well as a financial bottom line. This is apparent in both policy frameworks and emerging literature associated with new conceptions of commercial performance and global growth. The mid-1990s saw the emergence of measurement and management systems that sought to move beyond financial measures to assess the long-term value creation of both private for-profit and non-profit organisations (Kaplan, 2001; Kaplan & Norton, 1996). In 2003, Jed Emerson observed that the rise in anti-corporate globalisation protests, CEO attention to social and environmental performance, for-benefit organisations such as social enterprise, and discussions about impact investing were emblematic of a wider process of exploration regarding the true nature of value. In coining the term "blended value" Emerson (2003) suggested that " . . .the core nature of investment and return is not a trade-off between social and financial interest but rather the pursuit of an *embedded value proposition* [emphasis added] composed of both" (p. 37). Seeking to develop a new framework for thinking about business performance, Porter and Kramer (2011) propose the notion of "shared value", suggesting similarly that shared value creation focuses on identifying and expanding the connections between societal and economic progress.

These calls for conceptualising financial, economic and social value not as discrete elements, but as embedded, integrated and cumulative are similarly reflected in emerging public policy frameworks for social procurement. In the UK Public Services (Social Value) Act 2012, for example, social value is not prescriptively defined but rather articulated in very general terms as the collective benefit to the community of the awarding of a public sector contract (Social Enterprise UK, 2012). Such benefits refer to the wider added value that may accrue to communities through the ways that services are procured and delivered. For example, delivery of a construction project via a consortium that includes locally focused work integration social enterprises may result in the delivery of both the primary output of the construction task as well as increased employment of local people who face barriers to entry to the open labour market. In another vein, provision of social services that involve local volunteers via third-sector organisations may both deliver the service targets and increase social capital and related community cohesion through the increased social interaction afforded by such approaches to delivery. Emphasis on social value is purported to encourage public commissioners and service planners to consider the wider multiplier effects and benefits of service purchasing beyond the price value (Harlock, 2014) that accrue through the procurement process itself.

A prevailing assumption of scholarly, practitioner-led and policy-led conceptions of social and related forms of value is that they are measurable. Yet, one of the greatest practical challenges of social procurement – for both purchasers and providers – is determining and operationalising social value. This includes not just being able to "measure" social value, but also being able to determine priorities for stimulating social value creation and develop mechanisms by which different types of social value can be comparatively assessed. Financial currency is a long-standing and widely understood signifier of material value; such signifiers do not exist for social value. And, while social value creation includes the use and production of tangible resources, prevailing frameworks for understanding social progress – for example, the World Health Organisation's social determinants of health model (WHO, 2013) – increasingly recognise the iterative interplay between tangible (e.g., housing, employment) and intangible (e.g., social capital, cultural resilience) resources in the reduction of social inequities.

Cost-benefit analysis (CBA) – which monetizes and compares the benefits and costs of a particular intervention (Tuan, 2008) – has been traditionally used as a decision tool to determine the relative benefits of procurement and commissioning arrangements with regard to financial savings. Adaptations of CBA have been utilised in relation to place-focused social procurement initiatives in both the UK and Australia, to predict the savings on "reactive spend" – that is, costs of welfare payments, health inequities and crime management – effected by different social interventions (see Cox, Bowen & Kempton, 2012; Quinn, 2011). As noted in these studies as well as meta-analyses of methods for measuring social value (Tuan, 2008), lack of common measures for social value, combined with lack of quality data on costs, outputs and outcomes constrain the quality and comparability of CBA assessments of social value creation.

Limitations of existing measurement tools, combined with emergent debates about the nature and importance of recognising social value (Emerson, 2003; Nicholls, 2009; Porter and Kramer 2011), have stimulated concomitant growth of measurement frameworks and methods that seek to capture the intangible and holistic outcomes of social interventions, social benefit organisations and value-added activities. These methods include but are not limited to: social cost-benefit analysis; social accounting and audit; social return on investment (SROI) and local economic multiplier tools such as LM3. SROI has been perhaps the most dominant of new popular measurement approaches across a number of countries, and has influenced the development of a number of other alternative methodologies (Tuan, 2008). A meta-analysis of social impact measurement methods utilised between 2002 and 2012 found that SROI was one of the most widely utilised and discussed methods in the field (Krlev, Munscher & Mulbert, 2013). With its origins in the work of the Roberts Enterprise Development Fund in the United States and later popularised through the New Economics Foundation and SROI network in the UK, SROI applies accounting principles to a stakeholder-informed approach (Luke, Barraket & Eversole, 2013), using financial proxies to determine a ratio value for the (financial) costs versus the (monetised social) value created by particular interventions. In both single-case application and meta-evaluative studies of the use of SROI, researchers find an urgent need to standardise the application of financial proxies if the method is to have salience as a comparatively valid and decision-useful tool (Arvidson, Battye & Salisbury, 2014; Krlev et al., 2013). They also find that, despite its raison d'etre, the most underdeveloped aspect of the application of SROI is in the measurement of social value where the social is treated " . . . as a residual category that lacks definitional criteria . . . and is negatively affected by the urge of monetization" (Krlev et al., 2013, p. 5). In this sense, the application of SROI as a methodological tool has moved away from early promises in the literature regarding the measurability of the social dimensions of blended value, giving way to the use of a primary signifier – financial currency – to provide a veneer of certainty regarding absolute value and comparable value of different social interventions. Across the wider suite of methods and tools for measuring social value at the organisational or program level, lack of standardisation – and, therefore, lack of comparability – has been consistently identified as a major challenge to validity and reliability (Barraket & Yousefpour, 2013; Bull, 2007; Luke et al., 2013; Millar & Hall, 2013; Tuan, 2008).

Within the third sector, organisational decisions regarding what, when and how to measure social value are variously informed by organisational identity (Bull & Crompton, 2006), the purpose of measurement and the extent to which it is oriented towards meeting internal or external stakeholder needs, resources available and prior experience of impact measurement (Barraket & Yousefpour, 2013). In response to the limited accessibility and utility of prevailing measurement approaches, emerging third-sector responses have shifted conceptualisation away from measuring social impacts and towards demonstrating value. The Canadian Demonstrating Value initiative, for example, seeks to provide accessible tools for social purpose organisations to demonstrate their value, with a focus on what measures matter based on organisational purpose and context (Demonstrating Value, 2009). Such approaches eschew universalising assumptions about the nature of social value, while simultaneously seeking to establish common approaches and processes for assessment to allow for comparability required by social investors and purchasers.

Approaches to prioritising and assessing social value in social procurement processes

It is notable that, despite garnering popular attention in some jurisdictions (Millar & Hall, 2013), there is virtually no empirical evidence that any of the new social value evaluation methods just discussed have established practical legitimacy (Suchman, 1995) in the sense of stimulating greater purchasing from or investing in social impact organisations. Evidence on purchasing decisions related to social value remains scant. Recent UK studies have found that, on the one hand, public commissioning bodies are reluctant to employ tools or evidence arising from tools – such as SROI methods – that they view as untested

(Millar & Hall, 2013) while, on the other, third-sector organisations are reluctant to invest in performance measurement methods that they are not confident are significantly influencing public commissioning practice (Lindsay, Osborne & Bond, 2014; Munoz, 2009). Other research with public commissioners in the UK has identified that a lack of user-friendly assessment tools combined with the ambiguity of the concept of social value are major impediments to social procurement (Harlock, 2014). A recent review of the implementation of the UK's Public Services (Social Value) Act 2012 also found that defining social value was a major barrier to implementation (Cabinet Office, 2015). Uncertainty avoidance as an inhibitor of innovation in procurement processes is not limited to the pursuit of social objectives, with other public procurement research identifying familiarity – for both clients and industry – with particular procurement instruments, organisational culture and institutional norms as important drivers of procurement assessment decisions (Love, Davis, Edwards & Baccarini, 2008). As discussed in Chapter 4, rules, resources and relationships contribute to the legitimisation of practice in this emerging institutional field.

In practice, we can observe a number of dominant approaches to determining and prioritising social value in social procurement and commissioning processes. In the absence of definitive definitions of what constitutes social value and how to measure it, both public and private purchasers are guided variously by instrumental or procurer-centric approaches; reliance on proxies and standards for social value; and co-creation of indicators and frameworks (Table 7.1). Each of these locates authority for determining social value in different sectors and institutions. It should be noted that these approaches are not always mutually exclusive; for example, instrumental approaches are increasingly informed by transnational standards.

Table 7.1 Approaches to determining and prioritising social value in social procurement and commissioning processes

Approach	Source of Authority	Practices
Instrumental or procurer-centric approaches	Regulatory knowledge (government or industry standards)	Use of governmental and industry guidelines to determine priorities and methods
Reliance on proxies and standards	Expert knowledge and moral reflection (transnational civil society)	Preferred purchasing from third sector or social-benefit providers Adoption of transnational standards and policy instruments
Co-creation of indicators and frameworks	Network and local knowledge	Local priority setting and joint-value strategies

Instrumental or procurer-centric approaches

With authority located within regulatory knowledge, instrumental or procurer-centric approaches to social procurement are organised around compliance with top-down directives and utilisation of institutionally sanctioned processes for assessing social value. The focus here is on the stated rules, typically with regard to questions of competitive neutrality and price consistent with market logic. As has been widely discussed, market models of governance contribute to democratic deficits by concealing historically public accountabilities behind commercial in-confidence imperatives, and by constructing citizens as consumers of services (Ryan, 2001). Instrumental or organisation-centric approaches to determining social value(s) of social procurement are consistent with these observations, constructing procurement as a set of routine technical processes that occur inside the machinery of government. In constructing procurement thus, this approach also relegates decisions fundamentally concerned with the (contested) nature of social goods to administrators of routine procurement practices not typically engaged in such questions. A growing focus on the potential of all forms of procurement to drive strategic agendas within purchasing organisations (see Booth, 2014) is shedding light on new staff competencies required of contemporary procurement practices, which we consider further in subsequent chapters.

Reliance on proxies for social value

Early discussions of the most recent iterations of social procurement were driven largely by advocacy from the third sector, particularly amongst social enterprises. A number of working definitions of social procurement have thus positioned third-sector or social-economy organisations at the centre of social value creation. This has stimulated the use of third-sector and hybrid organisations – particularly social enterprises – as a proxy for social value in some procurement processes. Social enterprises are increasingly recognised as a class of providers in organisational supplier diversity policies, from the 2015 Pan Am and Parapan Am Games to the National Australia Bank, while public policy guidelines on social procurement in Scotland, Australia and England specifically nominate social enterprises as social benefit providers to be considered in social procurement activities. This approach to identifying and assessing social value vests legitimacy in a particular sector. It has also created an industry in identifying and legitimising providers – through certification standards delivered by second-tier third-sector organisations – particularly in countries which have a mixed economy of social enterprises regulated under a variety of legal forms. This mirrors earlier developments in supplier diversity initiatives discussed in Chapters 2 and 5, where third-sector organisations such as the National Minority Supplier Development Council in the United States and Supply Nation in Australia certify minority and Indigenous-owned businesses, respectively, as well as play an active role in stimulating and mediating supply chain relationships that include these suppliers.

In the UK, the Social Enterprise Mark was established to certify social enterprises and now is explicitly framed as a verification mechanism of the social value created by "genuine" social enterprises for public commissioners and procurement managers. As the UK social enterprise certification authority, the Social Enterprise Mark automatically demonstrates social value because the Mark independently proves that a business or organisation puts at least 50% of its profits towards social or environmental good. The Social Enterprise Mark makes it easy for commissioners and procurement managers to identify when social value is being delivered (Social Enterprise, n.d.).

With its origins in the United States, B Corp has also emerged as a framework for certifying "for benefit" businesses, although its stated focus is more on commercial responsibility and open market development than social procurement, per se. Each of these certification models emphasise different criteria in their determinations of the type and relative importance of social value produced by certified organisations. The normative principles that underpin these models have powerful consequences for determining – and, some suggest, potentially narrowing – definitions of social businesses and the types of social value they are able to create (Ridley-Duff & Southcombe, 2012). In each of these cases, the use of third-party certifications extend beyond industry self-regulation, placing third-sector organisations and networks in the position of outsourced regulators of the verification of proxies for social value (Hawkins, Gravier & Powley, 2011).

Most of these examples are contained within nation-states, although some have internationalised by establishing local chapters in other countries. Globalisation of markets, however, produces transnational supply chains, which have stimulated the development of transnational governance networks. Through these networks, there has been a rapid increase in the availability and use in procurement processes of all kinds of standards and related policy instruments, such as codes of conduct and certification schemes, over the past two decades (Boström & Karlsson, 2013). These instruments are typically generated through multi-actor deliberations and act as forms of "horizontal governance", particularly in transnational contexts where the nation-state lacks salience as a source of legitimacy (Mueckenberger & Jastram, 2010). As noted by Boström and Karlsson (2013), such standards derive their authority from expert knowledge and moral reflections. Their development is often, but not exclusively, located with global civil society.

In the domain of social procurement, transnational third-sector organisations and programs, such as the United Nations Environment Programme (UNEP) and the International Standards Organisation (ISO), have been active in developing frameworks for policy and practice. UNEP has been a long-time leader of sustainable procurement initiatives, launching the International Sustainable Procurement Initiative in 2012. ISO standards have been a reference point for corporate social responsibility since the 1990s; a new standard for sustainable purchasing – ISO/CD 20400 – is currently under development.

Co-developing indicators and frameworks

The post-liberal democratic literature notes both the constraining and ena-bling effects of distributed governance networks on democratic engagement. As Sørensen and Torfing (2005) note, distributed approaches to governing also provide opportunities for renegotiating points of democratic anchorage within governance networks. In social procurement, these negotiations may occur "upward" through transnational governance networks or "downward" through deliberations with local communities. Upward negotiations have already been discussed in relation to use of proxies.

In terms of downward negotiations, definitions and processes of determining social value that locate authority within the citizenry – requiring deliberative development of indicators that are given priority in procurement assessment weightings – generate new opportunities for democratic participation in local governance. This approach is particularly prevalent in the UK, where previ-ous commitments to "best value" procurement (Erridge, 2007) and third-way emphases on partnership working (Lawless, 2006) have emphasised stakeholder engagement and deliberation in local governance arrangements. Local gov-ernment responses to the UK's Public Services (Social Value) Act 2012 have included the development of joint social value strategies (Compact Voice, 2014). These are typically developed through cross-sector partnerships between local public agencies and third-sector networks, combined with consultation with local residents, to identify social outcomes and measures that meet the priority needs of local areas. Without legislative imperatives, similar approaches are emerging in Australia, with social procurement priorities embedded in local compacts aimed at improving place-based socio-economic equity in regions such as Geelong, which have been significantly affected by recent deindustri-alisation (Leach, 2014).

Measurement challenges

A common pragmatic observation of the challenges of measuring social value created in public goods is the problem of the interdependencies (Tuan, 2008). That is, it is difficult to distil the effects of specific interventions from other factors in the environment – including the presence of other services and ser-vice providers – when accounting for social change (Pawson, 2002). Beyond interdependencies between interventions, it is important to recognise that the performance of a service is not simply located in its effectual design but in the subjective experience of its users who are, in effect, co-producers of service quality (Osborne, Radnor & Nasi, 2013). For example, in terms of its outcomes, the quality of a local employment services program is affected not just by its intrinsic design, or by the relative performance of other local services, but also by the experiences, attitudes and expectations of the service's users, including individual clients and local employers. Taking this into account, the challenge of measuring social value is not simply one of distinguishing the effects of one service relative to another, but of recasting our understanding of the very mechanisms by which such value is (co)produced. A view of social value production as simply the aggregate of a series of discrete services or interventions is rather different to one that views such value as being produced systemically through the interaction of policy actors and the citizenry. As previously noted, different conceptions of social value and different approaches to the selection and legitimisation of particular iterations of social value permeate current social procurement practices.

Each of these conceptions of how social value is produced also leads to different measurement practices in social procurement. For example, a systems-based view of social value creation would lend itself to the measurement of integrated outcomes via higher-order indicators across service domains and/or across business units within a purchasing organisation. In contrast, a discrete elements–based view would lead to measurement of the outcomes of particular services or interventions in relation to one or more single-domain values, such as employment outcomes, financial value or specific environmental impacts, for example, carbon footprint reduction. It has been observed in the context of sustainable procurement that discrete element approaches can actually erode the central purpose of integrated value afforded by these procurement processes, where the outcomes of one discrete element undermines the outcomes of another. Policy approaches and strategic guidelines that utilise separate lists of indicators rather than integrated measures for each element of a triple bottom line approach thus lead to fragmented and compartmentalised decision-making in sustainability-related procurement processes (Meehan & Bryde, 2011).

These issues suggest that approaches to measuring social value are not simply instrumental tasks, but normative processes that shape both purchasing decisions and organisational cultures that interact with the procurement process more broadly. In the case of public procurers, for example, an Australian local government case of implementing a sustainable procurement strategy – with an explicit focus on triple bottom line returns – illuminates the implicit and explicit reshaping of organisational practice that occurs in line with policy implementation. In the development and implementation of its sustainable procurement strategy, Parramatta City Council (PCC) in the western suburbs of Sydney explicitly sought to recognise procurement as a strategic as well as an operational function of the organisation, with a view to stimulating greater local economic diversity within the region it serves. Explicit organisational changes required to enact the strategy included modifications to the staffing and procedural structures that underpinned procurement activity, and an ongoing process of culture change to shift from a siloed to an integrated approach to meeting environmental, social and economic objectives within the organisation. New intra-organisational relationships and new relationships with social economy suppliers developed as a consequence of restructuring are also affecting council practices implicitly (Dean, 2013).

We have observed in previous chapters and above that, at a macro level, the characteristics and practices of the third sector have been deeply influenced by service purchasing regimes consistent with NPM (Carmel & Harlock, 2008). In the case of organisations from which social and environmental value is purchased, mechanisms by which social procurement objectives are routinized in procurement processes can have powerful effects on the ways in which social and environmental value creation are embodied in wider organisational practice at the micro level. In relation to sustainable procurement processes in the UK, for example, Meehan and Bryde (2011) observed that a focus on compliance through tendering and contract criteria was favoured by public procurers over promotion of the sharing of sustainability values with suppliers through more relational processes. They concluded that this lack of engagement with suppliers constrained the sustainability agenda because it limited supplier engagement with the agenda's objectives to matters of compliance only (Meehan & Bryde, 2011). In the case of the emergence of hybrid financing instruments such as social impact bonds McHugh, Sinclair, Roy, Huckfield and Donaldson (2013) have cautioned that measurement logics can erode rather than increase social value creation, where measurement accountabilities drive third-sector providers away from interventions that are most needed and towards activities that are most easily measured.

Each of these examples reinforces the notion that evaluations of social value in social procurement processes are not "neutral acts of verification but actively shape the design and interpretation of 'auditable performance'" (Power, 2000, p. 114). Purposeful approaches to designing social and environmental value into procurement decisions also suggest a shift in the location of procurement from an operational to a more strategic function of procuring institutions (Preuss, 2009), both public and private.

Finally, the complexity of integrating strategic and operational commitments to triple bottom line imperatives can produce what Meehan and Bryde (2011) have described as "ontological anxiety" regarding the selection and privileging of indicators against which purchasing decisions are assessed. Again, the locus of decision-making and legitimation of what constitutes social value – both in absolute and relative terms – are significant here. Social and sustainable procurement agendas reframe the nature of routine administrative functions, placing new demands on commissioning and procurement professionals across sectors. These demands relocate decision-making accountabilities within organisations and require new workforce competencies, discussed further in Chapters 6 and 8. The logic of social procurement is one of relational co-creation. While it is clear that procurement has always been informed by relationships and interactivity within the supply chain (Carter & Jennings, 2002; Kwon & Suh, 2004), the institutional logics that underpin new approaches to social procurement suggest the need for new dialogic processes between upstream purchasers of services, providers and downstream beneficiaries of the value created.

Conclusion

In this chapter, we have considered the ways in which the construct of social value and its measurement has gained popular attention and the implications for social procurement practice. A prevailing tension of social procurement is the challenges of operationalising and measuring social value without access to established and collectively legitimated signifiers. In the absence of measurability, approaches to social procurement rely on proxies, narratives of good practice and legitimacy formed through the co-production of indicators and frameworks. We have argued in this chapter that approaches to assessing and comparing social value are not instrumental acts, but are both shaped by and contribute to norm-setting in this emerging institutional field. We have illustrated that in pursuit of social objectives, commissioners and procurement managers are simultaneously navigating vertical (in the form of legislative) and horizontal (in the form of standards and certifications) governance frameworks in the operationalisation of social procurement objectives (Boström & Karlsson, 2013). While this is particularly prevalent in the public sector, discursive constructions of social value creation and its measurement are also producing isomorphic effects within private organisations and their supply chain developments, both as independent purchasers and as suppliers to governments.

Note

1   It should be noted that there is relatively little evidence to date that outcomes measurement is actually guiding funding decision-making (Carman, 2009). Rather, the measurement of social outcomes appears to have gained symbolic legitimacy (Suchman, 1995) as a signifier of effective management amongst third-sector organisations, particularly funded non-profits, and their funders in recent years.

References

Arvidson, M., Battye, F., & Salisbury, D. (2014). The social return on investment in community befriending. *International Journal of Public Sector Management*, *27*(3), 225–240. doi:10.1108/IJPSM-03–2013–0045

Barraket, J., & Yousefpour, N. (2013). Evaluation and social impact measurement amongst small to medium social enterprises: Process, purpose and value. *Australian Journal of Public Administration*, *72*(4), 447–458. doi:10.1111/1467–8500.12042

Benington, J. (2009). Creating the public in order to create public value? *International Journal of Public Administration*, *32*(3–4), 232–249. doi:10.1080/01900690902749578

Booth, C. (2014). *Strategic procurement: Organizing suppliers and supply chains for competitive advantage*. London, UK: Kogan Page.

Boström, M., & Karlsson, M. (2013). Responsible procurement, complex product chains and the integration of vertical and horizontal governance. *Environmental Policy and Governance*, *23*(6), 381–394. doi:10.1002/eet.1626

Bovaird, T. (2006). Developing new forms of partnership with the "market" in the procurement of public services. *Public Administration*, *84*(1), 81–102. doi:10.1111/j.0033–3298.2006.00494.x

Bozeman, B., & Johnson, J. (2015). The political economy of public values: A case for the public sphere and progressive opportunity. *The American Review of Public Administration*, *45*(1), 61–85. doi:10.1177/0275074014532826

Brown, J. (2006). Equity finance for social enterprises. *Social Enterprise Journal*, 2(1), 73–81. doi:10.1108/17508610680000714

Bryson, J.M., Crosby, B.C., & Bloomberg, L. (2014). Public value governance: Moving beyond traditional public administration and the new public management. *Public Administration Review*, 74(4), 445–456. doi:10.1111/puar.12238

Bull, M. (2007). "Balance": The development of a social enterprise business performance analysis tool. *Social Enterprise Journal*, 3(1), 49–66. doi:10.1108/17508610780000721

Bull, M., & Crompton, H. (2006). Business practices in social enterprises. *Social Enterprise Journal*, 2(1), 42–60. doi:10.1108/17508610680000712

Burkett, I. (2010). *Financing social enterprise: Understanding needs and realities*. Brisbane: Foresters Community Finance. Retrieved from http://foresters.org.au/u/lib/mob/20131112141 609_2f919340f9710df47/2010_financingsocialenterpriseunderstandingneedsandrealities. pdf (Accessed 28th May 2015)

Cabinet Office. (2015). *Social value act review*. Retrieved from Cabinet Office website: www. gov.uk/government/uploads/system/uploads/attachment_data/file/403748/Social_ Value_Act_review_report_150212.pdf. (Accessed 28th May 2015)

Carman, J.G. (2009). Nonprofits, funders, and evaluation accountability in action. *The American Review of Public Administration*, 39(4), 374–390. doi:10.1177/0275074008320190

Carmel, E., & Harlock, J. (2008). Instituting the "third sector" as a governable terrain: Partnership, procurement and performance in the UK. *Policy & Politics*, 36(2), 155–171. doi:10.1332/030557308783995017

Carter, C.R., & Jennings, M.M. (2002). Social responsibility and supply chain relationships. *Transportation Research Part E: Logistics and Transportation Review*, 38(1), 37–52. doi:10.1016/S1366–5545(01)00008–4

Compact Voice. (2014). *Understanding social value: A guide for local compacts and the voluntary sector*. Retrieved from www.compactvoice.org.uk/sites/default/files/social_value_guid ance_2014.pdf (Accessed 28th May 2015)

Considine, M. (2001). *Enterprising states: The public management of welfare-to-work*. Cambridge, UK: Cambridge University Press.

Considine, M. (2005). *Making public policy: Institutions, actors, strategies*. Cambridge, UK: Polity Press.

Cox, J., Bowen, M., & Kempton, O. (2012). *Social value: Understanding the wider value of public policy interventions*. Retrieved from New Economy Working Papers website: www.ourlife. org.uk/silo/files/social-value-working-paper.pdf (Accessed 28th May 2015)

Dean, A. (2013). *Tackling long-term unemployment amongst vulnerable groups*. OECD Retrieved from www.oecd.org/cfe/leed/Tackling%20Long_Term%20unemployment_%20WP_ covers.pdf (Accessed 28th May 2015)

Demonstrating Value. (2009). *Developing the demonstrating value network: Detailed report*. Retrieved from www.demonstratingvalue.org/sites/default/files/basic-page-attach ments/DV_research_initiative_detailed_report.pdf (Accessed 28th May 2015)

DiMaggio, P.J., & Powell, W.W. (1983). The iron cage revisited: Institutional isomorphism and collective rationality in organizational fields. *American Sociological Review*, 48(2), 147–160. doi:10.2307/2095101

Emerson, J. (2003). The blended value proposition: Integrating social and financial returns. *California Management Review*, 45(4), 35–51. doi:10.2307/41166187

Erridge, A. (2007). Public procurement, public value and the Northern Ireland unemployment pilot project. *Public Administration*, 85(4), 1023–1043. doi:10.1111/j.1467–9299.2007.00674.x

Greenwood, R., Raynard, M., Kodeih, F., Micelotta, E.R., & Lounsbury, M. (2011). Institutional complexity and organizational responses. *The Academy of Management Annals*, 5(1), 317–371. doi:10.1080/19416520.2011.590299

Hajer, M.A., & Wagenaar, H. (2003). *Deliberative policy analysis: Understanding governance in the network society*. Cambridge, UK: Cambridge University Press.

Harlock, J. (2014). *From outcomes-based commissioning to social value? Implications for performance managing the third sector* (Working Paper No. 123). Birmingham: Third Sector Research Centre. Retrieved from www.birmingham.ac.uk/generic/tsrc/documents/tsrc/working-papers/working-paper-123.pdf (Accessed 28th May 2015)

Hawkins, T.G., Gravier, M.J., & Powley, E.H. (2011). Public versus private sector procurement ethics and strategy: What each sector can learn from the other. *Journal of Business Ethics, 103*(4), 567–586. doi: 10.1007/s10551–011–0881–2

Hood, C. (1995). The "new public management" in the 1980s: Variations on a theme. *Accounting, Organizations and Society, 20*(2–3), 93–109. doi: 10.1016/0361–3682(93)E0001-W.

Hopkins, L., & Thomas, J. (2002). *E-social capital: Building community through electronic networks*. Community Networking Conference. Monash University, Caulfield.

Jackson, E.T. (2013). Evaluating social impact bonds: Questions, challenges, innovations, and possibilities in measuring outcomes in impact investing. *Community Development, 44*(5), 608–616. doi:10.1080/15575330.2013.854258

Jacobs, L.R. (2014). The contested politics of public value. *Public Administration Review, 74*(4), 480–494. doi:10.1111/puar.12170

Jørgensen, T.B., & Bozeman, B. (2007). Public values an inventory. *Administration & Society, 39*(3), 354–381. doi:10.1177/0095399707300703

Julian, D.A. (2001). A case study of the implementation of outcomes-based funding within a local United Way system: Some implications for practicing community psychology. *American Journal of Community Psychology, 29*(6), 851–874. doi:10.1023/A:1012963415118

Julian, D.A., & Clapp, J. (2000). Planning, investment and evaluation procedures to support coordination and outcomes based funding in a local United Way system. *Evaluation and Program Planning, 23*(2), 231–240. doi:10.1016/S0149–7189(00)00004–5

Kaplan, R.S. (2001). Strategic performance measurement and management in nonprofit organizations. *Nonprofit Management and Leadership, 11*(3), 353–370. doi:10.1002/nml.11308

Kaplan, R.S., & Norton, D.P. (1996). *The balanced scorecard: Translating strategy into action* (1st ed.). Boston, MS: Harvard Business Review Press.

Katz, S.N. (2005). What does it mean to say that philanthropy is "effective"? The philanthropists' new clothes. *Proceedings of the American Philosophical Society, 149*(2), 123–131. Retrieved from www.jstor.org/stable/4598921

Krlev, G., Munscher, R., & Mulbert, K. (2013). *Social return on investment (SROI), State-of-the-art and perspectives: A meta-analysis of practice in social return on investment (SROI) studies published 2002–2012* (CSI advisory services). Heidelberg University, Germany: Centre for Social Investment. Retrieved from www.csi.uni-heidelberg.de/downloads/CSI_SROI_Meta_Analysis_2013.pdf (Accessed 28th May 2015)

Kwon, I.W.G., & Suh, T. (2004). Factors affecting the level of trust and commitment in supply chain relationships. *Journal of Supply Chain Management, 40*(1), 4–14. doi:10.1111/j.1745–493X.2004.tb00165.x

Lawless, P. (2006). Area-based urban interventions, rationale and outcomes: The new deal for communities programme in England. *Urban Studies, 43*(11), 1991–2011. doi:10.1080/00420980600897859

Leach, S. (2014). G21 region opportunities for work: *Employment and strategic procurement workshop*. Retrieved from http://grow.g21.com.au/wp-content/uploads/2014/11/Employment-Strategic-Procurement-Workshop-24-October-2014-Geelong-Presentation.pdf (Accessed 28th May 2015)

Lindsay, C., Osborne, S.P., & Bond, S. (2014). The "new public governance" and employability services in an era of crisis: Challenges for third sector organizations in Scotland. *Public Administration, 92*(1), 192–207. doi:10.1111/padm.12051

Love, P.E.D., Davis, P.R., Edwards, D.J., & Baccarini, D. (2008). Uncertainty avoidance: Public sector clients and procurement selection. *International Journal of Public Sector Management*, *21*(7), 753–776. doi:10.1108/09513550810904550

Luke, B., Barraket, J., & Eversole, R. (2013). Measurement as legitimacy versus legitimacy of measures: Performance evaluation of social enterprise. *Qualitative Research in Accounting & Management*, *10*(3/4), 234–258. doi:10.1108/QRAM-08–2012–0034

McCrudden, C. (2004). Using public procurement to achieve social outcomes. *Natural Resources Forum*, *28*(4), 257–267. doi:10.1111/j.1477–8947.2004.00099.x

McHugh, N., Sinclair, S., Roy, M., Huckfield, L., & Donaldson, C. (2013). Social impact bonds: A wolf in sheep's clothing? *Journal of Poverty and Social Justice*, *21*(3), 247–257. doi: 10.1332/204674313X13812372137921

Meehan, J., & Bryde, D. (2011). Sustainable procurement practice. *Business Strategy and the Environment*, *20*(2), 94–106. doi: 10.1002/bse.678

Millar, R., & Hall, K. (2013). Social return on investment (SROI) and performance measurement. *Public Management Review*, *15*(6), 923–941. doi:10.1080/14719037.2012.698857

Moore, M.H. (1995). *Creating public value: Strategic management in government*. Cambridge, MA: Harvard University Press.

Mueckenberger, U., & Jastram, S. (2010). Transnational norm-building networks and the legitimacy of corporate social responsibility standards. *Journal of Business Ethics*, *97*(2), 223–239. doi:10.1007/s10551–010–0506–1

Munoz, S.A. (2009). Social enterprise and public sector voices on procurement. *Social Enterprise Journal*, *5*(1), 69–82. doi:10.1108/17508610910956417

Nicholls, A. (2009). 'We do good things, don't we?': 'Blended value accounting' in social entrepreneurship. *Accounting, Organizations and Society*, *34*(6–7), 755–769. doi:10.1016/j.aos.2009.04.008

Nicholls, J., Sacks, J., & Walsham, M. (2006). More for your money: A guide to procuring from social enterprises. Retrieved November 20, 2009, from www.socialenterprise.org.uk/data/files/publications/sec_procurement_guide_final_06.pdf

Osborne, S.P., Radnor, Z., & Nasi, G. (2013). A new theory for public service management? Toward a (public) service-dominant approach. *The American Review of Public Administration*, *43*(2), 135–158. doi:10.1177/0275074012466935

Pawson, R. (2002). Evidence-based policy: The promise of 'realist synthesis'. *Evaluation*, *8*(3), 340–358. doi:10.1177/135638902401462448

Pol, E., & Ville, S. (2009). Social innovation: Buzz word or enduring term? *Journal of Socio-Economics*, *38*(6), 878–885. doi:10.1016/j.socec.2009.02.011

Porter, M.E., & Kramer, M.R. (2011). Creating shared value. *Harvard Business Review*, *89*(1/2), 62–77. Retrieved from https://hbr.org/2011/01/the-big-idea-creating-shared-value.

Power, M. (1997). *The audit society: Rituals of verification*. Oxford, New York: Oxford University Press.

Power, M. (2000). The audit society: Second thoughts. *International Journal of Auditing*, *4*(1), 111–119. doi:10.1111/1099–1123.00306

Preuss, L. (2009). Addressing sustainable development through public procurement: The case of local government. *Supply Chain Management: An International Journal*, *14*(3), 213–223. doi:10.1108/13598540910954557

Quinn, D. (2011). *A case for social procurement: Property cost management and advisory for AMES and Urban Communities*. Retrieved from http://socialprocurementaustralasia.com/wp-content/uploads/2013/09/Kensington-Cleaning-Social-Procurement-Report.pdf (Accessed 28th May 2015)

Rhodes, R.A.W. (1997). *Understanding governance: Policy networks, governance, reflexivity and accountability*. Buckingham, UK: Open University Press.

Ridley-Duff, R., & Southcombe, C. (2012). The social enterprise mark: A critical review of its conceptual dimensions. *Social Enterprise Journal, 8*(3), 178–200. doi:10.1108/17508611211280746

Ryan, N. (2001). Reconstructing citizens as consumers: Implications for new modes of governance. *Australian Journal of Public Administration, 60*(3), 104–109. doi:10.1111/1467–8500.00229

Salzmann, O., Ionescu-Somers, A., & Steger, U. (2005). The business case for corporate sustainability: Literature review and research options. *European Management Journal, 23*(1), 27–36. doi:10.1016/j.emj.2004.12.007

Sørensen, E., & Torfing, J. (2005). The democratic anchorage of governance networks. *Scandinavian Political Studies, 28*(3), 195–218. doi:10.1111/j.1467–9477.2005.00129.x

Social Enterprise (n.d.). Social enterprise mark. Retrieved from www.socialenterprisemark. org.uk/social-value/ (Accessed 28th September 2015)

Social Enterprise UK. (2012). *Public services (social value) act 2012: A brief guide.* Retrieved from www.socialenterprise.org.uk/uploads/files/2012/03/public_services_act_2012_a_ brief_guide_web_version_final.pdf (Accessed 28th May 2015)

Stoker, G. (2006). Public value management: A new narrative for networked governance? *The American Review of Public Administration, 36*(1), 41–57. doi:10.1177/0275074005282583

Suchman, M.C. (1995). Managing legitimacy: Strategic and institutional approaches. *The Academy of Management Review, 20*(3), 571–610. doi:10.5465/AMR.1995.9508080331

Tuan, M.T. (2008). *Measuring and/or estimating social value creation: Insights into eight integrated cost approaches* (final paper). Bill and Melinda Gates Foundation. Retrieved from https:// docs.gatesfoundation.org/Documents/wwl-report-measuring-estimating-social-value-creation.pdf (Accessed 28th May 2015)

Vromen, A. (2014). Campaign entrepreneurs in online collective action: Getup! in Australia. *Social Movement Studies, 14*(2), 1–19. doi:10.1080/14742837.2014.923755

Weber, O., & Geobey, S. (2012). *Final report: Social finance and nonprofits: The contribution of social finance to the sustainability of nonprofit organizations and social enterprises.* Ontario, CA: University of Waterloo.

World Health Organisation. (2013). *What are social determinants of health?* Retrieved from www.who.int/social_determinants/sdh_definition/en/. (Accessed 28th May 2015)

Wilkinson, A., & Kirkup, B. (2009). *Measurement of sustainable procurement.* Adam Wilkinson and Associates. Retrieved from www.enterprisingnonprofits.ca/sites/www.enterpris ingnonprofits.ca/files/uploads/documents/Measuring_SP_Report.pdf (Accessed 28th May 2015)

Williams, I., & Shearer, H. (2011). Appraising public value: Past, present and futures. *Public Administration, 89*(4), 1367–1384. doi:10.1111/j.1467–9299.2011.01942.x

8 Theoretical implications and practical portents

Introduction

Throughout this volume, we have explored developments in social procurement policy and practice in light of approaches to new public governance (NPG). We have observed that, while not new, social procurement is constituted in and by its institutional environment, suggesting that new models of governance produce social procurement in new ways. Early forms of social procurement reflected the bureaucratic governance frameworks and geopolitical contexts in which they were embedded. They emphasised command and control models of governmental purchasing of social services, and of mandating corporate behaviour in relation to affirmative action goals. The rise of new public management (NPM) heralded a more extensive role for social procurement, with an emphasis on decentralisation and marketization of public services. In an era of NPG—which adds to rather than eclipses earlier governance modes—social procurement is becoming one mechanism for the pursuit of public value creation, in which the relationship between state and civil society is being reconfigured.

In this chapter, we further consider the relationship between theory and practice of social procurement as a manifestation of NPG arrangements. We argue that social procurement is imbued with concerns regarding public value creation, which is consistent with NPG. We suggest that, in keeping with the hybridity of this mode of governance, there is an increasing focus on assemblage between old and new practices and languages, which require integrative devices to span their differences. We argue here that social procurement is a space that produces such boundary objects, and that their negotiation and implementation may lead to strong (integrative and transformative) or weak (instrumental and transferred) iterations of practice.

Beyond boundary spanning theory – which focuses on questions of coordination or translation – we are concerned here with transformation, which occurs where "merging" synthesising elements produces "a new whole" or new set of practices. In examining this link between theory and practice, we review dominant theoretical accounts, including institutional and practice theories, used to explain or "locate" social procurement. We observe that there are tensions in accounting for both structure and agency in these approaches to conceptualising social procurement and other practices of NPG. We further note that existing explanations typically focus on either macro or micro considerations, or are metatheoretical in nature, sometimes obscuring the link to practice. We thus return to boundary object theory to consider how the integration between structure and agency are embedded in practice.

New public governance, public value and hybridity: creating new spaces and imperatives for social procurement

As has been discussed throughout previous chapters of this book, a new public governance form is taking shape; it draws on the remnants of the previous governance modes as well as bringing some unique features of its own to the design. Its evolution represents the most recent iteration in an ongoing public governance transition that has shifted from traditional governance by governmental bureaucracy, to market-based approaches that coupled the adoption of business principles with completion and management of contracts, to an evolving governance form in which hierarchy and markets are supplemented, and even replaced by multiple, often multi-layered and diverse networks of interaction and negotiation. As Bovaird (2007) aptly noted, such an approach more adequately brings the public into public governance.

This NPG approach arises from a realisation that neither traditional government nor NPM has been able to fully resolve many of the persistent problems – such as entrenched poverty, poor health and education, drug and alcohol misuse and addictions – confronting societies and those who govern them in a global era. Indeed, layered upon these earlier problems are even more complex challenges, including: more frequent and widespread natural disasters; failures of economic systems as exemplified by the 2008 global financial crisis and its lingering impacts; increasing experiences of unevenly distributed wealth and social care support and deepening inequality of social, economic and civic participation across communities and nations. It has been long understood that these "wicked issues" are complex and intertwined, and therefore demand a coordinated contribution from a diverse set of actors (Clarke & Stewart, 1997; 6 et al., 1999).

In accordance with this emphasis on complexity and the need for coordination as an instrumental response, a defining feature of new governance regimes is a renewed emphasis on the creation of public and social value, both by government and by others active in the public sphere (Moore, 1995; Denhardt & Denhardt, 2000, 2011; Bozeman, 2002, 2007). While early conceptualisations of public value focused on the role of public administrators in enabling its creation (see Moore, 1995), further developments in the literature have suggested that public value management is consistent with networked inter-organisational and cross-sector modes of governance (Stoker, 2006). In this conception, public value includes efficiency, accountability and equity, as well as broader values related to democratic participation and process (Bryson, Crosby & Bloomberg, 2014). This has two implications. First, public value is produced, or inhibited, through all elements of public practice. Second, responsibility for public value creation is no longer held solely by governments, but becomes the responsibility of an expanded set of actors. As Jørgensen and Bozeman (2007) stress, such an extension does not absolve government of all responsibility:

> Public values and public value are not the exclusive province of government, nor is government the only set of institutions having public value obligations, [though clearly] government has a special job as guarantor of public values.
>
> (p. 447)

Mendel and Brudney (2014) suggest that much public value creation has its origins in public-private collaborations and that more must be understood about the direct and indirect actions through which civil society actors generate public value. As well as the increased involvement of third- and private-sector organisation participation, a wider role for citizens and citizenship is also central to this emerging style of governance. Citizens are elevated from users to co-producers, with their skills, expertise and experiential knowledge shaping them as contributors to problem and solution setting (Bovaird, 2007; Alford, 2002; Brandsen & Pestoff, 2006).

As an idea, social procurement is centrally concerned with public value creation. It is predicated on both equity and efficiency values in its assumptions that social as well as financial value can be stimulated through supply chain development. Efficiency and effectiveness are also stressed through the expected multiplier effects of purchasing behaviours. As a set of practices, contemporary approaches to social procurement seek to mobilise the relational value of cross-sector activity, through both public-private supply chain development and, as discussed in Chapter 5, private spending on social and environmental objectives. Those approaches in which citizens are engaged in determining indicators of social value are also concerned with democratic engagement, recognising that social value is not universal but a matter of contestation and deliberation in advanced liberal democracies. Each of these ideational and practical dimensions of social procurement demand new resource combinations, new skills and new relationships between policy and economic actors.

The nature of the interactions, the formation of joint goals and acts of reciprocity in terms of knowledge, expertise and resource sharing at play in these expanded governance networks challenge the essentially linear model of former policy and service approaches as unidirectional flows of transaction and influence. Instead, the emerging governance networks can be re-conceptualised as supply networks, in which a host of actors – located up, down and diagonally across the supply chain – are brought together, with their resources bundled up to generate shared or added value outcomes. Such outcomes are purportedly produced directly, through the instrumental and targeted effects of specific social purchasing endeavours (Hoejmose & Adrien-Kirby, 2012; McCrudden, 2004), and indirectly through changes in practice that arise from complex dynamic exchanges (Bovaird, 2006, 2007; Erridge & Greer, 2002).

It is important to remember that in these networked arrangements, members are mutually dependent for their goal achievement; that is, they need each other to participate and contribute in order for both individual and collective goals to be met. By working together, added value over and above the expected outcomes – such as innovation, extended scale and scope or capacity – potentially become possible. This added value is variously referred to as "collaborative advantage", "win/win" or "expanded pie", all of which refer to integrative processes which harness the synergistic properties of the network to increase efficiencies, product quality, sustainability and innovation (Fisher, Ury & Patton, 1991; Huxham, 1996). As Huxham (1996) argues, collaborative advantage moves beyond the sharing of existing value, to create new expanded benefits for all network members.

Allee (1997) describes this web of relationships as a value network, which generates economic and social value, indicating that, as well as producing tangible or physical benefits such as goods and services, such value networks facilitate intangible benefits such as good will and social capital. The value network conceptualisation becomes useful for its ability not only to describe the formal organisational structure of the network but also to map the informal networks, making the intangible values more apparent. Knowing where the value-adding connections within the chain are located helps managers to navigate and better manage these complex systems.

While such networked governance arrangements offer new promise for innovation and value creation, we are reminded that NPG is guided by a pastiche of logics and practices arising from earlier modes of governing (Osborne, 2006). As discussed in preceding chapters, procurement professionals engaged with social procurement – particularly in the public sector – need to navigate bureaucratic demands of probity, and market logics of price and competitive neutrality, while simultaneously fostering supply chain relationships consistent with network approaches. Further, while the locus of control in NPM rests most strongly with public administrators, NPG diffuses control and coordination in ways that may inhibit as well as stimulate innovation through loss of accountability for action and/or loss of institutional knowledge. In the case of social procurement, for example, the increasing role of civil society networks as quasi-regulators of "social purpose suppliers" raises particular questions about the decentring not just of supply through social procurement, but the procurement process itself.

Governing complexity: integrating diverse members

Bryson et al. (2014) point out that operating in these increasingly diverse and frequently changing conditions represents a governance as well as a management dilemma. That is, the various resources and expectations of the members first have to be brought into alignment, common direction agreed to, resources allocated and joint action engaged in order for a collective result to be possible. As Provan and Kenis (2008) prescribed:

> . . .some form of governance or direction-setting is necessary to ensure that participants engage in collective and mutually supported action, that conflict is addressed, and that network resources are acquired and utilized efficiently and effectively.
>
> (p. 231)

Accordingly, from this perspective, the task becomes one of choosing between an array of governance modes which best fit with the purpose and facilitate the levels and types of interaction required to meet goals (Keast, Mandell & Brown, 2006; Keast, 2011; Koppenjan, 2012; Raab & Milward, 2003). The selection of governance modes has thus been complicated by the growing complexity of the public systems in place and requires judicious crafting, particularly in regard to facilitation of interactions between more numerous entities. Geyer and Rihani (2010) persuasively argue that the complex reality of public service in contemporary society is best conceptualised as composed of a range of interacting phenomena, which are in a constant state of change. They further contend that, rather than controlling or nullifying these complex interactions, a governance mode that accommodates a mix of stability and interaction is required.

Following a similar line, Koppenjan (2012) notes that in "interaction-oriented" forms of NPG, the coordination of elements occurs through iterative processes of assembling and re-assembling different governance modes – hierarchy, market and networks and their associated integration mechanisms – to optimally meet objectives. Furthermore, in this interaction-oriented governance approach, Koppenjan (2012) stresses that designed governance modes ". . .should not be unilaterally imposed upon one party by the other party. Instead, they should be defined, applied, monitored, enforced and adjusted by mutual consultation and interaction" (p. 31). Thus, within the NPG context there is a growing understanding that governance and its implementation reflects a more pragmatic kind of rationality (Koppenjan, 2012; Osborne, 2010), which understands the changing nature of the operating environment, the requirement for more contingent responses as well as the application of new integration forms, located closer to the level of action. A challenge, as observed in the previous chapter, is that ontological anxiety (Meehan & Bryde, 2011) may be produced for those navigating multiple governance logics at this level.

Governance hybridity does not therefore stop at the macro level. Instead, as a number of theorists have posited, it increasingly impacts and shapes second-order or meso-governance levels and elements (Esmark, 2009; Kooiman, 2000; Meuleman, 2008). At this lower level of governance, the emphasis is on the design, care and maintenance of intuitions (Meuleman, 2008), and provides direction for management capacities, such as financial, personnel, information, organizational and contract management (Ingraham & Donahue, 2000; Meuleman, 2008). Esmark (2009) illuminates this mix of integration strategies and instruments and relies on the appropriation of different "mediums", programmes and scripts used by other functional systems. These include, for example, the grafting of communitarian tools and values onto business systems in the case of corporate social responsibility and stakeholder engagement, each of which opens business and business practices to a wider array of interactions, expectations and accountabilities. In the case of social procurement, efforts that link capacity building of micro-businesses, social enterprise and minority suppliers to procurement procedures exemplify these meso-level integrations and the challenges they pose as procurement professionals write or are in receipt of new scripts for practice.

The discussion thus far suggests an interaction between macro, meso and micro explanatory accounts and their implications for practice. Yet, NPG is arguably conceptually located at the meta level, providing analysis of the macro level of operation and the overall direction or steering for society or societies. Meta-governance refers to different ways of enacting the "governing of governing" (Kooiman, 2003, p. 170). In line with the emphasis of this book, we drill this concept down to describe it as the process of ". . . coordinating the actions of self-governing actors" (Sorensen & Torfing, 2007, p. 169). Thus, while useful in providing a background explanation for the formation of these multi-actor groups and providing the space in which forms of co-production, such as social procurement, can exist and thrive, NPG is limited in its ability to capture the detail of these interactions or contribute to the operational specifics facilitating social procurement practice and practices.

Similar to its Public Administration (PA) and NPM predecessors, NPG can thus be considered a partial theory. That is, while offering useful insights, NPG provides incomplete explanations of the phenomena that it is describing unless coupled with other theories (see Osborne, 2006). In the following section, we further consider the dominant theoretical frameworks informing – or with the potential to inform – understandings of social procurement and NPG at each of the macro, meso and micro levels. We then go on to consider how we might begin to advance a more integrative analysis of NPG across these levels, with social procurement as our practice exemplar.

Macro-analysis and institutional theory

Driven by concerns of regulatory and policy frameworks, and changes to the machinery of government under various paradigmatic shifts from NPM to NPG (see Bryson et al., 2014 for an overview), much of this discussion in academic literature has focused on the shifts in policy and practice, together with the underpinning values of these paradigms. The focus then is very much on the normative and regulative aspects of these changes, and is thus heavily influenced explicitly or implicitly by institutional assumptions on action occurring within, and being constrained by normative, regulative and cognitive frameworks. As interest in social procurement is dominated by public policy studies, this focus on the regulatory structures and institutions which frame action makes sense.

Drawing on sociological conceptions of neo-institutionalism (DiMaggio & Powell, 1983; Suchman, 1995), the function of isomorphism and legitimacy formation have been present in our accounts of the production of norms guiding new approaches to social procurement and their diffusion across jurisdictions and between sectors. In practical terms, institutional perspectives on social procurement lend themselves to positioning the locus of change in policy and regulatory regimes. This has been given recent expression in countries such as the UK, where substantial advocacy for changes in social procurement practice has concentrated on policy, contributing to the development of new legislation to support social procurement in the form of the Public Services (Social Value) Act 2012. Considerably earlier than this, the civil rights movement in the United States had substantial influence on the development of affirmative action policies that underpin early iterations of social procurement obligations upon private sector firms mandated by governments (McCrudden, 2004).

However, sociological conceptions of institutional theory, driven as they are by top-down understandings of how change occurs, historically have not allowed sufficiently for the role of individual actors or agents in bringing about change (Clegg, 2010). Clearly, any theoretical understanding needs to acknowledge that individuals can, and do, challenge institutional arrangements. From an agency perspective, change occurs from the bottom up, as individuals engage with and challenge the institutional status quo. An example of this would be advocacy, which has a special place in civil society activities, where individuals and organisations seek to challenge societal norms and related public policy. Strategic conceptions of institutionalism that have focused on how individual and collective actors purposefully legitimise their actions (Oliver, 1991) do present an account of agency (Suchman, 1995), yet the locus of attention has been on the stability of institutional fields rather than their disruption. As discussed in Chapter 4, much of emergent practice in social procurement is consistent with developing a new institutional field. This involves navigating existing norms of traditional procurement practices consistent with established governance logics, alongside instating new practices, new relationships and new professional competencies. Practice thus suggests the need for theoretical frameworks competent to engage with macro-, meso- and micro-analytic understandings of the field, and mechanisms by which integration between levels can be understood. We now move on to briefly consider both meso- and micro-theoretical accounts and their implications for understanding social procurement as an exemplar of NPG. We then turn to the question of integration, suggesting that understanding social procurement discourses as producers of boundary objects is one useful way forward.

Meso-accounts: network theory and beyond

To better elucidate and operationalise the relational aspects of NPG, its macro perspective has been bolstered and enlivened through the application of other, generally meso-level theories. For example, Osborne (2006, 2010) argues that NPG draws upon a suite of supplementing theories, which illuminate the relational aspects central to the emergent governance approach and the shift from expert, professional service delivery to co-production of services. Specifically, Osborne (2006) draws upon organisational sociology (Ouchi, 1979) and network theory (Powell, 1990) to describe and explain the emergence of more enduring, relationally derived inter-organisational networks as the vehicles for co-designed and co-produced services. Alongside the two pillars, he suggests applying insights derived from the complementary fields of relational marketing, and the organisational social capital literature held within strategic management literature (Tsai, 2000) to make clear and amplify the relational underpinnings of NPG.

In setting out his approach to NPG, Koppenjan (2012) also acknowledged the need for multiple theoretical streams to be applied to fully articulate the way in which NPG can be implemented and operationalised. Koppenjan's (2012) theoretical foundations are grounded in policy network and network governance theories. He contends that the network-level approach enables the complexities and dynamics of network interactions to be more accurately examined, and brings analysis down to the service delivery level (Koppenjan, 2012). In addition to focusing on the interaction processes, Koppenjan (2012) also proposes the inclusion of institutional theories to address the often overlooked institutional dimensions of networks, as evident in the layers of relationships and the institutional bundling taking place, as well as the interplay between institutional systems and behaviours.

Together, NPG and its attendant theories highlight the expansion of the array of groups involved in policy and service delivery and, as a consequence, the growing complexity of the decision-making processes. Arising from this is the need to design "edge" spaces and processes to facilitate the coming together of these diverse sets of actors, their different interests, needs and expectations and moulding these into a new collective agenda.

Micro-analyses and the role of agency

As explored throughout this volume, new approaches to social procurement may be understood as an emerging institutional field, in which the "rules of the game" are being negotiated by a variety of organisational and individual actors whose roles are themselves being recast by this emergence. Commonly utilised top-down approaches to explain these changes in systems are insufficient because they lack an account of the role of agency in such situations. As Suddaby (2010) notes in relation to institutional theory, institutions' "work, of course, is conducted by individuals and it is somewhat surprising to me how individuals often disappear from institutional research" (p. 17). In the case of social procurement, we have traced the role of collective actors – such as social movements and corporate networks – and individual actors, such as policy entrepreneurs, in the establishment of norms and the diffusion of practice across jurisdictions. These examples suggest that conceptual frameworks need to find ways of explicitly allowing for the role of agents in such processes.

Zucker (1987) has argued that "institutional theories of organisations provide a rich, complex view of organisations. In these theories, organisations are influenced by normative pressures, sometimes arising from external sources such as the state, other times arising from within the organisation itself" (p. 443). Further, institutions are both "a product of and resources for interaction and negotiation in everyday life" (Barley, 2008, p. 498).

Thus, while institutional theory has provided a macro view of how action is constrained, there is also an element of institutional theory which acknowledges the more micro-foundations. While it is not possible to review all the nuanced theoretical work in this area, the institutional "theories of practice" provide a useful place to start.

Feldman and Orlikowski (2011) note that, within practice theory, the focus can either be on: empirically examining how people act, a philosophical view on how practices produce reality, or theoretically understanding the relationship between action and structure. It is the latter which is the focus here. From this perspective, practice has been defined by Orlikowski (2002) as "recurrent, materially bounded, and situated social action engaged in by members of a community" (p. 256). Thus "everyday actions are consequential in producing the structural contours of social life" (Feldman & Orlikowski, 2011, p. 1241). If social procurement is viewed from a practice lens, then it could be seen to be a recurrent action, which occurs in a specific context, and these recurrent actions somehow influence structure. There is thus a duality inherent in practice theory (Feldman & Orlikowski, 2011).

Practice theory draws, in part, on the work of Bourdieu (e.g., 1999) on habitus, which is always practically orientated, and can be viewed as a product of historical collective practices. Bourdieu (1989) argues that there is a "twofold social genesis, on the one hand of the schemes of perception, thought, and action which are constitutive of what I call habitus, and on the other hand of social structures, and particularly of what I call fields and of groups" (p.14).

Both habitus and social structures interact, however. In terms of Bourdieu's habitus, Fuchs (2003) argues: "Cognitive structures are reproduced by actors engaging in social practices and relationships that reproduce society, social structures are reproduced by their production of cognitive structures of individuals that have social practices" (p. 399). This is similar to Giddens' (1984) structuration theory, which holds that agents are enabled and constrained by social structures, and also are involved in the production and reproduction of these structures (discussed further in this chapter). Indeed, both structuration theory and habitus are useful theories to explain how practices are reproduced (Morrison, 2005).

Practice theory also sheds light on how social procurement may be used to span boundaries and how different actors' actions can affect the adoption and implementation of social procurement. This is because practice theory conceives of practices as bundles of activity "centrally organized around shared practical understanding" (Schatzki, 2000, p. 11). Often this knowledge is structured by institutions, such as professional associations (Greenwood, Suddaby and Hinings 2002). This shared understanding sees "knowing as an ongoing social accomplishment, constituted and reconstituted in everyday practice" (Orlikowski, 2002, p. 252). Thus a specific practice is essentially social, and in this social practice, knowledge is shared, and may even be distributed geographically (Orlikowski, 2002).

Thus, from an institutional perspective, practice theory acknowledges that practices, such as social procurement, are structured by social systems, but also the ongoing micro-practices of social procurement are likely to create shared social understanding. A theoretical understanding of how this might actually happen, particularly for social procurement, remains unclear. However, there are recent developments within institutional theory which might provide a way forward. In particular, the micro-processes or activity-based perspectives approach holds promise.

The micro-processes approach examines how interactions at local levels can amplify meaning up to higher levels. Gray, Purdy and Ansari (2015) argue that cognitive understandings "laminate" upwards, and advance a number of theoretical macro patterns in which such change occurs. It is not surprising then that micro foundations of institutional logics is where much of the focus currently rests (Cloutier & Langley, 2013; Pernkopf-Konhäusner, 2014).

Currently there is no application of these new approaches to the micro-processes of institutional theory to conceptualising social procurement. However, this recent work holds promise for a useful research agenda in relation to the subject. Boxenbaum (2014) proposed three generic research questions that need to be answered in exploring bottom-up approaches to institutional theory. Applied to the social procurement context, Boxenbaum's (2014) questions might be:

- How do institutional norms, rules and understandings really constrain individual behaviour in social procurement?
- How do individuals involved in social procurement intentionally seek to change institutional norms, rules and understandings?
- How free are individuals involved in social procurement to engage in alternative sets of institutional logics?
- Following the work of Koppenjan (2012), other questions are more concerned with dynamics and structures, and might involve
- To what extent do networks serve as mediating structures between macro interactions and more meso structures?

Theorising social procurement: an integrative approach

While the macro theories canvassed earlier seek to explain larger or aggregate social occurrences, meso- and micro-theoretical accounts focus on networks, organisations, the individual and their interactions. If structures influence the actions of specific actors, and actors can influence institutional structures then, properly, the two perspectives are complementary rather than oppositional. Structures facilitate and inhibit action, and are the outcomes of interaction, as well as the framework within which actions take place (Giddens, 1984). Thus, institutions need to be seen as both "a product of and resources for interaction and negotiation in everyday life" (Barley, 2008, p. 495). This suggests that both the structure and individual experience and action are important to consider. This interrelationship, applied to social procurement, is depicted in Figure 8.1.

In his theory of structuration, Giddens (1984) seeks to integrate objectivist theories of social structure with subjectivist accounts that suggest that social reality is constituted in individuals' perceptions and experiences (Greenhalgh & Stones, 2010). Rather than treating institutions as separate from human action, Giddens' work on structuration posits that institutions, or structure, are "both a product of and a constraint on human action" (Barley & Tolbert, 1997, p. 97). As a process theory, structuration theory calls to attention the interaction between structure and agency, or what Giddens (1984) refers to as the "duality of structure". While a significant contribution, structuration theory has been critiqued for its level of abstraction (Barley & Tolbert, 1997) and associated limitations in suggesting useful ways of examining relationships between agency and structure (Mouzelis, 1989). While we have no argument with the meta-theoretical value of Giddens' foundational efforts to produce an integrative account of structure and agency, we suggest that conceptions of boundary spanning and boundary objects have greater explanatory power when considering both the function and effects of new efforts to make sense of and enact social procurement in the context of NPG.

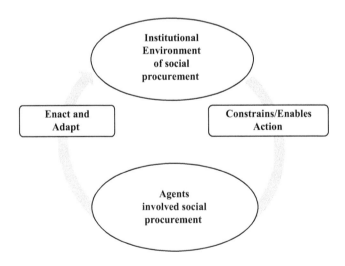

Figure 8.1 Structure, agency and social procurement

As several authors and theorists have stressed (Koppenjan, 2012; Osborne, 2006, 2010; Pestoff, 2006), NPG is at its heart about creating new opportunities and new interaction spaces to bring together the broader array of people and entities now engaged in public policy and its implementation. The effects of such interactions may also become uncoupled from public policy objectives as commitments to public value creation in the private sphere become embedded in practices beyond regulatory compliance and direct participation in public service delivery. As noted in Chapter 5, social procurement commitments in the private for-profit realm have their origins in regulatory compliance but have since diffused across jurisdictions and beyond policy and regulatory relationships between private providers and governments.

The action of bringing together people and resources from within and across boundaries of action is referred to as *integration*. Integration can take a number of different forms, occur at multiple levels and require different strengths of relationships depending on the type of task, the degree of dependency and the nature of the boundaries to be crossed (Keast, 2011). As Carlile (2004) notes, the more complex the boundary, the more complex are the integration tools and processes required to bridge the gaps in knowledge and relationships. Because such integration requires overcoming significant obstacles, organisations that are able to do so have a greater potential for producing innovative products and services (Kogut & Zander, 1996; Dyer & Singh, 1998).

Two key integrative processes and practices to facilitate boundary crossing have been identified within the literature: boundary spanners and boundary objects. Boundary spanners can be individuals or collections of individual actors, such as inter-organisational meetings, task forces or committees or teams who are "drawn from different ways of knowing or bases of experience for the purposes of coproducing [cross] boundary actions" (Feldman, Khademian, Ingram & Schneider, 2006, p. 95). Organisational literature defines boundary spanners as specific agents who, through a range of roles (e.g., gatekeepers, advice/trust brokers, information processing) (Friedman & Podolny, 1992), fulfil key linking functions between distinct groups at the intra-interorganisational levels (Tushman, 1977). Research on boundary spanners identified the multiple roles and the pressures and rewards of the people occupying the position, arguing that these pressures can lead to or generate psychological consequences – for example, role conflict and role ambiguity – which lead to stress and reduce job satisfaction and performance (Glavin, Schieman & Reid, 2011). At the same time, it has been argued that boundary spanners may use information and accumulated social capital to identify and leverage opportunities to advance their own interests (Jensen & Meckling, 1976). For some, boundary-spanning agents' self-interest, psychological discomfort, and temporal and physical limits constrain collaborative efforts.

Boundary objects were introduced as an alternative approach (Star & Griesemer, 1989). Star and Griesemer (1989) define boundary objects as "objects that are shared and sharable across different problem solving contexts" (p. 47). Boundary objects can include a wide array of artefacts (e.g., maps, network maps, decision support tools, prototypes, design drawings and scenarios) and to be relevant must be tangible, accessible and up to date (Carlile, 1997). Boundary objects thus are a relatively neutral item around which people with diverse views and understandings can gather. Boundary objects are typically important in helping people from multiple and often contested backgrounds create shared meaning (Star & Griesemer, 1989). More specifically Feldman et al. (2006) describe boundary objects as "physical objects that enable people to understand other perspectives" (p. 95). They function as ways of pinpointing different understandings of concepts and enable additional "neutral" information to be tabled to facilitate shared understandings and agreements on ways forward – for developing new routines and standardised procedures (Montin, Johansson & Forsemalm, 2014). Put another way, boundary objects create the space to see things from new perspectives and, while they might uncover some controversy or conflict, they can act to resolve this by use of new information and insights to reach agreement on certain defined points and establish common ground for joint action. Thus, boundary objects help us to shape practice in an agreed way (Carlile, 2002). Beyond that, boundary objects can facilitate the transformation of diverse views into shared knowledge and understanding (Carlile, 2002, 2004).

The concept of a boundary object becomes helpful in understanding and operationalising the dynamics of joint approaches and policy synergies required for social procurement to be designed and implemented. We see new discourses of social procurement as an emerging institutional field that produces a range of boundary objects that potentially "help participants make sense of their world, what they may want to do with it, and why; and, in doing so, . . . helps participants connect people, ideas and other kinds of actors into a way forward" (Crosby, Bryson & Stone, 2010, p. 205). As Crosby et al. (2010) citing Carlile (2004) note, boundary objects may be used to navigate syntactical differences in routines, codes and protocols, pragmatic problems arising from differing stakeholder interests, and semantic problems related to differences in meaning and context. Each of these navigable terrains has been touched on in previous chapters as we have traced the contexts in and mechanisms by which a variety of actors operating in the public sphere are both legitimising and practising new forms of social procurement. As a domain in which boundary objects abound, social procurement offers opportunities for integration and transformation through new (and new assemblages of) rules, actors and related modes of governance. These construct new sites of contestation as well as integration and, indeed, co-optation, about the nature of social and public value and the mechanisms by which it is produced.

Conclusion

Osborne's (2006, 2010) notion of a new public governance articulates a form of governance which acknowledges both a plural state, where multiple interdependent actors contribute to the delivery of public services, and a pluralist state, where multiple processes inform the policy-making system. This pluralism changes the dimensions of public governing and the actors within it. It requires integrative devices through which effective practice can occur. Social procurement is both a set of ideas and a field of practice in which such integration is under negotiation. In this chapter, we have considered the dominant explanatory frameworks that account for developments in social procurement. We have noted that, like practice, theory requires greater integration between macro-accounts of institutional norm setting and reproduction, and micro-accounts of practice. We note that an emerging literature on the micro-foundations of institutionalism has salience here. Ultimately, we suggest that social procurement spans boundaries, and that the concept of boundary objects has particular resonance in understanding both emerging discourses of social procurement and the practices and possibilities they construct.

References

6, P., Leat, D., Seltzer, K., & Stoker, G. (1999). *Governing in the Round: Strategies for Holistic Government*. London: Demos.

Alford, J. (2002). Defining the client in the public sector: A social-exchange perspective. *Public Administration Review*, 62(3), 337–346. doi: 10.1111/1540–6210.00183

Allee, V. (1997). *The knowledge evolution: Expanding organizational intelligence*. Burlington, MA: Butterworth-Heinemann.

Barley, S.R. (2008). Coalface institutionalism. In R. Greenwood, C. Oliver, K. Sahlin, & R. Suddaby (Eds.), *The Sage handbook of organizational institutionalism* (pp. 491–519). London: Sage Publications.

Barley, S.R., & Tolbert, P.S. (1997). Institutionalization and structuration: Studying the links between action and institution. *Organization Studies*, *18*(1), 93–117. doi: 10.1177/017084069701800106

Bourdieu, P. (1989). Social space and symbolic power. *Sociological Theory* 7(1), 14–25. doi: 10.2307/202060

Bourdieu, P. (1999). Structures, habitus, practices. In A. Elliot (Ed.), *The Blackwell reader in contemporary social theory* (pp. 107–118). Oxford: Blackwell Publishers.

Bovaird, T. (2006). Developing new forms of partnership with the "market" in the procurement of public services. *Public Administration*, *84*(1), 81–102. doi: 10.1111/j.0033–3298.2006.00494.x

Bovaird, T. (2007). Beyond engagement and participation: User and community coproduction of public services. *Public Administration Review*, *67*(5), 846–860. doi:10.1111/j.1540–6210.2007.00773.x

Boxenbaum, E. (2014). Towards a situated stance in organizational institutionalism: Contributions from French pragmatist sociological theory. *Journal of Management Inquiry*, *23*(3), 319–323. doi: 10.1177/1056492613517464

Bozeman, B. (2002). Public-value failure: When efficient markets may not do. *Public Administration Review*, *62*(2), 145–161. doi: 10.1111/0033–3352.00165

Bozeman, B. (2007). *Public value: public interest: Counterbalancing economic individualism*. Washington, DC: Georgetown University Press.

Brandsen, T., & Pestoff, V. (2006). Co-production, the third sector and the delivery of public services: An introduction. *Public Management Review*, *8*(4), 493–501. doi: 10.1080/14719030601022874

Bryson, J.M., Crosby, B., & Bloomberg, L. (2014). Public value governance: Moving beyond traditional public administration and the new public management. *Public Administration Review, 74*(4), 445–456. doi:10.1111/puar.12238

Carlile, P. (1997). *Transforming knowledge in product development: Making knowledge manifest through boundary objects.* Unpublished Dissertation. Ann Arbor: University of Michigan.

Carlile, P.R. (2002). A pragmatic view of knowledge and boundaries: Boundary objects in new product development. *Organization Science, 13*(4), 442–455. doi: 10.1287/orsc.13.4.442.2953

Carlile, P.R. (2004). Transferring, translating and transforming: An integrative framework for managing knowledge across boundaries. *Organization Science, 15*(5), 555–568. doi: 10.1287/orsc.1040.0094

Clarke, M., & Stewart, J. (1997). *Handling the wicked issues: A challenge for government.* University of Birmingham, Institute of Local Government Studies.

Clegg, S. (2010). The state, power, and agency: Missing in action in institutional theory? *Journal of Management Inquiry, 19*(1), 4–13. doi:10.1177/1056492609347562

Cloutier, C., & Langley, A. (2013). The logic of institutional logics: Insights from French pragmatist sociology. *Journal of Management Inquiry, 22*(4), 360–380. doi: 10.1177/1056492612469057

Crosby, B.C., Bryson, J.M., & Stone, M.M. (2010). Leading across frontiers: How visionary leaders integrate people, processes, structures and resources. In S.P. Osborne (Ed.), *The new public governance? Emerging perspectives on the theory and practice of public governance* (pp. 200–222). London: Routledge.

Denhardt, R., & Denhardt, J. (2000). The new public service: Serving rather than steering. *Public Administration Review, 60*(6), 549–559. doi: 10.1111/0033–3352.00117

DiMaggio, P.J., & Powell, W.W. (1983). The iron cage revisited: Institutional isomorphism and collective rationality in organizational fields. *American Sociological Review, 48*(2), 147–160. doi: 10.2307/2095101

Dyer, F., & Singh, H. (1998). The relational view: Cooperative strategies and sources of inter-organizational competitive advantage. *Academy of Management Review, 23*(4), 660–679. doi:10.5465/AMR.1998.1255632

Erridge, A., & Greer, J. (2002). Partnerships and public procurement: Building social capital through supply relations. *Public Administration, 80*(3), 503–522. doi: 10.1111/1467–9299.00315

Esmark, A. (2009). The functional differentiation of governance: Public governance beyond hierarchy, markets and networks. *Public Administration, 87*(2), 351–370. doi: 10.1111/j.1467–9299.2009.01759.x

Feldman, M.S., Khademian, A.M., Ingram, H., & Schneider, A.S. (2006). Ways of knowing and inclusive management practices. *Public Administration Review, 66*(s1), 89–99. doi: 10.1111/j.1540–6210.2006.00669.x

Feldman, M.S., & Orlikowski, W.J. (2011). Theorizing practice and practicing theory. *Organization Science, 22*(5), 1240–1253.

Fisher, R., Ury, W., & Patton, B. (1991). *Getting to yes: Negotiating agreement without giving* (2nd ed.). New York: Penguin Books.

Friedman, R.A., & Podolny, J. (1992). Differentiation of boundary spanning roles: Labor negotiations and implications for role conflict. *Administrative Science Quarterly, 37*(1), 28–47. doi: 10.2307/2393532

Fuchs, C. (2003). Some implications of Pierre Bourdieu's works for a theory of social self-organisation. *European Journal of Social Theory, 6*(4), 387–408. doi: 10.1177/13684310030064002

Geyer, R., & Rihani, S. (2010). *Complexity and public policy: A new approach to 21st century politics, policy and society*, Abington, UK: Routledge.

Giddens, A. (1984). *The constitution of society: Outline of the theory of structuration.* California: University of California Press.

Glavin, P., Schieman, S., & Reid, S. (2011). Boundary spanning work demands and their consequences for guilt and psychological distress. *Journal of Health and Social Behaviour, 52*(1), 43–57. doi: 10.1177/0022146510395023

Gray, B., Purdy, J.M., & Ansari, S. (2015). From interactions to institutions: Microprocesses of framing and mechanisms for the structuring of institutional fields. *Academy of Management Review, 40*(1), 115–143. doi:10.5465/amr.2013.0299

Greenhalgh, T., & Stones, R. (2010). Theorising big IT programmes in healthcare: Strong structuration theory meets actor-network theory. *Social Science & Medicine, 70*(9), 1285–1294. doi: 10.1016/j.socscimed.2009.12.034

Greenwood, R., Suddaby, R., & Hinings, C.R. (2002). Theorizing change: The role of professional associations in the transformation of institutional fields. *Academy of Management Journal, 45*(1), 58–80. doi: 10.2307/3069285

Hoejmose, S.U., & Adrien-Kirby, A.J. (2012). Socially and environmentally responsible procurement: A literature review and future research agenda of a managerial issue in the 21st century. *Journal of Purchasing and Supply Management, 18*(4), 232–242. doi: 10.1016/j.pursup.2012.06.002

Huxham, C. (1996). Collaboration and collaborative advantage. In C. Huxham (Ed.) *Creating collaborative advantage* (pp. 1–18). London: Sage Publications.

Ingraham, P.W., & Donahue, A.K. (2000). Dissecting the black box revisited: Characterizing government management capacity. In C.J. Heinrich & L.E. Lynn Jr. (Eds.), *Government and performance: New perspectives* (pp. 292–318). Washington DC: Georgetown University Press.

Jensen, C., & Meckling, W.H. (1976). Theory of the firm: Managerial behaviour, agency costs and ownership structure. *Journal of Financial Economics, 3*(4), 305–360. doi: 10.1007/978-94-009-9257-3_8

Jørgensen, T.B., & Bozeman, B. (2007). Public values an inventory. *Administration & Society, 39*(3), 354–381. doi: 10.1177/0095399707300703

Keast, R. (2011). Joined-up governance in Australia: How the past can inform the future. *International Journal of Public Administration, 34*(4), 221–231. doi:10.1080/01900692.2010.549799

Keast, R., Mandell, M., & Brown, K. (2006). Mixing state, market and network governance modes: The role of government in "crowded" policy domains. *International Journal of Organization Theory and Behavior, 9*(1), 27–50.

Kogut, B., & Zander, U. (1996). What firms do? Coordination, identity, and learning. *Organization Science, 7*(5), pp. 502–518. doi:10.1287/orsc.7.5.502

Kooiman, J. (2000). Societal governance: Levels, modes and orders of socio political interaction. In J. Pierre, (Ed.), *Debating governance: Authority, steering, and democracy* (pp. 138–166). Oxford: Oxford University Press.

Kooiman, J. (2003). *Governing as governance.* London: Sage Publications.

Koppenjan, J. (2012). *The new public governance in public service delivery: Reconciling efficiency and quality.* The Hague: Eleven International Publishing.

McCrudden, C. (2004). Using public procurement to achieve social outcomes. *Natural Resources Forum, 28*(4), 257–267. doi: 10.1111/j.1477-8947.2004.00099.x

Meehan, J., & Bryde, D. (2011). Sustainable procurement practice. *Business Strategy and the Environment, 20*(2), 94–106. doi:10.1002/bse.678

Mendel, S.C., & Brudney, J.L. (2014). Doing good, public good, and public value: Why the differences matter. *Nonprofit Management and Leadership, 25*(1), 23–40. doi: 10.1002/nml.21109

Meuleman, L. (2008). *Public management and the meta governance of hierarchy, markets and networks: The features of designing and managing governance style combinations,* Physica Verlag (Springer) Press, The Hague.

Montin, S., Johansson, M., & Forsemalm, J. (2014). Understanding innovative regional col-laboration: Metagovernance and boundary objects as mechanisms. In C. Ansell, & J. Torfing (Eds.), *Public innovation through collaboration and design* (pp. 106–124). New York: Routledge.

Moore, M.H. (1995). *Creating public value: Strategic management in government.* Cambridge, MA: Harvard University Press.

Morrison, K. (2005). Structuration theory, habitus and complexity theory: Elective affini-ties or old wine in new bottles? *British Journal of Sociology of Education 26*(3), 311–326. doi:10.1080/01425690500128809

Mouzelis, N. (1989). Restructuring structuration theory. *The Sociological Review, 37*(4), 613–635. doi: 10.1111/j.1467–954X.1989.tb00047.x

Oliver, C. (1991). Strategic responses to institutional processes. *The Academy of Management Review, 16*(1), 145–179. doi:10.5465/AMR.1991.4279002

Orlikowski, W.J. (2002). Knowing in practice: Enacting a collective capability in distributed organizing. *Organization Science, 13*(3), 249–273. doi:10.1287/orsc.13.3.249.2776

Osborne, S. (2006). The new public governance? *Public Management Review, 8*(3), 377–387. doi: 10.1080/14719030600853022

Osborne, S. (2010). Delivering public services: Time for a new theory? *Public Management Review, 12*(1), 1–10. doi: 10.1080/14719030903495232

Ouchi, W.G. (1979). A conceptual framework for the design of organizational control mech-anisms. *Management Science, 25*(9), 833–848. doi:10.1007/978–1–4899–7138–8_4

Pernkopf-Konhäusner, K. (2014). The competent actor: Bridging institutional log-ics and French pragmatist sociology. *Journal of Management Inquiry, 23*(3), 333–337. doi:10.1177/1056492613517467

Pestoff, V. (2006). Citizens as co-producers of welfare services: Preschool services in eight Euro-pean countries. *Public Management Review, 8*(4), 503–520. doi:10.1080/14719030601022882

Powell, W.W. (1990). Neither market nor hierarchy: Network forms of organization. *Research in Organizational Behavior, 12.* 295–336

Provan, K.G., & Kenis, P. (2008). Modes of network governance: Structure, management, and effectiveness. *Journal of Public Administration Research and Theory, 18*(2), 229–252. doi: 10.1093/jopart/mum015

Raab, J., & Milward, H.B. (2003). Dark networks as problems. *Journal of Public Administration Research and Theory, 13*(4): 413–439. doi: *10.1093/jpart/mug029*

Schatzki, T.R. (2000). Introduction: Practice theory. In T.R. Schatzki, K. Knorr-Cetina, & E. Savigny (Eds.), *Practice turn in contemporary theory.* (pp. 10–23). KY, USA: Routledge.

Sorensen, E., & Torfing, J. (2007). Theoretical approaches to metagovernance. In E. Sorensen, & J. Torfing (Eds.), *Theories of democratic network governance* (pp. 169–182). Basing-stoke: Palgrave Macmillan.

Star, S.L., & Griesemer, J.R. (1989). Institutional ecology, translations and boundary objects: Amateurs and professionals in Berkeley's museum of vertebrate zoology. *Social Studies of Science, 19*(3). 387–420. doi: 10.1177/030631289019003001

Stoker, G. (2006). Public value management: A new narrative for networked governance? *American Review of Public Administration, 36*(1), 41–57. doi: 10.1177/0275074005282583

Suchman, M.C. (1995). Managing legitimacy: Strategic and institutional approaches. *The Academy of Management Review, 20*(3), 571–610. doi: 10.5465/AMR.1995.9508080331

Suddaby, R. (2010). Challenges for institutional theory. *Journal of Management Inquiry, 19*(1), 14–20. doi: 10.1177/1056492609347564

Tsai, W. (2000). Social capital, strategic relatedness and the formation of intraorganizational linkages. *Strategic Management Journal, 21*(9), 925–939. doi: 10.1002/1097–0266(200009)21: 9<925::aid-smj129>3.0.co;2-i

Tushman, M.L. (1977). Special boundary roles in the innovation process. *Administration Science Quarterly, 22*(4), 587–605. doi:10.2307/2392402

Zucker, L. (1987). Institutional theories of organization. *Annual Review of Sociology, 13*(1), 443–464. doi:10.1146/annurev.soc.13.1.443

9 Conclusion

Throughout this volume, we have explored iterations of social procurement, both well-tried and emergent. We have observed that, although not new, social procurement practices both embody and extend the governance logics of their times. In most democratic countries, there is a long-standing relationship between state and civil society in the production and delivery of social services (Kendall & Knapp, 1993). Before the advent of the welfare state, charitable organisations played a major role in poverty alleviation and social protection in class-based societies (Lyons, 2001). In periods of bureaucratic ascendancy, social procurement has been characterised by state-centric purchasing of a prescribed set of social services, primarily from the charitable sector. The (r)evolution of new public management (NPM) and related emphasis on small government saw an increased focus on social procurement as an instrumental mechanism for purchasing social services from private for-profit and civil society actors. In the face of both contractions of public resources and the need to redress the democratic deficits of NPM and earlier governance regimes, social procurement is receiving new attention as a vehicle for producing social value while maximising the power of public expenditure on service provision. These dual roles resonate with the conditions of new public governance (NPG), which is essentially organised around new combinations and relationships in the design and delivery of public value (Bovaird, 2007; Osborne, 2006; Osborne, Radnor & Nasi, 2013). Typical of NPG, social procurement is also not confined to the practices of governments. Growing interest in social procurement in the corporate sector discussed in Chapter 5, and in organisation to organisation supply chains within the social economy touched on in Chapters 2 and 7, suggest that social procurement exemplifies the extension of the public sphere beyond relationships that directly involve government (Bryson, Crosby & Bloomberg, 2014).

We have argued that, although social procurement is an empirically observable phenomenon, examples of which we have explored, it is also emblematic of a set of ideas about the reality and nature of social value and the functions of governments, civil society (including third-sector organisations and communities) and private for-profit providers in its production. As a set of activities, the implementation of social procurement raises practical considerations which have been explored throughout this volume. In Chapters 6 and 8, we considered the challenges for policy design that seeks to address multiple and, in some cases, intangible value objectives. We examined the complications of public administration associated with new and emerging distributed approaches to social procurement, and the implications of these for the workforce capabilities and skills profiles of contemporary procurement professionals. Further, in Chapter 7 we examined in some detail the practical challenges of measuring social value, particularly in the context of public purchasing.

As depicted in Chapters 2 and 6, emerging approaches to social procurement – including new contractual instruments as well as policy frameworks – are relatively under-tested and lacking in clear protocols for implementation, although momentum is growing in some jurisdictions. An analysis across time and place suggests that the UK has been particularly active in the European context in linking public procurement with public value creation for more than 20 years (Erridge, 2007; Preuss, 2007). There has been particular leadership in North America from both the United States and Canada in the use of procurement to stimulate business diversity linked to affirmative action goals (McCrudden, 2004, 2007). With regard to diffusion of both policy and practice across national borders and world regions, we noted in Chapters 4 and 7 that private actors – specifically civil society networks and some multi-national corporations – have played a substantial role.

While policy that supports new approaches to social procurement is still in its infancy, practice is growing, and appears to be exceeding theory, with theoretical frameworks deriving from a number of perspectives and disciplines yet to be comprehensively developed. This uncertainty and under-development is symptomatic of the nature of the objectives and relational conditions of NPG. As persuasively put by Bryson et al., (2014, p. 448), ". . . What else can one expect in a shared-power, multisector, no-one-wholly-in charge-world?". It may also be viewed as a condition of functioning in complex adaptive systems, where leadership must be competent to operate in contexts of emergence and pattern identification rather than reliance on blueprints for best practice, which are artefacts of simpler systems approaches (Snowden & Boone, 2007). In Chapter 8, we suggested that the emerging approaches to social procurement produce boundary objects that act as integrative devices (Star & Griesemer, 1989). This may be useful in understanding the common ground for dialogue and joint action required in operationalising the increasingly dynamic (Bovaird, 2006) market and sectoral relationships constitutive of new approaches to social procurement.

In developing this volume, it has become apparent that integration is as imperative for scholarship as it is for practice. As we have navigated differences of language and theory between disciplines, we have found the literature on social procurement variously embedded in work on commercial, third-sector and public management, logistics, corporate governance and economic geography and law, in addition to public and social policy. While systematically reviewing and reconciling these literatures has not been a core goal of the text, we have drawn on them, identifying salient developments in social procurement and seeking to understand the logics that are driving these in the context of NPG. Where practice is exceeding scholarly accounts, we have also turned to the "grey literature" to better understand new approaches, and the norms and actors taking centre stage in this emerging institutional field. This volume is a contribution to the conversation, rather than the last word. While recognising the discussions that have preceded ours (see, for example, Bovaird, 2006; Erridge, 2007; Erridge & Greer, 2002; McCrudden, 2004, 2007), we hope that our analysis has presented new explanations and raised new questions about the nature and function of social value creation through procurement in an era of NPG.

References

Bovaird, T. (2006). Developing new forms of partnership with the "market" in the procurement of public services. *Public Administration, 84*(1), 81–102. http://doi.org/10.1111/j.0033–3298.2006.00494.x

Bovaird, T. (2007). Beyond engagement and participation: User and community coproduction of public services. *Public Administration Review, 67*(5), 846–860. http://doi.org/10.1111/j.1540–6210.2007.00773.x

Bryson, J.M., Crosby, B.C., & Bloomberg, L. (2014). Public value governance: Moving beyond traditional public administration and the new public management. *Public Administration Review, 74*(4), 445–456. http://doi.org/10.1111/puar.12238

Erridge, A. (2007). Public procurement, public value and the Northern Ireland Unemployment Pilot Project. *Public Administration, 85*(4), 1023–1043. http://doi.org/10.1111/j.1467–9299.2007.00674.x

Erridge, A., & Greer, J. (2002). Partnerships and public procurement: Building social capital through supply relations. *Public Administration, 80*(3), 503–522.

Kendall, J., & Knapp, M. (1993). *Defining the nonprofit sector: The United Kingdom.* (Working Paper No. 5). Baltimore, Maryland: The Johns Hopkins Institute of Policy Studies.

Lyons, M. (2001). *Third sector: the contribution of nonprofit and cooperative enterprise in Australia.* St Leonards, NSW: Allen & Unwin.

McCrudden, C. (2004). Using public procurement to achieve social outcomes. *Natural Resources Forum, 28*(4), 257–267. http://doi.org/10.1111/j.1477–8947.2004.00099.x

McCrudden, C. (2007). *Buying social justice: Equality, government procurement, & legal change.* Oxford University Press.

Osborne, S.P. (2006). The new public governance? *Public Management Review, 8*(3), 377–387. http://doi.org/10.1080/14719030600853022

Osborne, S.P., Radnor, Z., & Nasi, G. (2013). A new theory for public service management? Toward a (public) service-dominant approach. *The American Review of Public Administration, 43*(2), 135–158. http://doi.org/10.1177/0275074012466935

Preuss, L. (2007). Buying into our future: sustainability initiatives in local government procurement. *Business Strategy and the Environment, 16*(5), 354–365. doi: 10.1002/bse.578

Snowden, D.J., & Boone, M.E. (2007). A leader's framework for decision making. *Harvard Business Review*, (November 2007). Retrieved from https://hbr.org/2007/11/a-leaders-framework-for-decision-making (accessed 28th May 2015)

Star, S.L., & Griesemer, J.R. (1989). Institutional ecology, "translations" and boundary objects: Amateurs and professionals in Berkeley's Museum of Vertebrate Zoology, 1907–39. *Social Studies of Science, 19*(3), 387–420. http://doi.org/10.1177/030631289019003001

Index

Note: Italicized page numbers indicate a figure on the corresponding page. Page numbers in bold indicate a table on the corresponding page.

Abbott, Tony 19
agency role in new public governance 131–3
area-based initiatives (ABIs) 43
ARNOVA conference (2010) 22
auditable performance 83, 118
Australia 14, 16–17
Australian Institute of Health and Welfare 17
Australian Social Inclusion Unit 19

B Corp 115
Big Society notion 19
boundary spanning theory 124–5, 135–6
British Poor Laws (1573) 34
Brotherhood of St Laurence (BSL) 41–2
Building Lives social enterprise 78

Cameron, David 19
Canadian Demonstrating Value initiative 112
Carnegie UK Trust 14
Caterham Barracks Community Trust 43
civil rights movement 35, 130
coercive isomorphism 51
collaborative advantage, defined 127
commissioning approaches 41–4
Commonwealth Games in Glasgow (2014) 40
community-centric networks 91–3
Community Enterprise in Scotland (CEIS) 60
community services sector 22–3
corporate social responsibility (CSR): compliance responses 79–81, **80–1**; conclusion 84; ethical approaches 74; evolution of 70–4; factors driving 75–6; government regulation and **76**, 76–9, **79**; instrumental approaches **71**, 71–2; integrative approaches 73–4; overview 24, 70; political approaches 72–3; reporting and auditing 83–4; social procurement typology 74–84, **75**; social value chain 82–3; supply chain management 81–2
Cost-benefit analysis (CBA) 111
Council of Australian Government 5

Danish Ministry of Social Affairs 83
deliberative policy analysis 8
differentiated policy 95

embedded value proposition 110
emerging governance networks 126, 143
Enterprising Nonprofits 61
ethnic minority businesses (EMB) 78
European Commission 38
European Economic and Social Committee (2001) 75–6, 83
European Union (EU) 16, 62, 63
expanded pie, defined 127
Exxon Valdez oil spill 71

Federal Contractors Programme 35
fiscal crisis 17
for-profit organisations 110, 142

Global Impact Investing Network 109
globalisation narrative 7, 15–16
governance modes: changing sectors 21–2; meso-governance levels 128–9; prominent typologies of 90–1, **90–1**; regulation and corporate social responsibility **76**, 76–9, **79**; subsidization 92; *see also* network governance; new public governance; welfarism/welfare state

grant funding 92
green procurement strategies 36
grit of human relations 18

homogenisation of practice 51
"horizontal policies" 5
hybridity condition 58, 96–7, 124, 125–9

information and communication
    technology (ICT) 14–15
institutional and resource enablers: actors
    in relationships 53–4; conclusion 64–5;
    organisational roles/relationships 57–61,
    59; overview 50; perspectives on 50–2;
    resources 54, **64**, 79, rules for *52*,
    52–3; social procurement rules 54–7, **55**
integration, defined 135
"interaction-oriented" forms of NPG 128
International Integrated Reporting Council
    (2013) 83
International Standards Organisation (ISO)
    38, 115
intra-organisational relationships 117
IRIS metric 109
isomorphism: coercive isomorphism 51;
    function of 130; government regulation
    and 56, 108; homogenisation of practice
    51; mimetic isomorphism 51, 64, 78;
    normative isomorphism 51; social value
    creation and 119

Johnson and Johnson company 71

Koppenjan's theoretical foundations 131

Landmarc 79, 82
lesbian-, gay-, bisexual-, transgender-
    intersex-owned businesses 78
Local Government Authority 81

macro-analysis and institutional theory
    129–30
marginalised groups 35, 58, 107
market-centric networks 93–4
marketization of services 14
meso-governance levels 128–9
mimetic isomorphism 51, 64, 78
mixed economy 93, 114

National Australia Bank 82, 114
National Health Service (NHS) 44
National Minority Supplier Development
    Council 39, 114

network governance: institutional agendas
    and 58; introduction 3; Koppenjan's
    theoretical foundations 131; next-
    practice networks 89, 90, 94–8; social
    value measurement 108–9
New Deal for Communities 43
New Economics Foundation 111
new public governance (NPG): authority
    and accountabilities in 7, 9–10; corporate
    social responsibility 73, 84; emerging
    practices in 34, 142; governance in
    transition 89, 96–7; hybrid arrangements
    100; imperatives 106–7; institutional and
    resource enablers 51; introduction 2–3, 5;
    policy domains and policy actors 9; rise
    of 107–8
new public governance (NPG), theoretical
    implications: boundary spanning
    theory 124–5, 135–6; conclusion
    136–7; governing complexity 127–9;
    introduction 124–5; macro-analysis and
    institutional theory 129–30; network
    theory and 130–1; practice theory of
    132–3; public value and hybridity 125–9;
    role of agency 131–3; theorizing social
    procurement 133–6, *134*
new public management (NPM): auditing,
    monitoring and evaluation 106;
    emergence 36; governance in transition
    89; network governance 96; performance
    measurement demands 108; public-sector
    environment 93, 94; rise of 124, 125;
    service purchasing regimes 118
next-practice networks *see* third-sector and
    next-practice networks
non-profit organisations: higher-speed
    broadband for 14; long-term value
    creation of 110; procurement in 56, 57,
    60; social services 21, 22, 65, 82
normative isomorphism 51
Northern Ireland Unemployment Pilot
    Project 40, 77

Occupational Health and Safety Act
    (OSHA) 77
one-off contracts 94
organisational roles/relationships 57–61, **59**

Parapan AM Games in Toronto 40
Parramatta City Council (PCC) 117
Partnership Agreement on Indigenous
    Economic Participation 5
partnership-based commissioning 43

Plunkett Foundation 14
post-New Public Management (NPM) 4
practice theory of new public governance
132–3
private finance initiative (PFI) 44–5
private for-profit firms 1, 22, 23–5
pro-social actors 65
Public Administration (PA) 129
public-private partnerships 42, 93, 108, 126
public purchasing 45, 107, 143
Public Sector (Social Value) Act (2012) 5,
43, 60
Public Tenant Employment Program
(PTEP) 40
public value: creation 25, 106–8, 142, 143;
debates about 101; introduction 2, 4,
5; market-based service provision 38;
theoretical implications 124–6, 135

Reminiscent of Power (1997) 106
rules for institutional and resource enablers
52, 52–3
rules for social procurement 54–7, **55**

Scottish Procurement Directorate 39
Scottish Public Finance Manual 55
service purchasing regimes 118
short-term contracts 94
small-to-medium enterprises (SMEs) 56
Social Clauses Project 39
social enterprise: community care providers
and 19; introduction 3–6; procurement
relations and 45, 56; rise of 36–37,
39–41; third-sector advocacy 60, 63
Social Enterprise Canada 61
Social Enterprise Mark 39, 115
The Social Enterprise Networks (SENs) 60
social exclusion/inclusion 17–19
Social Firms Scotland 60
social impact bonds, 3, 22, 42, 62, 109, 118
socially responsible public procurement
(SRPP) 61
social procurement: approaches to 37–44;
commissioning approaches 41–4;
conclusion 45–6; defined 4–6, **6**;
early history 34–7; introduction 1–4,
13, 34; making sense of 9–10; new
approaches to 44–5; rules 54–7, **55**;
socio-economic and political drivers
13–26; standards, guidelines, norms 38–9;
theorizing in 133–6, *134*; traditional
contracting 39–41; typology 74–84, **75**;
understanding of 7–9

social purpose suppliers 127
social unrest 92
social value, assessment and measurement:
approaches in defining 110–12;
approaches in prioritising 112–16, **113**;
challenges to 116–18; co-developing
indicators and frameworks 116;
conclusion 118–19; drivers of interest
in 107–10; instrument/procurer-centric
approaches 114; introduction 106–7;
reliance on proxies 114–15
social value chain 82–3
Social Ventures Australia (SVA) 60
socio-economic and political drivers:
community services sector 22–3;
conclusion 27; economic conditions/
policy approaches 16–17; foci and
practices 25–6; globalisation 15–16;
government sector 21–2; private for-
profit sector 22, 23–5; problems with
21–2
sociological conceptions of institutional
theory 130
Sprout Ventures 82
SROI network 111–13
supplier diversity policies 114
supply chain management 81–2
Supply Nation 39, 114
sustainable procurement 25–6
systems-wide change 2

third-sector and next-practice networks:
community-centric 91–3; conclusion
100–1; governance modes 90–1, **90–1**;
management of 98–9; market-centric
93–4; mixed modes 94–7; negotiation
of goals and actions 100; network
negotiation 98; next-practice networks
97–100; in transition 89, 91–7
third-sector management 2–3
triple bottom line value creation 1
Tylenol poisoning 71

UK Department of Defence 79
UK Public Services (Social Value) Act
(2012) 110
United Kingdom (UK) 14, 16
United Nations 38
United Nations Environment Programme
(UNEP) 115
U.S. Green Buildings Council 77–8
US National Minority Supplier
Development Council 78

value chains 82–3, 95
Value for Money (VfM) 55
Vancouver Olympic Games (2010) 40
Victorian Office of Housing 40

welfarism/welfare state: charitable
    organisations and 142; costs of 111;
    embedded goals 77; establishment of 45,
91, 92; introduction 7, 17, 20; not-for-
    profit sector 35–6; responses to 43
Winnipeg Social Purchasing Portal 39
win-win, defined 127
World Health Organisation's (WHO) 111
World War I 92

Yarra City Council (YCC) 41–2

For Product Safety Concerns and Information please contact our EU
representative GPSR@taylorandfrancis.com
Taylor & Francis Verlag GmbH, Kaufingerstraße 24, 80331 München, Germany

www.ingramcontent.com/pod-product-compliance
Ingram Content Group UK Ltd.
Pitfield, Milton Keynes, MK11 3LW, UK
UKHW021610240425
457818UK00018B/474